NOT SO GOOD
A GAY MAN

NOT SO GOOD
A GAY MAN

Frank M. Robinson

TOR

A TOM DOHERTY ASSOCIATES BOOK

New York

Editorial Note: Within this memoir, the reader may note occasional errors, or that some of the recollections do not comport with all historical facts as they are now known. Because this is a posthumously published memoir, we chose to retain, as much as possible, the truth of Robinson's own writing. When in doubt, we either left Robinson's words as they were, or deferred to the preferences of his estate.

To the reader: Some names have been changed to protect the not-so-innocent if they're still living.

—The author

NOT SO GOOD A GAY MAN

Copyright © 2017 by Frank M. Robinson

A Tor Book
Published by Tom Doherty Associates
175 Fifth Avenue
New York, NY 10010

www.tor-forge.com

Tor® is a registered trademark of Macmillan Publishing Group, LLC.

The Library of Congress Cataloging-in-Publication Data is available upon request.

ISBN 978-0-7653-8209-2 (hardcover)
ISBN 978-1-4668-8576-9 (ebook)

Our books may be purchased in bulk for promotional, educational, or business use. Please contact your local bookseller or the Macmillan Corporate and Premium Sales Department at 1-800-221-7945, extension 5442, or by email at MacmillanSpecialMarkets@macmillan.com.

First Edition: June 2017

Printed in the United States of America

0 9 8 7 6 5 4 3 2 1

For Craig, Eric, Tom, David, Ron, Steven,
and others of the 636,000 who died of AIDS
because their government didn't give a damn.

ACKNOWLEDGMENTS

Richard C. Leo died in a car crash driving from Anchorage to Talkeetna the day before Christmas Eve 2013. He moved to Alaska thirty years ago, a land he came to love; married and raised his kids there. Recently he heard of a corporation planning on building the largest dam in North America in the middle of the Denali preserve, the last untrammeled wilderness in the United States. Rick rallied the opposition, wrote articles and gave speeches against it, and pressured the politicians who could do something about it. He won. The dam has been postponed for a year and there's doubt it will ever be built. Rick was an editor, a writer, and, in the best sense of the word, a rabble-rouser—a latter-day muckraker.

For the editors and writers who may read this: Richard Leo was one of you and attention must be paid.

If you don't know who you are, perhaps you've forgotten who you were.

—Harry Happening

NOT SO GOOD
A GAY MAN

❧ I ❧

BOB:

This is going to be a very long letter. I wanted to write it so you would know what it was really like to be a gay man before and after Stonewall and today, when same-sex marriage had become the law in California and a number of other states.

My mother was a saint—most mothers are, but my mother really did deserve sainthood in the pantheon of mothers. She had to divorce her husband after 1929, the start of the Great Depression, which left her alone with three children. Another marriage was probably the way to go, but during the Depression a single woman with three boys was not a hot marriage prospect.

She finally married a man who had a job at a bank and made real (though not much) money, which in the Depression made him golden. He had two sons of his own so it was a marriage of convenience for both of them. She would keep house for her husband and five boys, cook the meals, do the dishes and the laundry, make the beds, and sleep with a man she didn't love.

If she wanted to keep her family together, she didn't have much choice.

Her background was hardly a bed of roses. She had been

abandoned by *her* mother and "adopted"—not legally—by a retired opera singer, "Grandma" Edmonds, and her partner, Clara Mae Leighton. Miss Edmonds taught singing, Clara Mae the trumpet. My mother did the housework.

At seventeen, when she reached the age of "awareness" and began to suspect the nature of the relationship between Edmonds and Leighton, they married her off to a charming Canadian named Raymond Robinson. He was, probably, the first man she had ever fallen in love with. (Back then, at seventeen, a girl's experience with the opposite sex was usually not all that great.)

Happy ending, right? Not quite. Robinson was an improvident bastard and couldn't take care of his family. He fancied himself an artist and tried to make a living painting portraits of people based on their photographs. He wasn't very successful at it and my mother had to cook our meals over the gas jet in the living room.

Robinson tried to augment his income by visiting the local golf course, where my oldest brother was a caddy, and confiscating his earnings. Eventually he started forging the names of family friends on checks. A deal was struck: my mother's friends wouldn't press charges provided he went back to Canada so my mother could get a divorce on grounds of desertion.

Fortunately two of my mother's closest friends—Dorothy Hall, my "Aunt Dorothy," and her partner, Claudia—worked for the Institute of Juvenile Research in Chicago. They got my mother a job as a matron in the Lawrence Hall Home for Boys. Part of the deal was that she would work for next to nothing and the Hall would take in her children. The important advantage was that she would be close to her kids.

Except me. I was only three years old, and Mr. Houck, who ran the Hall, told my mother that he wouldn't take me in until I learned how to tie my shoelaces. I was farmed out to a family named the Bonifoys, and my mother would visit every Sunday and give me lessons in the mysteries of shoelace tieing.

I remember very little about my life with the Bonifoys except for one night when I stopped to admire myself in a full-length mirror, a skinny little boy in a nightgown that came down to his ankles.

I didn't sleep in my own bed. I slept with the Bonifoys in theirs.

When the day came that I mastered the art of knotting shoe-laces, my mother took me to the Hall. I was the youngest boy there but there were lots of other boys around and I could see my mother whenever I wanted. One time I hid in her room to surprise her when she came off duty. She started to change out of uniform and for the first (and only) time I saw my mother nude.

Four years old is much too young to see your mother naked.

At the Hall all us boys slept in a big dormitory where the rule was that we should sleep with our hands on the outside of the blankets. It was years before I figured out the reason for this requirement.

Nobody had much money during the Depression, least of all the Hall, and we ate day-old scraps. The Hall had a small truck that went around to the grocery stores to pick up any unsold produce. The findings would be spread out on a long table in the dining room, and the matrons would pick out anything that was edible. (Grocery stores back then didn't have their produce spread out on racks with overhead sprinklers to keep things fresh.)

One of the best attractions about the Hall was that one Saturday afternoon a month during the summer they'd line us up and march us down to the local theater. We would see a double feature, maybe two serials and half a dozen cartoons, and were given a candy bar. My favorite films were *Frankenstein* and *King Kong.* They're still among my favorite movies, though back then they gave me nightmares.

It was the theater's contribution to charity—they made money on Bingo nights and those nights when they gave away free dishes.

I saw my father again only once. One day I was called into the Hall's library and introduced to a rather stocky man. He didn't seem any more curious about me than I was about him. I was the last of the litter, and considering the tight finances of the family at the time, I might have been a mistake. The first-born is always the one parents *ooh* and *aah* about, and the second is insurance to make sure the first won't become spoiled. The third is frequently an afterthought. Few parents pay much attention to him—the kid is usually left to raise himself.

A girl might have made a difference—but another boy?

Much later I realized as far as I was concerned my father had functioned as nothing more than a sperm donor—he might as well have been the milkman. The meeting in the Hall was the last time I would see him. But it wouldn't be the last time I had contact with him.

I didn't see much of my brothers at the Hall, and it wasn't until my mother remarried and set up a private household for the family that I got to know my brothers better. "Red" (for his hair) was eight years older than I and five more than Mark. As the oldest, Red became something of a father figure, more so for Mark than for me, though I always felt indebted to him for teaching me how to ride a bicycle, trotting behind me as I pumped the pedals and making sure I wouldn't fall. When he got married, he more or less abandoned the family. Mark never forgave him. On the other hand, Mark and I were fairly close and made the perfect pair—he was a bully and I was a snitch.

I lived in the Hall from ages three to eight and barely made it through alive. I must have been about five when I came down with double pneumonia. I was so sick they didn't dare risk a journey to the local hospital—I wouldn't have survived the brief trip. Most of the time I just slept in the Hall's infirmary. When I was awake the night watchman, a middle-aged, badly hunchbacked man, would read me the *Mother West Wind* stories printed on Coca-Cola serving trays. He kept a careful watch over me and I have a hunch I wouldn't have survived otherwise.

The best thing about the Hall was that it had a summer camp on Little Blue Lake, near Holland, Michigan. It's difficult to remember everything when I was four and five, but little things stand out. At summer camp it was putting a tomato on my mother's sewing machine as a surprise but she never saw it when she closed the cover of the machine. A week later she discovered a small pool of dried spaghetti sauce in the machine.

We hiked in the woods, slid down the banks of a creek we called "marrow beds" because of the slippery clay sides, and were very proud of the older boys who frequently had to hunt for Boy Scouts from a nearby camp who got lost in the forest. We were pretty familiar with the woods around Little Blue Lake—we spent the whole summer wandering through them. The Scouts spent only a week or two, not long enough to learn all the trails.

My mother married for the second time a few years later. Unfortunately it meant no more summer camp at Little Blue Lake, no more splashing around in the water, no more tramping through the woods, no more sliding down the banks of marrow beds and dirtying my shorts.

For the first year of my mother's remarriage, Aunt Dorothy tried to fill the summer gap. I got permission to spend the summer with Dorothy, who had a little cabin—the "Dinghy"—on the shores of Lake Michigan near Macatawa, midway between Holland and the resort town of Saugatuck. My favorite recreation was curling up in a window nook and leafing through the pages of old issues of *The Saturday Evening Post* and *Fortune* magazine that were lying on shelves near the windows. I couldn't read the articles, but the ads for Chevrolet and Studebaker (one red, almost modern two-seater), Packard, the Arrow Collar Man, Kuppenheimer suits, and Florsheim Shoes fascinated me. The house ad in early issues of *Fortune* featured an almost completely nude statue of a young woman with the slogan "The Perfect Gift for the 'Friend Who Has Everything.'" A precursor of the "Petty Girl" to come a few years later.

The next summer Dorothy got me two weeks at a camp for disadvantaged kids. The first week, we decided to "put on a show" (we were years ahead of Mickey Rooney and Judy Garland). I found a beat-up top hat and an old cane and did a really bad imitation of Fred Astaire. The applause was terrific. Unfortunately, my ease behind the footlights didn't last. In grammar school I had the lead in the eighth-grade play and forgot every single line.

Aunt Dorothy was a heroine to me. She picked up her Mercury at the factory and broke the speed limit driving back to Chicago. Family legend had it that Dorothy of *The Wizard of Oz* was modeled after my aunt. Not true—after her retirement Dorothy gave an interview to the local paper and said she'd been much too young at the time. But author L. Frank Baum, Macatawa's leading citizen, was a friend of her grandfather and used to dandle young Dorothy on his knee when he came to visit. Dorothy may have been too young to be the model for the main character in the book, but I'm pretty sure she supplied the name.

(My mother broke with Dorothy years later—why, I never knew—but I kept in occasional touch. The last time I visited her I wanted to ask her about the things that really bothered me in life. She evaded the questions but assured me I came from "good stock." My last view of Dorothy was her standing in the door of her retirement home in Chicago, watching as I disappeared in a cab. I waved at her and she waved back. I considered it a benediction and started to cry.)

Robert Knox, my mother's new husband, worked as an accountant in the largest bank in Chicago, was a single parent (his wife had died a few years previous), and had two boys in the Hall. Gene was five years older than I was, Bill was a year and a half. I was friendly with Bill, closer to my own age, and later got to know stepbrother Gene a little too well.

During the courtship Mr. Knox romanced me by teaching me how to play checkers, then letting me win a few games. He was a nice guy but to us Robinson boys he was always "Dad Knox," never simply "Dad." He was hunchbacked, not badly, and had gone through hell as a kid. He was a farm boy, injured in an accident that had broken his back, and his father had strung him up by his arms in the barn to try to straighten him out. It hadn't worked.

The marriage was much more of a financial arrangement than it was a romance. Robert Knox wanted a mother for his two sons, and my mother wanted a father for her kids. Dad Knox would support the new family, and my mother would be the chief cook and bottle washer. He would discipline his kids, she would discipline hers. Family routine was that he would come home, eat supper and help with the dishes, then settle in the easy chair in the living room and read every stick of type in the *Chicago Tribune*—he believed every word of it—before falling asleep. My mother always called him "Bob," never "dear" or "honey" or any other affectionate name. My mother's maiden name was Leona White, and he always called her "Leona."

"Dad Knox" was never the image of the typical father for us Robinsons. He was partly crippled, which meant he never took us fishing, was never interested in sports, and couldn't horseplay with us.

My first outing with him was when he took me to the bank where he worked, showed me the huge ledgers in which all the accounts were entered by hand, and proudly took out a savings account for me. I wasn't much impressed.

The second outing was a good deal more enjoyable. It was Christmas, and the owners of homes in River Forest, a nearby wealthy suburb, went all out in decorating their houses. The time to see them was at night, when all the lights in the decorations were on. We had an ancient roadster at the time complete with a rumble seat, which meant you would get soaked in a rainstorm.

This particular night it wasn't too cold and it was snowing just enough to make the houses look like Christmas cards. Dad Knox and my mother bundled Bill and me up in blankets and gave us a tour of River Forest.

It was a beautiful night with the lights twinkling through the falling snow, Santa Clauses on almost every lawn, and even a few plaster reindeer. After an hour I fell asleep, Dad Knox carried me inside, and my mother put me to bed.

Many more outings like that and I probably would have referred to Dad Knox as "Dad," but the mutual affection didn't last, and within a week he was "Dad Knox" again.

We boys always considered ourselves blessed because we were good middle-class Americans—not "niggers" or "kikes" or "shanty Irish."

Some prejudices die hard. Mark always thought of himself as the athlete in the family, and when drafted into the army made the mistake of picking on a Jewish kid. (All Jews were moneylenders, they couldn't fight, right?) This prejudice died after the Six-Day War, but for my brother it vanished when the Jewish kid—a Golden Glover from New York—beat the crap out of him. Mark spent three days in the camp hospital. After that I never heard a derogatory comment from him about a minority group—any minority group.

(I learned a lot about prejudice in the United States when I was in high school in Chicago and asked the black kid sitting next to me if he'd like to go swimming at the YMCA. He got angry—didn't I know that blacks could swim only at the Englewood YMCA, the segregated Y for blacks on the South Side? And it was the Jewish kid down the block who showed me how to throw a baseball—my brothers used to humiliate me by shouting "You throw like a girl!")

My mother had a piano and used to gather us kids around to sing. But we broke up into groups of Robinsons and Knoxes and she soon realized she had five kids to raise and a husband to feed and sleep with but she didn't have what she had wanted most—a family. She finally sold the piano and it broke her heart.

Our first house was very old and very huge, in Forest Park, Illinois. We lived kitty-corner from an equally big, old house occupied by a Gypsy family, complete with an old man and his traveling bear plus a cherry tree in the backyard.

We picked cherries for my mother to make pies, watched in fascination as the old man went through his tricks with the bear, and built forts in the backyard and had snowball fights during the winter. (We outnumbered them by one and usually were victorious.)

During the height of the Depression in the middle '30s my mother used to keep a small stack of sandwiches by the back door for hungry homeless men. She wasn't the only housewife who did that. The photographs of veterans selling apples on street corners were real. Some towns and small municipalities (and large ones) issued their own currency, called "scrip," with which to pay municipal employees. The scrip was accepted by shopkeepers, who in turn used it to buy the supplies they needed, and so on.

All the boys in the family worked. One of us had a *Saturday Evening Post* route—the magazine was distributed to subscribers door-to-door like a newspaper. During the summer months we loaded our wagon with a box full of dry ice and ice cream bars and sold them before the Good Humor truck showed up. When the war began in 1941 I peddled popcorn at the Parichy Bloomer Girls stadium in Forest Park—the home of a women's softball team that had replaced male players who had been drafted.

About this time I asked my mother if she thought I was handsome (standard question from a teenage boy). She made two mistakes. The first was to take a minute to think about it. The second was to say "You're very nice-looking." It took me a few decades to appreciate the wisdom of this. A handsome movie star whose career depends on his looks had a lot more to lose as he grew older than I did.

A few years before, I learned that kids are sexual at an early age even though they don't yet know what to do with the sensations. In sixth grade I usually sat in the back of the room with a young girl and we'd tell each other dirty jokes. When one of us didn't get it, the other would explain it.

By the seventh grade all us boys sweated for fear we'd be called to the front of the class to diagram a sentence on the blackboard or do a simple problem in math. Our pants would rub against our legs and we would get an erection. We used to bite our lips as an antierection aid. And then there was the problem of taking a shower after gym class. Those boys who had matured early usually flaunted the evidence and the rest of us would stare at them with envy and admiration.

My favorite comic strip at the time was *Tarzan of the Apes*. Artist Burne Hogarth, for reasons I suspected later, had Tarzan swinging through the trees in leopard-skin Speedos, which gave him the most attractive butt in comics. I mentioned this to friends, who looked puzzled and said "So what?"

By thirteen I was introduced to more serious forms of sexuality by stepbrother Gene. We had a table tennis setup in the basement and we started playing games together. He was a much better player than I was and after a few volleys always managed to hit the ball directly into my crotch—with the expected results.

Things became embarrassing one Thanksgiving when I excused myself from the table to go to the washroom to take a pee. I wriggled my penis once or twice, got an unwanted erection, and then very strange things happened. My family began to holler at me, asking if I'd died in there, and finally I emerged, sweaty and flushed.

Everybody stared at me for a long moment and I realized that now they all knew about my coming of age. The Ping-Pong games became more serious now, and after a dozen volleys stepbrother Gene and I would end up in the coal pile.

At the time, we boys slept two to a bed. One of my stepbrothers and I in one, Mark and Gene in another. One night I completely lost it and tried to climb into bed with Gene, even though Mark was already there—hopefully sound asleep. A week later Mark and stepbrother Gene got into a fight when my folks weren't home and sprayed blood all over the upstairs hallway. That scared both of them and they spent all afternoon trying to wash it off.

Neither ever admitted the reason for the fight, but I suspected it had been about me. I was Mark's little brother, which automatically made him my protector. A few months later Gene was drafted and a year or so after that so was Mark.

For a long time I hated my stepbrother for "turning me gay," but a few decades later, in therapy, I discovered I hadn't hated him at all. I'd loved him. Our Ping-Pong games had become sexual, but to me physical touch, a rarity in the family, had translated as affection, sexual or not.

Mark and I became much closer the year he got his driver's license and almost killed us both. We were driving along a country road paralleling a train track when we heard a train whistle in the distance. My daredevil brother decided to beat it to the next crossing. He floored the gas pedal and I started to sweat as the warning whistle of the train got louder. We just made it. On the other side of the crossing my pale-faced brother abruptly stopped the car. I flew forward and bumped the windshield with my head, raising a welt. Once home, my mother asked what had happened, how come the bump on my head.

For once in my life, I kept my mouth shut.

⊰ II ⊱

SOME YEARS LATER I had lunch with director Tom O'Horgan (*Hair, Lenny, Jesus Christ Superstar*) and during the conversation discovered that for my first two years of high school, at the start of World War II, we'd both gone to Proviso Township in Maywood, Illinois. We'd taken the same classes, had the same instructors, and knew the same students.

The big difference was he knew all the gay students. I knew some of them but had never known they were gay.

I had started reading science fiction when I was eleven. I usually stayed up in my bedroom reading science fiction magazines while my brothers played baseball in the empty street (few people had cars in those days) or shin hockey in the alley (roller skates, cheap hockey sticks, and a tin can for a puck). I graduated from high school when I was sixteen—I was a smart kid and had skipped a grade—and by this time I was a dyed-in-the-wool science fiction fan. I carefully saved all the magazines and joined a magazine correspondence club (so had Hugh Hefner, who joined "The Weird Tales Club" in 1943) and was starting to make friends across the country.

Locally my friends were Ronald Clyne and Charles Beaumont (originally McNutt, but he took a lot of kidding from classmates and while living in Beaumont, Texas, had changed his last name to that of the city). Ron was an artist and Chuck wanted to be a writer (so did I), and in our senior year the three of us decided to put out an amateur magazine titled *Parsec*. That never happened, but Clyne went on to design most of the jackets for Folkways Records, and Chuck ended up selling stories to *Esquire* and *Playboy* while I was still mucking around in the penny-a-word digest magazines.

My mother had hired a private eye to find her own mother, and while none of the family had much in common with our bedridden Grandmother Proctor, we always liked her husband, Fred, who covered sports for the *Chicago Herald-Examiner*.

Fred got me a job as a copyboy at INS (International News Service—both it and the *Examiner* were owned by Hearst) and took me to hockey games and down to the locker room, where he introduced me to "Mush" March and Johnny Gottselig of the Chicago Blackhawks as the "great white hope." That got a laugh out of the players—at 140 pounds sopping wet I wasn't the great white anything.

Hockey wasn't my favorite sport, but I went with Fred to the games, where he would dictate his story to me, I'd write it down and hand it to the telegrapher, who'd send it to the sports desk. (Fred had palsy and couldn't hold a pencil.)

After six months of picking up the morning reports from the Chicago livestock yards for INS and feeding rolls of paper to their teletype machines in the afternoon, I got a dream job working in the mail room of Ziff-Davis, then publishers of *Amazing Stories*, *Fantastic Adventures*, *Mammoth Mystery*, and *Mammoth Detective*. The fiction magazines did well, but the real money-makers were *Flying*, *Popular Photography*, and *Radio News*.

Between delivering mail to the various departments, I'd hang out with a diminutive hunchback, Ray Palmer, head of the fiction department, and Howard Browne, who handled the mystery magazines. Howard was a pretty good mystery writer himself and introduced me to novels by Raymond Chandler. Years later, in journalism school at Northwestern, I combined the mystery genre with the fantasy genre and wrote one of the first "thrillers" (*The Power*). I hit it big—magazine serialization, television, a George Pal movie, and more foreign editions than anything else I've ever written.

I owed Howard a lot.

(I also owed Palmer a lot, though I didn't realize it until much later. If you write what you think is a great line, kill it—it will throw the rest of your piece off balance. The same advice was given by the writing teacher in the movie *Kill Your Darlings*.)

As an avid magazine collector, I was also something of a thief. The mail room held the original two years of *Amazing Stories*, bound in thick, black volumes, six magazines to a volume. "Sydney Gernsback" was printed in gold at the bottom of the spine (Sydney was the brother of Hugo, the original editor and publisher of *Amazing*.) Nobody ever looked at the volumes; nobody had in years. But to a collector they were pure gold. It was winter and my overcoat was very big and floppy. I smuggled the volumes out, one at a time, beneath the coat. The only time I was almost caught was when the treasurer of the company rode down with me in the elevator, staring at me, wondering how his office boy had gained so much weight.

The most horrifying thing that ever happened in my life was when I was walking to work one spring morning. A stockbroker in the building next to 540 North Michigan—the home of Ziff-Davis—had leaned too far back in his swivel chair by an open window and toppled out of the fifth floor. If I had gotten there ten steps sooner I would have been beaned by him. I was one of the first to arrive at the scene—no police, no ambulance, no shocked pedestrians, just myself.

My first thought was what science fiction writer Robert Heinlein had once said: a human being was just a bag of liquids. What would a grapefruit—which had a much thicker skin than a human being—look like if it had fallen from five stories up? It would have splattered on the cement, which is what our broker had done. Year, later I would wonder what a soldier would look like if he had been driving his Humvee in Iraq and hit an IED? I wouldn't wonder long—I already knew.

I could hear the police sirens and an ambulance in the distance and hurried through the gathering crowd to the offices of Ziff-Davis. I got there just in time to lose my breakfast when I hit the john.

My sexual life was nonexistent. By now I was familiar with "faggot," "queer," and "dirty Commie faggot." I didn't want to be any of them, knew I had no choice, and started building a social closet so nobody would know. I was pretty sure I was unique—I knew of nobody else like me. Talk about it to a minister or a priest? You've got to be kidding. Living at home, my mother knew everything about me—after all, she did the laundry. I could have confided in her, but what young boy ever talks to his mother about his sex life (or lack of it)?

The Trevor Project, the hotline for young, troubled gays, had yet to be created. Like many other young gays I thought of suicide but didn't have the courage—or, when it really came down to it, the desire. It seems silly to say it now but the serials in the science fiction magazines were a big help. What was going to happen in the next installment of *Second Stage Lensman* or the new novel by Robert Heinlein? I'd stick around long enough to find out.

I knew a few gays—along with some nongays—who lived in a small science fiction commune in Battle Creek, Michigan, called "Slan Shack." (A "slan" was a superhuman mutant in a popular novel by A. E. Van Vogt.) One was an older man who had actually served time for being gay. Another one became one of my best friends: Walt Liebscher (the only one in science fiction "fandom" who knew I was gay at the time but never talked about it).

Slan Shack used to throw its own small conventions, notable for their auctions, to which Ray Palmer contributed some of the artwork from *Amazing Stories*. (An original cover painting by J. Allen St. John, the doyen of cover painters at the time, might go for $25. Today it would go for more than twenty-five grand.) At one of these conventions I developed a crush on a fellow teenager from Buffalo, New York, who traveled all the way in for the convention. If I had made a pass, he probably would have agreed—much later I learned that many late teenagers are sexual experimenters. (Some members of Congress learned it before I did. It's probably a toss-up whether the congressmen preyed on the page boys or some of the teenage page boys preyed on the congressmen.)

When Slan Shack broke up and Walt moved to Los Angeles, he and a local gay man, Jimmy Kepner, were promptly "outed" by another fan when outing could frequently have tragic consequences. Walt became a recluse. Jimmy Kepner, on the other hand, became a leader in the gay rights movement, one of the founders of *ONE* and largely responsible for its archives.

I had become a serious collector of old magazines, which by now led to my last contact with my father. I and two collecting friends discovered a large second-hand magazine store on Chicago's South Side. We were flipping through handfuls of *The*

Shadow and *Adventure* magazines when one of us spotted a locked glass cabinet at the rear of the store. Behind the glass doors we could see the spines of the old *Amazing Stories*, *Wonder Stories*, *Weird Tales*, and others—probably several hundred or more. We dropped the magazines we were holding and made a dash for the cabinet.

"How much for all of them?"

"I'm not going to sell anything to you guys," the owner said with a snarl. "You dropped my magazines on the floor."

We romanced the old man, we listened to his tales of World War I, we bought hamburgers for his dog. Finally he relented. We could have the cabinet. For $150. Split three ways, that was $50 for me, a lot of money for a kid. I asked my mother for a loan— she now had a job in a defense plant and was making serious money for the first time in her life. I'll never know why, but she lent me the $50.

Once home, we spread the magazines out on the kitchen table and started divvying them up. My friends were in love with the garish Frank R. Paul covers on *Amazing* and *Wonder*. For reasons I didn't understand, I picked out all the copies of *Weird Tales*— by comparison, a drab-looking magazine with stories by authors I'd never heard of.

My mother came out to see how I'd wasted her money and turned pale. While my father painted portraits from photographs, she had read to him from his favorite magazine: *Weird Tales*. She was now looking at some of the identical covers. (It turned out my father was also a fan of Edgar Rice Burroughs and *Tarzan*. So was I.)

I have no explanation, but I would like to think it was genetic. Recently I was offered close to a quarter of a million for a complete file of *Weird Tales*—I had kept upgrading over the years and by now it was probably the only mint-condition set in the country. My old man had bequeathed me something after all.

I spent a year at Ziff-Davis in the early '40s, then the draft caught up with me. I'd tried to enlist but was classified with "compound myopic astigmatism." That settled that, I thought—I was safe. When I went for my draft physical my handicap was downgraded to simple myopia, and in 1943 I was cannon fodder.

I had my choice of services and chose the navy—my best friend in science fiction had enlisted in it. And besides, I liked the uniforms, thirteen-button flies and all. Not the equal of leopard-skin Speedos, but they had their own appeal.

Electronics school started at Great Lakes, but the last seven or eight months were spent at Navy Pier in Chicago. A great town for liberty—the best music town in the country. Pickups were easy, and those who wanted to get laid had no trouble finding companionship. One guy we felt sorry for—he was slender and had a walk that would've put any Hollywood starlet to shame. Most of us wondered when the navy would get around to discharging him. One liberty, a member of the division followed him and returned looking awestruck. It had been an act. The suspect sailor would make friends with a likely prospect, have a few drinks, tell her about his lonely gay life, shed a few tears, and the girl would promptly decide to save him from himself.

He scored every time, our spy said.

(When it came my turn to relate my own sexual adventures during the weekend, I lied.)

The dropping of the atomic bomb on Hiroshima in 1945 was the first indication that maybe we wouldn't have to invade Japan after all. Another one followed on Nagasaki, and shortly afterward came the surrender. We had originally been scheduled for assignment to the "working navy"—troop ships, attack cargo ships, LSTs, etc. We'd be anchored off Japan, supply ships for the invasion. Considering the Japanese suicide planes, we probably wouldn't be anchored there for long. One sadistic chief even told us that in the cold Pacific water, our life expectancy would be something like twenty-seven minutes or less.

The surrender was a huge stroke of good fortune for us. And atomic power! The newspaper ads said that atomic power would be so cheap it wouldn't be worth the cost of measuring it. I was the science fiction buff ("Frequency Modulation Robinson") in the division, which meant I was an authority and knew about such things. I was swamped with questions. Most of my answers were courtesy of Dr. E. E. Smith, the author of the *Lensman* series. Apologies to the memory of Doc Smith, but I'm sure I was wrong every time.

None of us thought about the civilian casualties in either Hiroshima or Nagasaki, which numbered in the hundreds of thousands. All we knew was that the war was over and we had a new lease on life.

The war might be over, but the navy decided to ship us overseas anyway. The railroad trip from Navy Pier to San Francisco took two days and nights. In the sleeper cars we slept head to toe, two to a bunk. They bed-checked us every hour, and I prayed that my bed partner was fat and ugly.

The few days I spent in San Francisco settled all my doubts about the city being a mecca for gay sailors. My first night in, I drew shore patrol with a first-class officer and we checked out the waterfront bars—forbidden to navy personnel. In the first one we entered, all the drinkers at the bar swiveled their heads in unison to stare at us. Two bars later we gave up and concentrated on finding drunken sailors roaming the street.

Late that night, when I went off duty, I stripped down to my skivvies and crawled into my cot, dead tired—the navy had filled the gym floor of the Embarcadero YMCA with cots right next to each other—two rows of cots, then an aisle, then another two rows of cots. About two in the morning I felt somebody's hand reach under my covers. I froze. I knew the penalties for gay behavior. A dishonorable discharge and maybe time in the Portsmouth Naval Prison (or so I had been told). Then I relaxed, figuring I had the perfect alibi. I hadn't felt a thing—I'd been sound asleep.

The next morning I got up early to check out what I hoped was a friend in the next bunk. (He'd left early.)

Later on that afternoon I went up to the weight room to work out. It was deserted except for one guy who had completely stripped, then hung a towel on the end of his erection.

I wasn't sure what I wanted to be in life, but one look and I knew for damned sure what I didn't want to be.

We were assigned to a troop transport bound for Japan the next day. It was jammed to the gunnels. Along with several friends I stood at the railing and watched San Francisco recede into the distance. I reassured my friends that seasickness was all in the mind. Then we hit the rollers outside the Golden Gate and I promptly vomited over the side.

The trip to Japan took two weeks and I shed twenty pounds—from 140 to 120. By popular acclamation I was made compartment cleaner, since I did the most to dirty it up. I couldn't help it—I'd go to the head (bathroom) in the morning, and the first thing I saw was a mix of seawater and vomit sloshing back and forth in the bathroom trough. I'd promptly lose my breakfast. On inspection day, I'd sit on the edge of a bottom bunk with a bucket between my knees, stand up and salute when the captain came through, then go back to holding my head over the bucket.

I probably could have gotten out of the navy because of chronic seasickness, but then I discovered if I went topside, on the bridge where the cold wind could catch my face, it would help a lot. I spent as little time belowdecks as possible.

Another week and we were anchored off Yokohama. It was now a few weeks after the surrender. Some days later I was transferred to a small ship going upriver to Nanking, China, to pick up half a dozen women, White Russian refugees, and take them to Shanghai. Once on board the captain gave them several cabins near the bow, then posted guards to make sure that no members of the crew wandered forward to try to make friends with the women.

I pulled one afternoon liberty, about which I remember very little except that I had never seen so many Chinese in all my life.

The trip back to the States was uneventful, except for the "thrill" of standing at attention on deck in the hot summer sun going through the Panama Canal. A week or so later we docked at Norfolk.

The day I got my discharge papers and was walking to the train station to go home I was picked up by the police for "being out of uniform." It had been a hot day and I was wearing whites instead of travel blues. I spent the afternoon in jail.

"Sailors and dogs keep off the grass."

The people in town meant it.

I was looking forward to civilian life. I never in my worst nightmares thought that in a few years I would be back in the navy.

❧ III ❧

MY MOTHER HAD worn a small pin with four stars on it—one for each of her and Dad Knox's sons in the service. She put it in her jewelry box when we came home. Gene and Mark were lucky. Both had served in the Pacific and both came home without a scratch—though neither ever talked about the war. Bill wasn't so lucky. He had been in the Battle of the Bulge and lost several toes to frostbite. I, lucky fellow, had never seen any action at all.

Gene and Mark went looking for jobs. Bill had been a star in math class in high school and I thought sure he would go to college. He didn't—he drifted from job to job and eventually went into the antiques business.

I spent my time looking for a college. Two years in the navy had bought me four years of the GI Bill. I finally picked Beloit College in Beloit, Wisconsin, just over the state line from Rockford, Illinois. It was small—the GI Bill didn't exactly cover you if you wanted to go to Harvard or Yale—and close enough so I could go home on the weekends if I wanted and also send my laundry home and get it back the same week.

Beloit was a quiet, midwestern college—probably one of the best small colleges in the country.

I lived with the other returning veterans in "huts" the college had built just off the campus proper. Maybe eight or ten to a cottage, all of us ex-marines, sailors, or air force personnel.

My major was physics—my hero had been Robert Oppenheimer, one of the creators of the atomic bomb, and one of the few who regretted it. I aced my freshman physics class—my education as a navy technician helped a lot. It was a different story a few years later, when I was struggling with calculus and physical chemistry. The smartest students in the college were majoring in physics, and I was out of my league.

During the second-year summer break I took a short-lived job at Western Electric, working the line, assembling telephones. It was repetitive, low-pay work where you punched a time clock and your only break was lunch in the company cafeteria. I knew I was a fish out of water, that as a college student I didn't belong, but I decided to make the effort—at least to the point where I'd try to "butch it up," become one of "them."

I bought a pack of cigarettes and stuck it in my shirt pocket, and a pack of condoms, which I carried in my wallet.

After lunch I lit up, and tried to talk with the people around me. I didn't get much more than a suspicious glance and monosyllables. In the cashier's checkout line I stubbed out my cigarette—I had been careful not to inhale, of course. (I had started with nickel cigars when I was a kid and never got past the first one, which made me violently sick.)

I pulled a five-dollar bill out of my wallet to pay for lunch, and unfortunately the pack of condoms stuck to it. Without thinking I gave the bill a flip, and the condoms landed on the floor. Everybody around me glanced down and then at me.

I wasn't one of them and I never would be. They knew I was a fake, and they were contemptuous of my act. (In the late thirties there was a gulf between college kids, whose families presumably had money, and those who worked the line whose families didn't. It was a while before the GI Bill evened out the difference.)

With the start of the regular school year I was "rushed" by some of the fraternities. The students were split into two groups—younger students who had never been to war, and us veterans, older and more cynical. I pledged Pi Kappa Alpha, known as the "old soldiers' home" because most of the members were vets.

Come Halloween I discovered that of all the colleges I had considered, I may have picked the right one. Halloween night it was an unofficial tradition for the freshmen boys to knot their clothes tightly around themselves and go out to the grinder, an open field where the sophomore boys—stark naked—would meet them and try to tear off their clothing.

When we heard of this a photographer in the house grabbed his camera and ran to chronicle the festivities. He came back with a fine selection of X-rated photographs. I was sorry I hadn't gone with him.

By my sophomore year, I was beginning to suck wind in my major of physics, though I was a straight A student in my minors. Anthropology I aced—it was a class I loved. There were a number of Indian mounds near Beloit, and the anthro majors would make periodic trips to excavate them and examine the bones. (They wouldn't get away with that now.)

Another minor that interested me was English composition. I had applied for a course in article writing, but the class was full, and fiction was the only thing available. I hadn't wanted to sign up for it at first for fear I would discover that I wasn't capable of doing what I really wanted to in life.

One session we had a teaching assistant who assigned us to write a horror story. The best ones would be read in class.

I rewrote my effort at least a dozen times and was not too happy with it. But it was read aloud in class and halfway through it I noticed something strange. It was deathly quiet in the classroom; everybody had been caught up by my story.

Fuck physics. I had just found my profession.

The process of storytelling was exciting—I thought I might even be able to make money doing it. And it was a lot more fun than learning formulas in physics.

My other minor was history. One day the captain of the diving team, Don, asked if I would like to come over to the Phi Psi house and cram for a history test. I was flattered. Don was a top member of the swim team, a reliable man in relays, and a standout when it came to diving.

I went over that night and thought for a moment that nobody was home. I rang the bell and a few moments later Don opened it. As I recall, he was starkers—obviously the only one home. I hid my surprise and followed him to his room, the only one lit in the entire house. I sat on the other side of his desk, stuck my nose in a history book, and kept it there, looking up at Don only to answer questions.

I had no idea what he wanted, but the feeling was growing that he wasn't that much interested in history. I was frozen; I couldn't have done anything, not even touch him.

After graduation in 1950 I heard that Don had gotten a job at the American School in Beirut, Lebanon, teaching English to the sons and daughters of oil engineers. A year or so after that, word came that Don had committed suicide. It had run in the family, friends said.

Much later on, when I was called back into the navy, I chose the Mediterranean as my theater of operations, and one of our ports of call was Beirut. On my first liberty I took a cab to the cemetery to pay my respects.

The cabbie showed me the bluff above Pigeon Rocks, where Don had taken his last dive. I walked to the edge of the cliff and looked down at the Mediterranean crashing against the rocks a hundred feet out.

I felt like shit.

It was in the family, people had said. I didn't believe it. I wished to hell that that night I had closed my history book and just talked to him.

Both of us were lost, I thought. Of the two of us, he had been the unlucky one. I was desperately unhappy but I was still alive.

Later that year I tried once again to break out of my closet. The fraternity had pledged a young basketball player, and he became my roommate. He was a nice kid, a well-built basketball type. One night we were studying and he had to use the pencil sharpener behind where I sat at my desk. He had on a floppy bathrobe, and I started to make a pass. He didn't move but continued sharpening his pencil—a nub by now. He was waiting but I chickened out. He returned to his desk and both of us resumed studying as if nothing had happened.

Michael was a member of the Newman Club, a Catholic group that met once a week. When he went to confession, I was afraid he would tell everything to a priest. In retrospect he probably would have been told "say twenty Hail Marys and what are you doing tonight?"

What locked me further in the closet was meeting Barry Westlake, a man I liked and learned to love. He was an independent (no fraternity) and had a freedom of outlook that I admired. Both of us had gone to summer school, and one night we walked out to the college's football stadium and sat in the bleachers and just talked.

After half an hour of trading family history he was silent for a long moment, then began to talk about the highly personal things he had done in his family. They weren't easy for him to say. Once his father had even threatened to throw him out of the house if he didn't shape up.

It was hard for him to talk about them, but at that moment I was his best friend. I'm sure he felt like he could tell me anything.

What struck me later was a quote from the comic strip *Peanuts*, where Lucy has a little booth from which she's peddling advice. The sign on the booth was "Sympathy is next to love."

What I felt was an overwhelming sense of sympathy and a sudden rush of love. I didn't have enough experience to know when to sympathize and when to stop. I massaged his back, then slipped his shirt off. I was unsure what I wanted to do or how to do it but I was sure nature would take care of things like that.

He turned when I got to his belt buckle, and the look on his face was a mix of anger and loathing. We were best friends but I had never had the courage to tell him I was gay, and what was worse, I had reduced his confiding in me to something physical.

He put his shirt back on and started walking back to campus. I followed, not knowing how to apologize, not knowing what to say.

There was no doubt in my mind that my life was now over. He would report me to the campus authorities, I would be kicked out of college, my faculty adviser would drop a note to my parents, and I would lose my family and my home.

I didn't sleep that night, running the scene over and over in my head and feeling worse every time I did so. The look on his face was etched in my memory. I started packing my suitcase in the morning, prepared to leave without a word. I was halfway through the packing when a pledge came up to the attic and said somebody wanted to see me.

At the door Barry said quietly, "You okay, Frank?"

The look on his face this time was one of deep concern. I wanted to bust out crying. I didn't know what he thought of the previous night, but to me it meant a good deal more than just sex. I had offered him what I thought was the best of myself— the love I felt for him, my sense of pride. I swore that I would never lose my pride again.

(I did, of course—and more than once.)

Barry and I became even closer than before and went on long bike rides over the Wisconsin hills (you haven't lived if you haven't tried pedaling a balloon-tired bike over thirty miles of rolling hillside). We went fishing once and stayed at Barry's home that night. His mother offered us the spare bedroom. The bed was big enough for two but I didn't trust myself and, oddly, I didn't trust Barry, either.

That night I slept in my sleeping bag on the floor.

With time we drifted apart but I would see him sporadically and once flew down to San Jose for the wedding of his son. When I started back to the airport after it was over, Barry asked if he could come to the airport and wait for the plane with me. He and I sat in the airport lounge and talked and suddenly Barry was confiding in me again, telling me his problems at work and life in general. It got more personal and I began to feel the same surge of sympathy that I had felt so many years before.

I wrote a long letter to him when his wife died. He told me afterward he had cried for months. The last time I saw him was a few years ago, in the early 2010s, when we met at the Monterey Bay Aquarium—he, his son and his son's wife, and me. Barry had worked in the Forest Service most of his life, and the sun had weathered him. He was much older now, his hair white and the skin on his forearms not just tan but tanned, like leather. He said he skied and even had a kayak he used during the summer.

When we left we said good-bye, and then his son turned to him and said quietly, "Go ahead, Dad—you know you want to."

Barry walked over and hugged me, saying, "How can I thank you? You've done so much for me all my life."

I wanted to remind him about the time he'd saved my life so long ago. I didn't; I was afraid I would embarrass him.

But my feelings for him then and my feelings for him now hadn't changed a bit.

I felt very good about that.

I sold my first short story when I was a junior at Beloit in the late 1940s. It didn't sell right away—editor John W. Campbell of *Astounding* liked it but said, regretfully, that he was overstocked with stories of that length. I showed Chad Walsh, my composition instructor, Campbell's letter. He suggested I cut a few thousand words out of it and resubmit the story.

I did and this time Campbell took it and sent me a check for $200. I immediately told everybody on campus that I was now a published author.

Well—not yet. Campbell was still overstocked, and the story never appeared that year. Most of my friends now looked at me with suspicion. I was sure they thought I was a status liar.

That year was also the year I was elected president of Pi Kappa Alpha. For a variety of reasons, besides the obvious one, I was woefully unsuited for the job. My major supporter was a muscular ex-marine named Jeff Richards, but that was support enough.

(I was not the only gay man at Beloit. After graduation, the president of the senior class became the lover of a Chicago puppeteer with an early TV show. We never knew each other in college but met briefly afterward. In college, both of us were in the closet.)

It was expected that the president of the fraternity would play on our basketball team during the intramurals. I knew better than to even show up. (It turned out I was a pretty good right-handed handball player, but I didn't discover that until years later.)

My last summer break I got another low-pay job at a metal job shop. Once again I was a fish out of water but didn't try to pretend otherwise. My job was simple enough—grind irregularly shaped pieces of metal until they were roughly smooth on both sides.

I ran into my first Neanderthal at the shop, or at least a man who could qualify as one. He was short—about five-six—with relatively short legs and extremely thick, muscular arms. A stumpy man who probably weighed 225 or 250 pounds. I'd throw the finished lumps of metal into a barrel until it was almost full and then look around for a cart or something to move it over to a different part of the shop. I didn't have to bother. My stumpy friend would trundle over, put his arms around the barrel, lift it, and carry it over. The barrel had to weigh 300 to 400 pounds.

(Anthropologists have now figured out that all of us have somewhere between 1 and 2 percent of Neanderthal genes. My muscular friend had more than his share.)

By now I was becoming a minor VIP on campus. I had become the news editor of the weekly campus newspaper, *The Beloit College Round Table*. (In 1972, Don Bolles, the editor in chief, became part of the investigative beat of *The Arizona Republic*. He was killed when six sticks of dynamite exploded beneath his car as he went to meet a contact. Don became an early hero of mine.)

The other major social activity on campus at which I was woefully inept was dating.

Occasionally the college had a dance, and the various presidents of the fraternities were expected to attend, especially the senior prom. At that time many girls going to college considered it the happy hunting ground for marriage prospects.

My date had had few boyfriends, and she was enthusiastic about the prom. I danced with her only a few times (I dance badly). Afterward, you were expected to walk hand-in-hand back to the sorority house, telling her how gorgeous she was and proving it when you got to the sorority house, sealing the evening with a tight squeeze and a hot and sexy kiss.

I flunked the course. I kissed her briefly, then turned and left. I'm sure it was the worst date she ever had in her life, and to be destroyed on prom night had to be too much to bear. When I was back in the house I had trouble remembering her name. My guess was that she also had trouble remembering mine—or perhaps forgetting it.

In May of 1950, a month before graduation, the June issue of *Astounding* came out with my story in it. I ran to downtown Beloit and bought all the copies I could find, then hurried back to campus and distributed them to people that I knew had never believed I'd sold a story and had been public about their doubts.

Once out of college I asked my stepfather for a loan of $500 to support me during my apprenticeship as a writer. His answer was a polite "No." If you weren't working nine to five or punching a time clock, you really weren't working.

I lived at home and holed up in the kitchen typing away on my trusty typewriter, my most prized possession. The Christmas before I had worked a few weeks delivering gift baskets for Stop & Shop, an upscale Chicago grocery store—the precursor of Harry & David. The route covered Chicago's wealthy North Side suburbs and included such notables as illustrator George Petty, the creator of the "Petty Girl" for *Esquire*. One thing I learned early: Poor people can't afford to tip, the middle class is usually generous, but forget the upper classes. The maid who answers the door is not authorized to tip tradesmen.

I earned $50 that winter—just enough to buy a secondhand Model 5 Underwood typewriter. (Every time my computer goes out—which is often—I really miss the old manual.)

One of the many magazines I was submitting to included Bill Hamling's *Imagination*, a local science fiction digest. I had first met Bill when he and a writer friend shared an office on Chicago's North Side, where they ground out stories for *Amazing Stories*. I used to drop by and sell Bill my cigarette rations when I was in the navy. I don't think he ever realized how envious I was of his being a writer. The office was small and cramped with a broken-down couch, and I imagined Sam Spade might walk in at any moment.

One day Bill asked me to fill in as bartender for a party he was throwing in his rec room the next week. The party was a rousing success, but I noticed a man standing quietly in a corner who didn't talk much to the people there. It turned out that he'd worked with Bill when they had both been employed by a publishing company in a North Side suburb. He was a would-be cartoonist, Bill said, and had self-published a book of his own cartoons titled *Chicago, That Toddling Town*. As a favor Bill had bought several of his cartoons for *Imagination*, though he never planned to publish them. I think I poured a beer for the man and promptly forgot him.

That was the first time I met Hugh Hefner, though it wouldn't be the last.

I was also going to a number of local conventions those days (back then few women attended, and almost all of the men were young and skinny—a lot different nowadays on all counts), and at one of them I thought my double life was blown.

Bob Bloch—author of *Psycho* and one of the most talented and nicest guys in the business—asked me how I was doing. I gave him the financial report: what stories I had written, who had published them, etc. He looked at me for a long moment, then asked quietly, "And how's Frank?"

He had guessed everything about me, I thought, and I felt sick. Later I realized he wouldn't have given a damn but at that moment in time I was a sexual paranoid. You could be arrested if you were caught in a gay bar, and your name, home address, and the name of where you worked printed in the morning newspaper. (More than one gay man hanged himself in jail.) If you picked up the wrong man in a bar or on the street you could have the crap beat out of you and people would think you deserved it. If you were really unlucky when you took a trick home, you might be robbed and murdered—and your pickup would get off scot-free if caught. It was called the "homosexual panic defense"—your would-be sex partner had panicked when you touched him and momentarily lost control.

Being a "faggot" or a "queer" put you beyond the pale. You weren't human.

My writing career came to an almost complete halt when Shasta Publishers, a local publisher with whom I was friendly, announced a contest for the "Best Science Fiction Novel." Pocket Books would put up the prize money for the contest. Shasta would publish the hardback and Pocket Books the paperback.

First prize would be $4,000, and there would be six second prizes of $2,000 each (a lot of money then). I would be one of six lucky second-prize winners. (I was good buddies with one of the owners of Shasta—all I had to do was write a novel.)

I did. It took me a week of eighteen-hour days. I had to keep reminding myself that with two grand, I could get my own apartment and write stories and novels in my own kitchen. Suddenly there were problems. Shasta took Pocket's prize money and invested it in publishing a book titled *The Westmore Beauty Book*—makeup tips from Perc Westmore and his brothers, popular Hollywood makeup artists of the period. With the expected proceeds from the book, Shasta would then go back to the science fiction book contest. They were so sure of the plan they even had a publicity photo taken of the president of Shasta handing the winner—Phil Farmer—a huge, oversize check for four grand.

The Westmore Beauty Book actually came out, and I took one look and realized my kitchen and small apartment had suddenly vanished. The book was in black-and-white, and no way could a black-and-white book show the variations in shades of color for lipstick and face powder or the colorful three-dimensional beauty of a woman's face.

There were no second prizes—nor was there a first prize.

I had my own problems at the time, but they had nothing to do with Shasta's default. I came home one day and found my mother holding a letter and crying.

The Korean War had just started in the early '50s, and the government had panicked and called up the reserves. Upon my discharge from the navy at the end of World War II, I had been talked into joining the "Inactive Reserve." Just a formality, I'd been assured, but in case of a war or police action I would keep my rank, etc., etc.

I glanced at the papers and wondered why the hell my mother was crying. It should have been me who was bawling.

The Inactive Reserve had just been activated, and what my mother was holding out to me were seventeen—count them—copies of orders to report.

THERE WERE AT least twenty of us in the navy doctor's waiting room. One was a young student with two months to go before he got an engineering degree, another was an older first-class radioman whose son was in the army, his daughter was in the WACs, and his wife was rolling bandages for the Red Cross.

Others in their late twenties and early thirties sat in chairs around the wall, looking glum. I was probably the only one there who had no excuse to evade serving my country—the nation would never miss a struggling science fiction author.

A few minutes later a doctor in a stained white smock stuck his head in the doorway and looked quickly around to see if anybody there could qualify as being lame, halt, or blind. He smiled. All of us had managed to make it under our own steam.

"Anything wrong with you guys?"

A dozen hands shot up.

The doctor smiled again and said, "Welcome aboard."

Three days later I was on a rust bucket out of Norfolk. Civilian life with all of its problems and duties was now left behind. I wasn't entirely unhappy about it. I liked the smell of fuel oil in the shipyard, the slow roll of waves against the bow and sides of the ship, the sounds from other ships, and the faint echoes of shouted commands.

I felt right at home on the USS *Alshain*.

They had asked me which theater of operations I would like, and since the war was in the Pacific, I had chosen the Atlantic. I would take Italy and France and the rest of Europe over Korea any day. At the very least, nobody would be shooting at me.

A few days of loading supplies and then we got under way. I watched the land slowly slip over the horizon, and this time my seasickness really was a case of mind over matter.

Our first Sunday out was a day off from holding various watches, drills, and inspections. Some of us slept in and the rest of us flaked out on the deck to enjoy the entertainment. Somebody had brought a record player on board and a few records.

I made myself comfortable against a bulkhead, and after a few records, members of the crew began dancing. With each other. I watched with more than passing interest. There was going to be competition for the cute-looking guys on board.

(Every time we got new additions to the crew, we'd line the railing to check out the new arrivals. I put it down to just curiosity, though I may have been wrong.)

The entertainment wasn't limited to the Sunday dance. The most popular man on board was a first-class yeoman in the ship's office who had a flair for writing pornography. He'd turn out stories three or four pages long, single-spaced, on yellow second sheets, staple them, and give them to friends to pass around. He had a commercial eye and quickly learned the trick of breaking a story in two—the first half the buildup, the last half the wildly explicit sex, where our hero would lay the women in the aisle—literally. Within a day, the stories would be dog-eared, some pages only half there. My guess was some members of the crew tore out the hottest scenes and saved them for future reference.

One rumor was that actual sex might also be available. Younger crew members suspected of being gay would be approached and bet twenty bucks they wouldn't go down on a shipmate. Ten minutes or less later the horny member of the crew would button his fly, hand the kid the money, shrug, and say, "Gee, I lost the bet."

I considered that rumor more wishful thinking—a certain amount of privacy would be required, and navy ships were notoriously short of private spaces.

It wasn't all fun and games. Shortly after I reported on board, the ship took on a contingent of marines for an operation off Vieques Island, Puerto Rico. The island was small, with about ten thousand inhabitants. The navy owned half the island and used it over the years for simulated landings, bombardments, etc. The natives who lived on the other half of the island, of course, hated the navy.

We weren't entirely without amusement—one of them was watching the marines muster on deck in the morning. Their company clerk responsible for the roll call was slightly built, somewhat girlish, all spit and polish, and with a high-pitched voice. At another time in another place he would have been known as a "screamer" (an obviously effeminate man). On liberty one day some sailors cornered him, a few marines noticed it, a fight followed, and the sailors went back to the ship nursing bruises and missing a few teeth.

The company clerk may have been a screamer, but before he was anything else, he was a marine—and marines protected their own.

The *Alshain* took part in training exercises at Onslow Beach,

North Carolina, headed back to Norfolk, and then to the Mediterranean, where Naples became our home port. Most of the bars and whorehouses were along the waterfront. Sightseeing tours were available for members of the crew who had culture on their minds, but some of the crew never got beyond the whorehouses. When liberty was over they staggered back to the ship and reported to the "clap shack" for inspection and shots from the ship's corpsmen.

My first tour was of the ruins of Pompeii, a city near Naples and in the shadow of Vesuvius, which had erupted in A.D. 79 over a period of two days. Many of the people left the town the first day Vesuvius let go. Those who stayed behind were buried in eighteen feet of ash the next day. (If the wind had been blowing in a different direction, scientists might be excavating the ruins of Naples.)

What was of immense interest to us sailors was the erotic nature of the city. Paving stones had phalluses chiseled in them like arrows, pointing the way to the nearest brothel so visitors wouldn't be embarrassed by asking where it was. At the entrance to the "House of the Vetti" (the Vetti were merchants) there was a large statue of Priapus weighing his huge phallus against a bag of gold. Our guide said that since we were sailors and obviously more sexually sophisticated than the average tourist, he would open up a room usually closed to visitors. The Vetti had provided their guests with a private room for entertainment, with frescoes on the walls depicting naked Pompeians cavorting and having various forms of intercourse.

We were fascinated to see that what they did two thousand years ago wasn't that much different from what people did today. At least I didn't see anybody taking notes.

The next two stops were a little south of Pompeii, along one of the most beautiful coasts in the world. Sorrento and

Amalfi—if I could have, I would also have included Capri, but that was an island close ashore, a favored resort area.

Both towns still showed the effects of World War II, when the Nazis and the Americans fought over them. Shell holes in buildings, walls here and there still partially knocked down. But what you were really aware of was the sheer beauty of the place, our bus driving along the narrow highway with the Mediterranean a sparkling blue below us.

A few weeks later came the tour most of us had been waiting for. Rome—which had been an open city during World War II—was disappointing. A relatively modern city, it was still spotted here and there with an ancient statue or an equally ancient building shouldered by a building of the twentieth century. The trick was to ignore anything modern and try and see the city as the Romans had.

Part of the enormous Colosseum was falling down, and I was inclined to view it as a tumbledown ruin. There were dozens of them throughout the city, though none as large as this. Then I visualized the stone benches crowded with forty-five thousand spectators cheering on the gladiators, holding their thumbs up when they wished to save one of the vanquished, or gossiping with one another as they ignored the cries of the Christians being fed to the lions.

Aside from the classical ruins, the two most striking buildings in the city were Mussolini's railroad station—all modern, all huge—and the basilica of St. Peter, the largest church in the world.

St. Peter's was an architectural fantasy, the product of the talents of Michelangelo, Bernini, and dozens of other artists, sculptors, and architects. It took almost a thousand years before it finally assumed its present form. On the inside, the space under the huge dome was vast, the altar in the middle framed by four twisted columns and capped with a golden cupola. The number of tourists crowded inside had to be limited—as large as the space was, it couldn't accommodate them all. Crowded or not, you could see figures in black robes and red hats scurrying through the corridors.

The enormous building and its art treasures were overwhelming. If someone were to put a value on it, it would have run into the billions of dollars.

I—and a thousand other sailors—had an audience with Pope Pius XII in his consistory. It was short, the pope waving his hand and blessing us and the rosaries we had brought along for friends.

I'm not especially religious, but as I was leaving I stood in the entrance for a moment and tried to imagine Jesus, a Jewish man of thirty or so wearing sandals and dressed in a simple robe that swept down to his feet, looking around, puzzled, and feeling desperately out of place. Would he have felt at home in the basilica built in his honor with all its gilt and statuary and the imposing high altar flanked by its fantastic columns? I doubted it. The Jesus I had read about had thrown the moneylenders out of the Temple. What would he have thought of the pope and the gaudily dressed priests?

And if the pope and priests could see me for the would-be sexual outlaw that I really was, would they have welcomed and accepted me? I thought Jesus might have, but I felt a lot less sure of his worshippers.

There was more to see in the Mediterranean than Rome and Pompeii. I pulled liberty in Crete, and what impresed me the most was the utter poverty of the country. What symbolized the capital city of Heraklion for me was a little girl relieving herself in the gutter as people wandered by. (It gave me great pause years later when the stores along San Francisco's Castro Street wouldn't let an old bag lady in to use the john. Her only choice was to lift her skirts and squat over a nearby sewer grating.)

Athens was to prove something of a relief from the poverty of Crete. Like Rome, Athens was a relatively modern city dotted with classical ruins, the most famous of which is the Parthenon, a slim, simple building with classical pillars holding up its roof. Built hundreds of years before St. Peter's, at various times it served as a temple, a treasury, and a storehouse for ammunition in the various wars that severely damaged the building.

The appearance of the Parthenon was further marred when in the early 1800s some of the sculptures around the top of the building were removed by the British. (You can see the "Elgin Marbles" in the British Museum in London—they're gorgeous.)

We pulled more liberties at cities along the Mediterranean, but the last one I remember was Cannes, famed later for its film festivals. I was looking forward to flaking out on a beach and watching the boats in the harbor, but the beach wasn't a beach at all, at least not like the sandy stretches I had ever walked on. It was covered with stones and what looked like dark gray shingles. You could, of course, buy a chaise lounge or a mattress, so you had something soft to lay on as you watched other beachgoers pick their way over the rocks.

A tour of the different towns and cities that bordered the Mediterranean would have cost me thousands of dollars through a regular tourist agency. I'd had it, courtesy of the US Navy (with only minor inconveniences), free of charge. I had seen Italy's beautiful coast along with Amalfi and Sorrento, Rome and Athens, Cannes, and far from least, Beirut, where I had paid my final respects to my friend on Beloit's swimming team.

And there was the Colosseum, the Basilica of St. Peter, the Parthenon, and, of course, the private room in the House of the

Vetti in Pompeii that I doubted was on any tourist company's list of things you shouldn't miss.

The first thing most of us did that first liberty back in Norfolk was to buy a pint of milk and chug-a-lug it. On board ship we ran out of fresh milk in two days; after that, it was all powdered. The second thing we did was buy a pint of real ice cream (same reason).

After that the rest of the crew went looking for entertainment or momentary companionship. I searched out a store that specialized in magazines and paperbacks. I noted with envy that one entire table was covered with copies of Mickey Spillane's *I, the Jury*.

Almost hidden in a corner was a small stack of *Astounding Science Fiction*. I flipped open the cover and just gaped. There it was—"Untitled Story" by Frank M. Robinson.

What the hell . . .

Then I remembered that one of the last stories I had written before returning to the navy was the result of a conference between Bill Hamling, then editor of *Amazing Stories*, and myself. *Amazing* always changed the title the author had given a story, so I had let it go as simply "Untitled Story."

I found out later from Fred Pohl, my agent, that the editor of *Astounding* had a twelve-thousand-word hole in the magazine and that "Untitled Story" would just fit. At three cents a word (*Amazing* paid one), Bill Hamling was pissed but I was delighted, though somewhat confused. *Astounding* had the reputation of being the thinking man's science fiction magazine; *Amazing* was for kids.

What puzzled me more was that my story was rated second in the issue by the readers. (Just goes to show you why so many adults read the Harry Potter books and love them. The stories appeal to both kids and adults—a good trick for any author to pull off.)

While I was in the service, the family had moved to Beverly Shores, Indiana, relatively close to the steel town of Gary, but I decided to stay in Evanston, a suburb of Chicago, and study journalism at Northwestern University.

I got in without any trouble—I had written and sold short stories and been the news editor of Beloit College's weekly paper, the *Round Table*. The Medill School of Journalism was rated one of the tops in the country, right after the University of Missouri and Columbia. At Medill I learned how to set type by hand from a tray of tiny metal letters—I failed to realize the importance of that—and how to take photographs with a Speed Graphic and develop the prints myself. (In a few years, the Speed Graphic would become a museum piece.)

There were, however, two advantages. The course on reporting would be important for its mantra of who-what-how-when-and-where. I knew that learning how to interview people for news stories and articles would be invaluable. Most important of all, Northwestern was close to home.

Making money by writing stories for one or two cents a word for science fiction magazines began to lose its glamour.

What was worse was that I had begun to buy into the popular attitude toward homosexuality. It was dirty, it was sinful, it was a crime.

My self-esteem was rapidly sinking, and there was nobody in whom I could confide, nobody who could offer real-life advice. I was on my own, and if I didn't do something I would go off a bridge, as Tyler Clementi was to do generations later.

I had to bite the bullet and do what I knew had to be done. I didn't succeed, but in the process I managed to fuck up the lives of two other people.

THE NORTHERN CAMPUS of Northwestern was in Evanston and stretched along the shores of Lake Michigan. A cramped but beautiful campus and one that I fell in love with. Unfortunately, it would take two years to get a master's degree in journalism—my undergraduate work at Beloit was of little help (they were not impressed by my major in physics nor my minor in anthropology).

It was also expensive, and my government aid wouldn't cover it. My brother Mark—probably making up for all the times he'd hit me on the arm or belittled my prowess when it came to throwing a baseball—offered to send me $100 a month. If I were frugal, I could just make it.

My first job was to find a place to live, and the first stop was the Pi Kappa Alpha fraternity house. They weren't interested in anybody from a hick school in Wisconsin, or maybe I had the fraternal grip wrong. At the door it felt like I was shaking hands with a freshly caught trout.

I finally ended up on the top floor of a three-story rooming house run by a more-than-friendly middle-aged woman. How friendly I found out when I went to the basement to take a shower. The shower stall was made of wooden slats with a lot of space—maybe two inches—between them. I had just soaped down when my landlady came bustling into the basement with a load of laundry. The first time was maybe coincidence. The second time I realized she was checking me out through the slats. After the third shower she knew everything there was to know about me. From then on I turned my back to the slats and mooned her when I heard her coming down the stairs.

One of the few advantages was that the local campus hangout, the Hut, was just a few blocks away. Everybody who was anybody dropped in there—meaning many of the students in drama and journalism, as well as the usual townies trying to make friends and influence people, especially the girls.

It was a great hangout. One of the girls I briefly knew was a child prodigy in theater, fifteen years old when she entered Northwestern (she left after two years). A number of the Hut regulars razzed her because of her age and doubted she could act her way out of a paper bag.

Karen Black grew up and won critical praise playing opposite Jack Nicholson in *Five Easy Pieces*. She won an Oscar nomination for Best Supporting Actress and a Golden Globe for the same film. (She also appeared in *Nashville* and *Come Back to the Five and Dime, Jimmy Dean, Jimmy Dean*, both Altman films. I liked *Dean* the best because it promised so little and delivered so much.)

One time my brother's check was late and I was flat broke. I didn't want to borrow any money, but a Canadian student, Bob Vallance, a Hut regular I'd met, glanced at the starved expression on my face one morning and said, "Hey, Frank, how about I spot you to a breakfast or two?"

Eggs, bacon, toast, coffee, and a small bowl of peaches. The waiter forgot the peaches for the second breakfast, so I took the bowl back to the pass-through from kitchen to dining room and did my best imitation of "Please, sir, may I have some more?"

Jerry Orbach, the temporary short-order cook, stuck his hand in a #2 can of peaches, pulled up a handful, and plopped them in the bowl. I never got to know him well but attended a few college plays he was in and went backstage once to compliment him on how he carried his spear or whatever. He was a very good actor, but part of my visit was just to thank him for the peaches.

(Next time I heard of Orbach he had a long-standing role in the Off-Broadway play *The Fantasticks* and went on to win nominations and Tonys for *Guys and Dolls*, *Promises, Promises*, *Chicago*, *42nd Street*, etc. On television, he played the lead for years on *Law & Order*. The day of his death, Broadway theater marquees were dimmed in his honor.)

Journalism school was an almost all-white school back then. No Chinese or Latinos that I remember and only one black, a friendly guy named Arthur France. One time I asked him why he wanted to be a reporter.

He hesitated, then blurted, "Because then people won't have to look at me."

He was going to spend his whole professional life hiding his face behind a byline. I hope Art lived long enough to see Eugene Robinson, Don Lemon, the Reverend Al Sharpton, and dozens of other black anchormen or experts being interviewed on TV today. I hope that on some station Art had been one of them.

One night Art and his wife invited me to dinner and I went shopping for groceries with his wife. They lived on the very segregated South Side of Chicago, where there were only mom-and-pop stores; no supermarket had located down there. When the elevated trains emptied out, everybody headed for the stores. It was hard not to notice that there were few blacks behind the counters, that few blacks owned the stores where other blacks bought their groceries.

On the black South Side everybody shopped meal to meal. The iceman had long vanished, and few families owned a fridge. At one meat market, Art's wife picked out some chops for supper and asked the clerk to turn them over so she could see the bottom. She told me that a lot of the stores dyed their meat so you had to watch out for chops that were green on the bottom.

In journalism school, I fumbled my way through print shop, did moderately well in reporting, and loved special projects. I had started a novel and spent most of my evenings working on it. One day, out of curiosity, I looked up the bona fides of the instructor who was teaching the course. So far as I could find, he had sold one story to *The Saturday Evening Post*—and that was it. Google didn't exist back then so there was no way I could easily check him out for books or articles. I suspected there hadn't been many.

I hung out at the Hut and met most of the regulars, including Big George (six-four at 225 and a regular in the weight room of the Evanston YMCA). I also worked out at the Y, determined to match the physiques of my brothers, all of whom had exercised with weights. (Stepbrother Bill could do a stomach isolation—it was all I could do to suck it in.) I could bench-press 225—once—but no matter how much I worked them, I never got an abdominal six-pack.

I was getting further along with my novel, which I had titled *The Power*, after a few lines in the movie *The Bachelor and the Bobby-Soxer* (screenplay by Sidney Sheldon).

You remind me of a man.

What man?

The man with the power.

The publisher subtitled it "a novel of menace," which much later would be referred to as simply a "thriller."

I was very proud of what I had written so far, and the instructor asked to see it. He was not nearly as delighted as I was and called me into his office. Had I ever read *Man and Superman* by George Bernard Shaw? I said I hadn't, though of course I knew of Shaw.

He claimed that my lead character's name—William Tanner—was the same as the name of a character in Shaw's book. And both books dealt with "supermen." I don't think I convinced him, and the manuscript earned an A minus. I checked later, and decided he probably hadn't read Shaw's book, either. For Shaw it was "John Tanner," for me it had been "William Tanner." As close as "Jim Jones" and "Bob Jones."

My personal life by this time was nonexistent. Why the hell was I interested in men, not women? There was nobody to tell me; I had to find out for myself.

There was one kid who hung out at the Hut who seemed to have few friends. He was somewhat effeminate, and rumors were he was probably a "faggot." He became the object of an experiment for which I was never to forgive myself.

One night I asked him up to my apartment and stripped him of all his clothes, including socks and shorts. Without saying a word I then gave him the male equivalent of a gynecologic examination, inspecting every external organ and every orifice, trying desperately to find out exactly what attracted me.

After twenty minutes, I gave up. I sat there staring at him as he put his clothes back on. As he was leaving, he turned at the door to look at me with hatred. He was crying.

"I was looking for somebody for a long time," he said. "I was hoping you might be him."

I was badly shaken. I looked for him after that but he never came to the Hut again, nor did I ever see him on campus. Effeminate or not, he was what I had always wanted. Somebody I could talk to and compare notes and maybe even sleep with. I finally realized that whatever I had done to him I had also done to myself.

⋘ VI ⋙

I LIVED AT home during the summer in Beverly Shores, Indiana, a short distance from the steel mills of Gary. I got there too late to get the usual college summer job of reading meters in the main building. The only job open was manual labor as an assistant in Central Mills maintenance. I surprised them and took it.

I had no idea what I was getting into. Every day one of the five mills would close down and we would go in to fix anything that needed fixing—primarily replacing the huge links on the conveyor belts that carried ingots of steel from one part of the plant to another. The links that were broken or worn, we'd take off the belt and replace with a new one. The links weighed a good twenty-five pounds, and I carried the comealong—a device for hoisting the heavy links—on my shoulders. Once the new link was in place on the belt my job was to "buck" the rivets that were inserted through the link to make it part of the belt while a workman on the other side flattened the rivet with a sledgehammer. If they missed the rivet, the only thing in the way of the sledgehammer would be my head. On Monday, when some of the workers showed up either drunk or with hangovers, I'd hide until somebody sober reported in.

The best and most reliable worker was an avowed socialist. The company would have canned him, but he was the best man on the gang. If something went wrong, he was the one they called on to fix it.

The supervisor took me aside and warned me that Scotty was a socialist and I should be wary of him. Scotty and I, of course, became good friends.

I joined the steelworkers' union when two very large union men showed up in the locker room where we boiled our overalls, thick with grease, in kerosene. They suggested I join the union and I readily agreed. (I would have joined even without the muscle showing up. I was a dyed-in-the-wool union man.)

Working in the mills was hard work. I'd go home and sleep for an hour before I had strength enough to eat supper.

It was a different sort of danger the few times I worked out in the Gary YMCA gym. I was showering one Saturday getting ready to go home and there were only two of us in the shower room. The other guy, about my age, was semierect and studying me, making sure I knew he was available.

I ignored him, feeling the sweat pop out on my forehead. I didn't know him from Adam, and he didn't know me. Entrapment, I thought. If he were genuinely interested he would have started a conversation as I was getting dressed, or offered me a lift home. I left the Y but not without regrets. What if he had been for real? There were ten years missing out of my life that I desperately wanted to make up for. But this time I was sure the closet had saved me.

At the end of my last year at Northwestern, my master's thesis was titled "Pornography and the Law," and I dropped in on the one man I thought would know the most about it. Hugh Hefner had first proposed a "sophisticated men's magazine" to his publisher at PDC in Cicero, but there was room for only one genius in the shop and his name wasn't Hugh Hefner.

Hefner gave his magazine a new title, pasted it up on his kitchen table, and used a near-nude photograph of Marilyn Monroe as his first centerfold. The rest of the issue he filled with cartoons and fiction. He printed fifty thousand copies of the first issue (so I was told), which he planned as a bimonthly publication.

The first issue sold out; so did the second. He went to monthly publication, and by the end of a year had a small office on Chicago's near North Side and enough spare cash to buy himself a Mercedes with gull-wing doors (at least so the rumors went), and his friend and former fellow employee at PDC, Bill Hamling, reportedly turned green with envy. So did everybody else who knew Hefner.

He didn't recognize me as his former bartender of a few years back and waved me to a chair. There were maybe a dozen female assistants who came in and out of the office while we talked—most of them wore tight sweaters with "Hef" printed on the front. (This is from memory, so forgive me if I'm wrong.) Hugh Hefner was a slender, handsome man and the women in the office were definite knockouts. Whatever else might be said, Hefner had great taste.

He was friendly and told me everything I wanted to know. In the back of my head was the idea that if I'd asked him for a job, he would have given me one—he could have hired me for stamp money. But along with being an overage virgin, I was also something of a prude. Work for a magazine that featured naked women? No way.

One major insight into myself was offered by a psychology major in casual conversation. You were programmed to do certain things in life at certain times, he said. If you failed, you'd spend the rest of your life playing catch-up.

He didn't know me that well, but I felt that everything he said applied to me.

I finished the novel that semester and went running to the post office and sent it off to my agent. Two weeks later I heard back. Lippincott wanted some minor changes, but they offered an advance of $500. I immediately called my mother (collect) and told her the good news, slapping the side of the phone booth (they had them then) as I talked. She was excited but I could detect a trace of doubt in her voice. She'd believe it when she saw it.

When the books came in, I spread them out on my bed in the Y and looked at them with great pride and satisfaction. Ten copies of a book with my name on it. Then came the letdown, and I realized I was just as unhappy as I was before.

The book was dedicated to my mother, and she got the first copy of the ten. She put it proudly on the coffee table so all her friends would see what her son had done.

She never read it.

My friends at Northwestern promptly threw a party for me, and I was the man of the hour. It was the first book I ever sold (a dozen more were to follow), and like a lot of things in life, there's nothing like the first time. And this turned out to be a home run—paperback, television, magazine, a dozen overseas editions, and a lousy movie.

I got mildly plotched at the party and so did a pretty, slender Irish girl named Cathy McGill, a fellow journalism student. She felt mildly ashamed and hid under the piano, afraid she would spoil the party. By this time most of those at the party were drunker than she was and I assured her there was nothing left to spoil. Since then we became good friends.

One time she gave me a book—*Now We Are Six*, by A. A. Milne, detailing the adventures of Christopher Robin in verse.

Now I am six and I'm clever as clever,
So I think I'll be six now for ever and ever.

On the book jacket Cathy had carefully printed "to Eeyore," Christopher's grumpy and pessimistic donkey friend. (She had that right.)

I got my degree in 1953, needed work, and ended up working on a new magazine with Bill Hamling. He had started his professional life as a science fiction fan, become a writer, eventually edited *Amazing Stories*, then left Ziff-Davis and started his own magazines, *Imagination* and *Imaginative Tales*, because he loved the field. They did well and then began to slip in circulation along with the rest of the field. At one time, to keep them going, Hamling found work at Publisher's Development Corporation in nearby Skokie, where he met Hugh Hefner. They became friends and went to each other's parties, though later Hefner denied ever becoming really close friends.

At PDC Hefner was in promotion and drew cartoons on the side. Hamling bought a few for *Imagination* but strictly as a favor; he had no intention of publishing them.

When *Imagination* and *Space Travel*—formerly *Imaginative Tales*—started to really fail, Hamling and I had a bull session and I suggested changing the title of *Space Travel* to *Caravan*, a digest version of *True*, *Argosy*, *Stag*, and the other men's adventure magazines, hot sellers at the time. Hefner, by this time very successful with *Playboy*, gave Hamling an introduction to his distributor. The lunch that followed was a disaster. Hamling talked about his plans for *Caravan*, at which point the distributor put down his cigar and asked acidly, "What's it going to be about—camels?"

Hamling immediately changed his approach, saying he also had an idea for a sophisticated men's magazine to be titled *Rogue*, something like another *Playboy*. He was a very fast man on his feet or had intended to suggest it all along.

The distributor okayed it, which came as a shock to Hefner. He had thought he was helping Hamling change one of his science fiction digests to a men's book and find a distributor for it. He'd had no intention of setting Hamling up as a possible competitor. He immediately set restrictions on the new *Rogue*. Hamling could not print the magazine on slick stock, use four-color reproduction, full-page cartoons, and definitely no centerfold.

Hamling had no choice—Hefner could have killed the project immediately. Hamling went ahead with a crippled *Rogue*. He was editor and publisher; I was managing editor; and Henry Bott, a friend of Hamling's, was associate editor.

Hamling's feelings toward Hefner were now somewhat mixed. He owed Hefner for the help so far given but was irritated by the restrictions. Rumors were that Hefner had offered Hamling a piece of the action in his projected *Playboy* and Hamling had turned him down. If true, Hamling was probably also somewhat jealous. (The rumors never suggested where Hamling, nearly broke at the time, would have found the money.)

Rogue was now anything but a class publication—Hefner had killed that possibility—and after three issues I left, looking for another job.

First stop was *Iron Age* magazine, a publication for the steel industry that was looking to beef up its midwestern office. I thought I was admirably suited—I had a degree in physics and had actually worked in the steel mills. The one-year gap didn't seem to bother the senior editor, Keith Bennett. "I used to write science fiction," he mused.

All the tumblers suddenly fell into place. "You wrote 'The Rocketeers Have Shaggy Ears' in the Spring 1950 issue of *Planet Stories*," I blurted.

We science fiction fans never forgot a cover, a title, or an author. I was one of the very few people in the entire United States who would have remembered his story (actually a poem).

I didn't get the job. The midwestern office had three people—one senior editor and two advertising men. The admen thought my $1 sport coat and my tennis shoes that flapped when I walked would give the wrong impression of *Iron Age* and black-balled me. All of that could have been fixed with my first paycheck, but I wasn't given the chance.

The next stop was a Sunday supplement titled *Family Weekly*, which circulated to small-town newspapers. I had checked out the editor—Ben Kartman, a hard-bitten type who had once been a makeup editor for the *Chicago Daily News* and an associate editor of *Coronet* magazine. (He also taught night school at Medill, but I never knew that until much later.) I slid my degree from Northwestern across his desk and he glanced briefly at it, not impressed, then asked, "Can you write?"

My next offer was the contract for *The Power*. He spent a little more time looking at that, then said, "When can you start?"

With my first paycheck I replaced my sport coat and gym shoes, though I don't think anybody in the office noticed or cared. Regina Gruss and I, both associate editors, became fast friends despite my almost having set her hair on fire demonstrating magician's flash paper.

I loved doing interviews for the paper and was good at it. One time Jan Peerce, a leading tenor at the time, showed up in the office surrounded by his retinue of half a dozen. I remarked on this and he motioned me over to a corner and said, "There are two things they cannot do for me—they cannot sing for me and they cannot go to the bathroom for me."

It was the greatest one-line quote I ever got, but I couldn't use it because *Family Weekly* was a "family" paper.

Another time I did a piece on "a day in the life of an intern" and got a tour of Cook County Hospital. What I was never to forget was the morgue. The bodies were laid out on individual tables complete with drains. All of them had their head, hands, and feet wrapped with white cloths. I asked why and the guide said, "They're the most distinctive parts of the human body. When they're covered, you're working on an anonymous body. If you took the coverings off, then you'd be working on a human being."

I noticed one of the interns eating his lunch on the chest of one of the bodies and hurriedly left.

After a few months of turning out articles and interviews and acting as fiction editor for the occasional story we ran, I was very full of myself and asked Ben why he'd never complimented me on the obviously sterling pieces I was writing.

He looked at me as if he couldn't quite believe what he'd heard, then said with a growl, "I pay you, don't I?"

Editors are not in the business of giving out compliments.

My social life sans any sexual encounters had taken an upturn. Most of my friends at the Hut had graduated, and I changed my hangout to a coffee shop a few blocks north. I was also working out at the Evanston YMCA, managing to add muscle mass without much definition. I had worked up to doing squats with 225 pounds (once) and took off my gym shorts—they bound—and did the squats in my jockstrap. Nobody made any witty comments—hey, 225 was a lot of weight, and if that's what it took, that's what it took.

NOT SO GOOD A GAY MAN · 71

I had learned some wrestling holds in college and ended up wrestling a kid named John Mallman, who became one of my best friends. I always thought John cheated—he wore about six layers of sweats and I never knew if I were holding him or merely a handful of cloth.

Most of my spare time I hung out in the coffee shop, run by Joe Moore and his wife a few blocks from campus. It was also a hangout for a group of sports-car racers. Not my interest, but they were nice guys, and at least one was young and drop-dead handsome. He was devoted to racing, which was all he ever talked about. All of his friends were fellow drivers.

One day he didn't show up at an event, but it was a few more days before some of the drivers went to his rooming house to see if he was sick.

He had hanged himself in the closet. There was no note, nothing. Nobody knew if he had any relatives they could notify or girlfriends they should contact. Nobody could remember if he had any.

A chill settled over the coffeehouse, and I waited for what I knew was coming. It probably ran in the family, somebody said, and everybody shook their heads wisely.

I knew better.

Nine months after I had started at *Family Weekly*, a fraternity brother who worked for *Popular Mechanics* (then published in Chicago) told me there was an opening at *Science Digest*, a small companion magazine. It was slanted for high schoolers, and the idea was we would "digest" science articles, carefully taking out all the hard science but leaving in the general thrust of the article.

It was a dream job, partly because it fit in with my educational background but primarily because I would be working with Fritz Leiber, a fantasy writer who was a literary hero of mine. (J. K.

Rowling would match him, but she was generations away.) The interview with Fritz went fine, and I was told to show up in two weeks.

When I came to work I was shown to Fritz's office, which would now be my office. I didn't understand, and they told me Fritz had been a drinker who had gotten drunk once too often and fallen asleep in the john. To interview his successor for the job was a polite gesture on their part.

For years I thought I had taken Fritz's job away from him. Intellectually I knew better but emotionally I felt I had stolen it.

Working at *Science Digest* was the best job I ever had. The work was easy and interesting and I have dim memories of condensing articles by Isaac Asimov (I might be wrong but I'd like to think that I did) for the high school readers.

The money was good but there was more involved than that. The magazine had four employees—the chief editor, a makeup man, another associate editor, and myself. H. H. Windsor, the owner of the company, took three-week vacations and felt so energized by them that he decreed all his employees should have three-week vacations.

Science Digest was already overstaffed by half a man, and a three-week vacation was frosting on the cake. We now had time to put our feet up on the desk and take an afternoon snooze.

Shortly after I'd come to the *Digest* I got a call from a secretary at *Playboy* inviting me to a party at their offices. I was properly impressed and said, "What should I wear?" I could hear her laugh as she said, "Clothes will be enough." (Dumb question, smart answer.) Their offices were midsize—larger than when I had interviewed Hefner for my master's thesis, not nearly as large as when they hit their stride, rented a number of floors in the old Palmolive Building on Michigan Avenue, and renamed it the Playboy Building.

I wandered through the offices, drink in hand, and ended up in their almost empty conference room. Seated in the chair at the head of the table was Hefner's distributor (he also distributed *Rogue*, which is where I'd first met him). He waved his hand around the office and said, "You know, if I wanted, all of this could be mine." Magazines in general, not just *Playboy*, had hit a serious slump on the newsstands. Hefner apparently needed cash and had gone to his distributor (the banks, of course, were out).

I stared at him, wondering if, of all the conferences he must have had with Hugh Marston Hefner, he really knew who he was talking to. His chance for a takeover never came. Several months later the "Playmate of the Month" was Jayne Mansfield, and *Playboy* sold out.

Once I caught a glimpse of Cathy McGill in the hallway just outside the door to *Science Digest* and ran out to meet her. She was on her way up to the next floor to apply for a job. I took her to lunch and after that she was a more or less my regular luncheon companion. I introduced her to the other staff members, all of whom were charmed. She was Irish, beautiful, and a Quaker who tithed 10 percent of her salary to the church. She was offbeat in her approach to life—something that always fascinated me in people—and once took her two-week vacation by going to Iceland in the middle of winter. I asked why and the only answer she had was that she was curious.

It was the kind of answer that made complete sense to me. I started to see more of Cathy, though there was nothing that could be construed as an honest-to-God date.

That is, until the night she came up to my apartment to sauté some shrimp and fixings. We were both comfortable with each other and she told me about her boyfriend at the University of Chicago who was making her increasingly nervous. He was possessive and there was something about him that was making her wary.

In the back of my head was the growing thought that maybe I should try to go to bed with a woman whom I genuinely cared about. I was unsure of the physical end of things, but I was also pretty sure that could be worked out. The least that could happen was that I would end up with a very good friend of the opposite sex.

(This was not all wishful thinking. I was to have close relationships with three or four men who were later to marry and raise families and be perfectly happy—most of them happier than a lot of straight couples I knew. Only one ever called me every few years to ask if I were happy. He'd had to make a choice and made the one that society and the church had dictated for him. Over the phone, at least, he sounded distinctly unhappy and wanted to know if I were also. Misery, apparently, demanded company. But he was the one who had taken the road less traveled.)

Before Cathy left I suggested that she dump the boyfriend at U of C who made her uncomfortable. On the inside, I was already grooming myself as his replacement.

There was one more thing in the equation that I wanted to settle. My three-week vacation was due, and I planned on heading out to Los Angeles, where a friend of mine was going to introduce me to the L.A. gay community. If I wanted to choose sides, I owed it to myself to see what the other side had to offer.

The answer was—not much. Everybody dressed to the nines (preferably in white), called each other "Mary," and when they went to a film festival it was usually a Betty Grable film festival. Their idea of gay liberation was to have a beer at Barney's Beanery while sitting underneath his banner that said "No faggots allowed."

I was underwhelmed. (Things would change drastically a few years down the road, but we weren't there yet.)

I came back to San Francisco filled with plans for things that Cathy and I could do together. Good restaurants, Off-Broadway plays—Chicago was next only to New York when it came to Off-Broadway, and to friendly bars where we could just sit and talk and get to know each other better.

I still had the apartment above the Hut, and as I was unloading from the airport a friend of mine hollered, "Did you hear what happened to Cathy?"

I hadn't, but my friends at *Science Digest* had saved me the newspaper clippings.

Cathy had taken my advice and dropped her nutty boyfriend.

He had returned the next night, dragged her out to the parking lot and shot and killed her.

Then he'd shot and killed himself.

❧ VII ❧

I DIDN'T GO back to work for a week. What I finally did was visit my mother and tell her what had happened.

She didn't believe me.

In years past she had been the typical mother when it came to romance: Who was I dating? When was I going to get married? Who was going to take care of me when I got old? From my answers—or evasions—she probably figured I was growing up gay. She had nothing against gays—if it hadn't been for her lesbian (she never used the word) friends, her family would not exist.

Her oldest son had left the family as soon as he could find a job so he could get married. Mark had rejected her in an effort to protect himself emotionally. Dad Knox and his sons had never really been a part of her family.

I had been the only family confidant she had. I was the one who listened in silence while she told me the details of being brought up and taken care of by her close friends. I was the one to whom she confided her personal tragedies.

Now I was telling her a tragic story about a woman I had never mentioned before, a woman she had never met. She was con-

vinced I was lying because I was getting ready to leave her emotionally as well.

She had no sympathy for me; the look on her face was stony.
I took the newspaper clippings from my pocket, tore them in
two, and dropped the pieces in the wastebasket. If she wanted
to piece them together, she could.

It took me a long time to forgive her.

I went back to work, and it was business as usual. Nobody
said anything about Cathy. There was nothing to say, though
I caught the occasional glimpse of sympathy.

A few weeks later I was shaving before going to work and
stopped in midstroke.

I didn't know whose face I was shaving. I didn't really know
anything about myself. I knew what I ought to feel, I knew what
I ought to do, I knew what was expected of me in life. But I
didn't know what I really felt, I didn't know what I wanted to
do, I didn't know if anything at all was expected of me in life,
and if so, what the hell was it?

The trouble with the closet was that it had not only kept other
people out, it also had kept me in. I'd had no open relationships with people, none of the real-life experiences that formed
people, that made them what they were, that made up their
lives.

I didn't know who I was and neither did anybody else. I finally realized what my swimmer friend and the sports car driver
had gone through and exactly what my experiment with the gay
kid from the Hut had cost him and what it had cost me.

I made a few calls and found out that it was possible to enroll
as a patient in the psychiatric clinic at the University of Chicago.
I would be a guinea pig for a future shrink to work on.

I went down the next day and ended up in a sparsely furnished room with a desk and chair and a tape recorder on the desk so the would-be psychiatrist's instructor could monitor the session. There was a box of Kleenex next to it.

I had been given an instuction sheet on exactly what would happen. The process was called Rogerian therapy, and I would do most of the talking. The future shrink would prompt me from time to time, but he would never tell me what I should do or offer any suggestions. It would be a case of self-analysis, and he would be a sounding board.

I was disappointed. I thought it would be a two-way conversation and he would tell me where I had gone wrong in life and what I should do about it. But the position of this therapist was to be accepting, nonjudgmental, interested, and yet never cross the line between therapist and friend.

There was a wooden chair in front of the desk, and I sat down and tried to make myself comfortable.

After a few minutes the student shrink came in and we shook hands. I had expected an older man, a man with a lot of experience. I was convinced I needed somebody who could disassemble and then reassemble me into a more functional human being.

He looked in his early thirties (one strike against him) and stared at me with mild curiosity. He settled back in his chair and waited for me to start talking. I had thought he would start by asking me questions, but it was going to be up to me.

My first question was how many patients he had who were like me. I was still convinced I was unique.

"None," he said. "You're my first patient."

I stared at him for a long moment, wondering if I should get up and walk out or what. Then I realized this was the end of the line, I had no place else to go. But I already knew one thing: he would never lie to me.

For the first three or four sessions I babbled on about my work and what it was like to be a writer. (I learned later that his father owned a newspaper in San Diego—he knew everything there was to know about writers.)

Eventually I told him I was a closeted homosexual but hadn't really indulged in it much. He showed no reaction and after a few more sessions I told him about the kid who had been my experiment, and eventually about Cathy. I hadn't cried at the time. This time I did.

The real breakthrough came about the tenth or fifteenth session, when he finally asked a question that he was curious about.

"Frank, I know everything about you. How would you react to me if you met me outside this office, on the street?"

I looked at him blankly and said I didn't know. A few sessions later I was to find out.

We were about five minutes into the session and he suddenly held up his hand, frowning. For just a moment he was no longer a therapist but an ordinary human being with something on his mind.

"I was at the Coronet Theater the other night with my date and we ran into you and a girlfriend. I said 'hello' but you didn't respond. I thought you hadn't heard me and I repeated it. You still wouldn't respond. Why?"

I was totally shocked.

"I never saw you," I said. I was absolutely honest and he looked puzzled, then once again he was the therapist. He and his instructor would have a long conversation about me.

He said nothing more, and it was up to me to figure it out. I had been so desperately afraid that somebody would find out that I was gay, that my mind simply blanked—it wouldn't accept their presence. They didn't exist; they weren't there.

From then on I was no longer going through the motions;

I really needed therapy. No more bullshit about my job or where I worked or anything else that would put off the session.

It was hard, it tore me apart. I was looking at all those things that had frightened me, that I'd thought separated me from everybody else.

My sessions with the student therapist lasted for two years. At the end of the last session—I didn't know it would be the last—he said he wouldn't be seeing me anymore. We shook hands and he walked out of the room. I don't remember whether he ever told me his name.

I was assigned to another student therapist, but this time it didn't work. He was nervous, uncertain of himself, and there wasn't the rapport that had existed with the first man.

I left, not completely happy with myself but a good deal more confident than I had been before. I wasn't about to "come out" to members of my family, to the people where I worked, nor to strangers. With other gay men, there would be no problems. With close friends—it was worth a try.

Big George didn't seem to care one way or the other. He was casual about it. "If I ever go gay, Frank, you'll be the first person I'll look up."

Big George wasn't my type, but the realization that I even had a type surprised me.

The next person I told was something of a setback.

Jeff, another workout friend, stared at me for a long moment, then said, "It's not your fault you're sick, Frank."

At one time I would have been crushed. I wasn't, and a few years later I was glad it turned out that way. Big George had gotten married, it had failed, and his ex-wife ended up in San Francisco dancing topless at a club on Broadway. Jeff was in town for a trade show. I was living in San Francisco then; he looked me up and talked to me about how much he wanted to go to the show and see the "tits" of George's ex-wife. He was obsessive about it.

Being "sick" was a matter of interpretation.

One day Big George said he wanted me to meet somebody—a millionaire he knew on Chicago's South Side, near the University of Chicago, whom he thought I would like to know. His name was Herb.

Herb's mansion was small but it was still a mansion with a huge living room, large kitchen, and a dozen small bedrooms upstairs. Herb himself was about my size and age with fading red hair and with something of the air of a company vice president. I wasn't that far off—he had his own bond company downtown and was a small-time trader. He owned a Rolls-Royce, complete with a chauffeur who was a stunning blond, and there were two or three other good-looking young men hanging around the house.

Herb dealt in more than just stocks and bonds, but I was in no position to be judgmental. He liked young men, was what you would call an "A" gay, and knew the other wealthy gay men in Chicago. (One of them was rumored to have bought an entire high school football team. I didn't believe it.) Another rumor was that being gay would save you from the venereal diseases that were prevalent with straight sex. It didn't take me long to find out that was a lie, too. Herb also knew the hustlers who hung out around Bughouse Square on the near North Side and sometimes he'd swing by the bus station downtown and wait for the runaways to get off. A friendly man in a Rolls willing to give you a lift, buy you a meal, and put you up for a night or two? There weren't many runaways who were naive. They knew the payment required and few hesitated to pay it.

Herb was cynical; his comment on young hustlers was "If you can't fuck them, what the hell good are they?" My first reaction was why did I want to spend any more time with this guy? Shortly afterward he proved he was at least as complicated as I was. He gave me a tour of his house and on the bureau in his bedroom I noticed a large framed photograph of a young woman in her twenties. She could have been a twin of Cathy's and in many respects probably was.

Aside from his chauffeur—whom he set up with a bar when the relationship grew thin—his other love (unwanted) was a young Yugoslavian kid who worshipped the ground Herb walked on. No money was ever exchanged—the kid wouldn't accept it. He loved Herb for who he was, for his hidden generosity, for his knowledge and general grasp of the workings of the world.

The kid adored Herb and finally Herb threw him out. He couldn't stand adoration—it eventually requires that you live up to certain standards, which Herb certainly had no intention of ever doing. In Herb's world you did things for money, not for love.

One of Herb's closest friends, Max, was a stylist on the North Side of Chicago who was Herb's personal pimp. He knew a lot of the older kids in the neighborhood and sooner or later Max would let some of them know there was an easy way to earn a quick $50 so they could take their girlfriends out on a Sunday date.

Max was always subtle—there was no way you could legally pin him down. The word spread that the kids wouldn't have to do much to earn their $50 (sometimes, surprisingly little). These weren't the type of rent boys you met in bars in New York or posing on Polk Street in San Francisco. They weren't druggies or alcoholics, and it would have been difficult for a TV show to feature them as kids without a home or with abusive parents or who had been driven into prostitution for a few bucks.

For the most part, they came from good Irish families on the North Side. A few of them went to night school or college (more common than I might have thought in later years).

I now knew two types of gays—those who bought and those who sold. I was in no position to make judgments, but for the most part, the sellers seemed to be a better breed.

In any event, therapy had taught me that this was my world, the one I had to live in.

A few weeks after meeting Herb, he invited me to a party. I asked Big George if he were going and he laughed and said, "I'm not their type."

It didn't take me long to figure out what kind of party it was going to be.

Herb had beer and soft drinks set out, and that was about it. His living room was gradually filling up with older men who bought and younger men who played for pay. There was one small group of them who obviously weren't there to sell themselves. They stayed by themselves and didn't talk much to anybody.

I asked Herb about them and he said they were from the Chicago Theological Seminary, a few blocks away. They were there to buy. (I knew about the priest scandal long before it hit the front pages.)

The master of the revels was Max, who would match up pairs, and if both parties agreed, they'd disappear upstairs to one of the bedrooms.

He tried to match me up and I shook my head. It was nothing complicated—I was just shy.

The party broke up in an hour or so and one of the hustlers gave me a lift home. Neither one of us had much to say. He eyed me once or twice but he'd made his fifty bucks for the evening and wasn't really eager for any more action. I wasn't either, for different reasons.

I didn't see Herb for a few weeks and I didn't particularly want to. I hadn't found my first glimpse of gay life in Chicago that inviting.

It was the middle of winter and I was getting ready for bed when there was a knock on the door. It was obvious from the whispering that there was more than one person outside. I looked through the glass peephole in the door and was surprised to see Herb looking back. What the hell . . .

I opened the door and all three came in. Herb, Max, and the rent boy who had given me a lift a few weeks before.

"This is on the house," Max said. He looked for the light switch and flicked it off. I froze. The rent boy started with the buttons on my shirt. He was much better at taking my clothes off than I had been with the kid from the Hut.

We found the bed and suddenly there was light. Both Herb and Max had brought flashlights to watch the action.

It didn't last long—the kid was very professional—and soon they were on their way out. Max had the last line.

"I told you this was on the house; usually you tip."

I sat there in bed, the covers wrapped around me. All I could think of was that I had just lost my virginity before an audience of two guys with flashlights.

I had wanted it to happen sometime, though not like this. But if I'd had any doubts about being gay, I didn't have any now.

❧ VIII ❧

MY WORLD TURNED upside down a month later. *Popular Mechanics* and *Science Digest* were sold to Hearst (based in New York). They actually wanted *Popular Mechanics*; *Science Digest* was just part of the package. H. H. Windsor, the original publisher, had printed the magazines on his own presses—editorial was on the fourth floor and we could hear the rumble of the presses all day but now those were sold.

Science Digest was eventually turned into a glossy science magazine to compete with *Omni*, a very thick, popular science magazine (with a little science fiction), which sold a million copies as soon as it hit the stands. The newsstands were quickly glutted with pop science magazines, most of which soon died.

I'd left *Science Digest* with the New York move and went back to writing science fiction. My fortunes shifted again when Hefner sold his distribution contract of *Playboy* for a reported $1 million, which left his old distributor with no "sophisticated men's magazine."

Except *Rogue*. It was successful in its own right but could hardly be called "sophisticated." The distributor promptly gave Hamling permission to go to slick paper, print color photographs and full-page cartoons, and most important of all, he could print a centerfold.

Hamling was the editor and publisher; his wife, Frances, was executive editor; and I held down the spot of associate editor. Lead fiction was by a hot science fiction author, Harlan Ellison, who was to become associate editor with the third issue—probably one of the smarter moves Hamling made. Ellison was an offbeat and very prolific writer who "thought outside the box." (At one point he became the editor of Regency Books—a legitimate paperback imprint published by Hamling.) It was Ellison's idea to bring Lenny Bruce aboard as a columnist for *Rogue* and also to publish stories by Charles Beaumont under the pseudonym of "C. B. Lovehill."

Beaumont was a frequent contributor to *Playboy*, and it occurred to Harlan that maybe Beaumont had a few stories lying around that *Playboy* might have rejected or thought were too unusual for the magazine. I was designated as the one to call up Lovehill to see what the situation was.

I did, and the voice on the other end of the line said, "Frank, don't you remember me?" My childhood friend—Charles McNutt.

After a few months at *Rogue* and Regency (both as an editor and frequent contributor), Harlan left; the once-friendly relationship between him and Hamling had broken.

The argument may have been about money, though Harlan was always well paid, but more likely about Ellison's reluctance to edit more of Hamling's erotic paperbacks. Ellison also wanted to try his luck in Hollywood and was very successful, writing scripts for *Burke's Law*, *Route 66*, *The Outer Limits*, and *Star Trek*, among others. He wrote what was probably the best script for *Star Trek*: "The City on the Edge of Forever."

Rogue went slick about the time that Hamling discovered the answer to something that had bothered him much of his life. At one time, at lunch some years before, Hamling admitted, "If I had one dollar, I'd want ten, and if I had ten, I'd want a hundred, and if I had a hundred, I'd want a million." He said it as something he didn't quite understand and didn't quite approve of.

It took a while for Hamling to learn a very bitter lesson. Money made the world go around, and despite working his butt off, he had ended up with not much. Despite the restrictions, *Rogue* had been a minor success, but even going slick was not a sure thing when it came to money.

One story of how Hamling started his line of stroke books is that he saw some sexy paperbacks out of New York and thought of taking them a step further. The other is that a writer already in the field approached Hamling with the idea of raunchier books. The possibilities that more explicit books offered were obvious. The investment would be cheap, the returns could be . . . huge. He started two lines of books to be published by the Blake Pharmaceutical Company, at the back of the same building as *Rogue*.

Two officers from the local state's attorney's office once came looking for Blake and first stumbled into the offices of *Rogue*. When asked about the Blake Pharmaceutical Company, Patty, our secretary, drew herself up and acidly asked, "Does this look like a drugstore to you?"

Nightstand Books and Midnight Readers quickly built up an audience. There was no price on them—they were sold to stores and dealers for whatever the traffic would bear, which in turn sold them under the counter for a hefty markup. The books were cheaply printed by a small printer in Ohio owned by two deacons in the local church; their usual product was children's books with colorful, religious covers. The ladies of the congregation boxed up the stroke books for shipping, apparently unaware of just what the books were about (or more likely were paid well enough not to care).

One of the books became a million-copy-plus bestseller. Titled *Song of the Loon*, it was about a love affair between a horny cowboy and an Indian (or maybe a lot of Indians).

Everybody made money off *Loon*—except for the author, who was paid the standard price of $800, while Hamling made millions and the store owners who sold them made thousands.

My job at the new *Rogue* was to be somewhat varied. Once I was asked to edit one of the stroke books, did so, and then told Hamling that was it. I had enough problems with my sex life outside the office; I didn't need to work editing books about variations of the old in-and-out as part of my job.

Aside from that one incident, I didn't pay much attention to Blake and its sex books, although some of the editors were to become my friends. I was enchanted by the possibility of competing with *Playboy*, a dream that took years to die (it was doomed from the start but I really did think we could become number two).

Hamling published the stroke books for money. He never read them, never labored over them as he once had over *Stardust* (a glossy, printed semipro magazine) or *Imagination*, his professional science fiction digest magazine), and no longer had much of an interest in science fiction, though every now and then the occasional science fiction story would crop up in *Rogue*. The stroke books were strictly cash-and-carry and no problems.

Hefner published *Playboy*, which had now become a not-so-small gold mine, as a labor of love. He picked the covers, he picked the centerfold girls, he passed judgment on the cartoons, and came up with the ideas for the "*Playboy* philosophy," which the editors for the "front of the book" turned into English. Fiction was left largely to Ray Russell and his successor, Robie

Macauley, while articles and interviews were left in the more-than-capable hands of A. C. Spectorsky.

Hamling became a multimillionaire, though he never did catch up to Hefner nor did he ever receive the satisfaction that *Playboy* gave to Hefner.

Hugh Marston Hefner was a respected publisher, even though he published a magazine that was criticized by women's groups and had an occasional run-in with the law. Hamling never achieved the same level of respectability. Young men—and frequently older men—fell in love with *Playboy*'s centerfold girl and the model on the cover. And then there were the interviews and the fiction and the fashion tips. Teenagers and lonely men took Hamling's books to bed with them, but love had nothing to do with it.

In one case, Hamling was a hero. A clerk was picked up by the police for selling some of the Nightstand books, and Hamling paid his legal bills. The case went to the Supreme Court, and Hamling won on a somewhat curious point. (Stanley Fleischman, legal counsel for most of the sex book and magazine publishers in California, was the lawyer. A badly crippled hunchback who walked with canes, he had the sympathy vote the moment he stepped before the Court.) Those with money and culture could go to museums and admire the nudes by Rubens and others, but the poor and culturally uneducated could not. It was a case of discrimination.

Afterward, *Playboy*, which had been denied a mailing permit, applied again and got it with no hassle, quoting Hamling's case as the precedent. I don't think Hefner or other publishers of "sophisticated men's magazines" or stroke books ever thanked Hamling for his efforts.

FOR ME, *ROGUE* became an obsession. I realized it would always live in the shadow of *Playboy*, but at the same time I thought maybe it could become a runner-up. We carried fiction by Graham Greene and Charles Beaumont (under the pseudonym of C. B. Lovehill), most of which were *Playboy* rejects, though Ray Russell, fiction editor of *Playboy* at the time, admitted that some of our best "Lovehill" stories should have appeared in *Playboy*. And we published a number of offbeat stories by editor Harlan Ellison.

We ran articles by Arthur C. Clarke (he of *2001*) and a few by Hunter S. Thompson before he became the Hunter S. Thompson we all knew and loved. Except for me. In a cover letter accompanying his first submission, Thompson wrote that his recreation included taking potshots with his BB gun at the gays going to the bathhouse at the bottom of his hill in Big Sur. (The article itself was a love story to Big Sur.) I had to grit my teeth when we accepted his second piece, a short story about murder at sea. The hero was no Travis McGee, but the story wasn't bad. Thompson's skill with a BB gun I chalked up to a reflection of American attitudes at the time, and besides, an editor should never let his personal life interfere with his professional one. (So much for embryonic gay liberation.)

We published articles by big names (for the period)—Ben Hecht, William Saroyan, and Philip Wylie, among others—but the articles I was proudest of were those that were in-your-face and that I thought *Playboy* would never publish. They were the ones that were both offbeat and showed great bravery by the writer. Jerry DeMuth, a staffer for Regency Books (Hamling's legitimate line), wrote a first-person article on SNCC—the Student Nonviolent Coordinating Committee—when it was involved in registering black voters down South. Jerry was never shot at or roughed up, but that wasn't because he wasn't exposed; he was just lucky.

Despite the high quality—in my opinion—of our fiction and articles, we had two built-in handicaps. One was the size of the magazine. We had 80 pages, while *Playboy* was constantly increasing in size, to 120, 150, etc.

The other one were the centerfold girls we ran. Frankly, I was a little bit at sea in picking girls who would appeal to our presumably heterosexual and very masculine readers. Hamling was a happily married man (a handicap under the circumstances) and had a physical difficulty—he was addicted to wearing sunglasses. This was most apparent when we went to the printing plant to inspect the initial copies of our centerfolds just coming off the press. The object was to call for color corrections. Much to the hilarity of the printers, who hid behind the presses to smother their laughter, Hamling never took off his sunglasses while calling for corrections.

A younger and considerably more randy Hugh Hefner suffered from none of these handicaps. He loved women and was an expert at picking out those models who typified the girl next door in the first blush of youth. The public obviously agreed with him.

When Harlan left I inherited Lenny Bruce, who was almost always late with his column. One time I had made up his column by excerpting some of his comments about our gatefolds in his letters to Hamling.

Lenny Bruce was a man ahead of his time. The cops used to roust him at various clubs for routines they claimed were obscene (today you can see and hear much more obscene material on television and your computer—and without paying a cover charge). There was only one time when I saw Bruce at a loss for words. He had a gig at a nightclub in Chicago but the day before, its liquor license had been revoked. Bruce's audience that evening were high school kids out for a night before their prom. Bruce knew he couldn't use his usual routines, so he had to wing it. He flopped—badly. It was obvious then that he had worked on most of his routines beforehand and that this night his usual audience had been pulled out from under him.

We lost Bruce a few issues after that. He had sold his autobiography to *Playboy*—the same autobiography from which we had excerpted a column months before. What *Playboy* printed was exactly the portion that we had, word for word.

When I heard that *Playboy* had bought it, I told A. J. Budrys (formerly of Regency Books but who had defected to *Playboy*) that Rogue had published part of Bruce's autobiography previously, but he didn't believe me. When I finally saw it in *Playboy* I sent AJ the copy of *Rogue* and he in turn showed it to A. C. Spectorsky, head of the magazine division. The ever-phlegmatic Spectorsky simply shrugged and said, "I guess they'll have to sue us."

I never told Hamling about it—AJ was a friend.

Lenny Bruce died a few years later. The police found him

sitting on the toilet, a needle still stuck in his arm. The word was that the police had put it there so the news photographers would know the cops were busy upholding the morals of the community.

Myself, I suspected that there wasn't a more moral man in show business than Lenny Bruce.

(We ran a photo feature on Lenny Bruce and his ex-wife, Honey, in our December 1960 issue. Bruce had written the caption for a partial nude shot of Honey: "I still think that Honey can cut most of the Woolworth clerks you guys seem to favor." He was absolutely right.)

Garry Marshall (a very popular film producer later on and an acquaintance from Northwestern) and his sidekick Fred Freeman both had articles on humor in the same issue. Years later, when *Rogue* was a fond memory, I dropped in on Marshall and Freeman at their offices on the Desilu lot in Hollywood—they were producing *Hey, Landlord* at the time—and applied for a writer's job. I got turned down, but as second prize they give me several free tickets to *I Love Lucy*. It was an act of mercy—when it came to writing sitcoms I would have been horribly out of my depth.

❧ X ❧

THE FIRST FEW issues of the new *Rogue* came out in 1959, and we tried for a more serious bent than *Playboy*. One of our major efforts along those lines was when we reviewed the movie *The Intruder* in an early 1960s issue (to the best of my knowledge, we were the only publication that did). We had run the article by Jerry DeMuth about his adventures with SNCC, and we thought this would be a good follow-up. We had some terrific photographs from the film and a great article by O. C. Ritch. It was also one piece I was intimately connected with. We ran it in the back of the book, but in retrospect, we should have splashed a blurb on the front cover.

We decided to review the movie based on the book by Charles Beaumont ("C. B. Lovehill"). It concerned a northern rabble-rouser who goes down South to the little fictional town of Caxton, Missouri, which had just started to desegregate its schools. Adam Cramer (played by William Shatner) claims he is a representative of the "Patrick Henry Society" and is intent on stirring up trouble between blacks and whites embroiled in the desegregation of their high school.

The film was shot in two towns in southern Missouri, and the actual desegregation of some eight years before was still a sensitive subject in the minds of the townspeople. The only filmmakers willing to produce the movie with no changes to Beaumont's text were the Corman brothers, who had never read a classic horror story they didn't want to film. This was to be a switch for them, their first serious endeavor in filmmaking. They had approached the majors for funding, but no one was interested in as hot a property as *The Intruder* promised to be.

The budget was pared to the bone, less than a hundred grand—most of the money coming from the Corman brothers themselves, who mortgaged their houses. To save money they decided to shoot on location in an area that if it weren't for the occupation by Northern troops in the Civil War, would have joined the South.

The natives never forgot it, and at the start, the desegregation of the schools was strictly token. Two blacks in a white high school were one too many.

Whether or not the Corman brothers realized how dangerous the shoot would be, I don't know. But they soon found out. Hard looks and lack of cooperation were the order of the day. Many of the actors were locals, and as a precaution the script was handed out daily—page by page.

Charlie Beaumont called me and asked if I wanted to be in his film. He didn't go into details but hinted it might be on the dangerous side. (I found out later that he carried a tear gas canister disguised as a fountain pen for personal protection.)

I asked Big George to come along—hey, an adventure, he was all for it! We packed some overnight bags, and George found a baseball bat he thought might come in handy if there was trouble. Hours later we drove into Charleston, Missouri, site of most of the shooting. From the looks people gave us on the street, we were more of those damned northern types coming into town.

We found a motel, grabbed a sandwich at a luncheonette, and hit one of the local bars—all white, of course. About two beers later a drunk sitting on a stool next to George wised off, and George grabbed the edge of his bar stool and spun it around so the drunk went flying off. A moment later it was our turn to go flying out of there—the other patrons didn't like us.

It was late and we headed for the motel. George put the bat by the side of his bed and we finally dropped asleep. The next morning we discovered that while George had remembered the bat, he had forgotten to lock the door.

The shooting was done in sections, and the last three—the most inflammatory—were scheduled for that Saturday. They included a Ku Klux Klan automobile parade through the center of the "badlands" (the other side of the tracks, or "niggertown," as some of the locals called it), followed by the burning of a cross and blowing up the front of the local black church. Big George was cast as one of the Klansmen burning the cross; I rode in the automobile parade and later shoveled the debris off the top of the church when they blew off the false front.

William Shatner, immortalized a few years later as the intrepid Captain Kirk, played the smooth-as-silk Adam Kramer. (It was Shatner's best role—he'd had stage experience and it showed.) Two of Charlie Beaumont's friends—George Clayton Johnson and William F. Nolan—had also been invited to appear in the film. All three had frequently written scripts for *The Twilight Zone*. Beaumont played the principal of the local high school being integrated, Nolan portrayed a southern "cracker" and Johnson a psychotic version of the same. (George could have made a career out of playing psychotics.)

Whether any of them knew what they were getting into, I didn't know. Shatner was a Canadian and ignorant of a lot of American politics. Johnson and Nolan thought it would be a hoot until they got down there.

The KKK drive through the badlands had struck all of us as

highly dangerous. What would happen? A riot? Stoning? We were genuinely frightened. I was sitting in a car with a sheet over my head, running every five minutes for the gas station on the corner because my bladder had sprung a leak. At one point a curious black man poked his head through the car window and asked if we were in some kind of "pee-rade." "Yeah," I mumbled, "some kind of pee-rade."

We were totally unprepared for what actually happened. "Hey, they're shooting a real movie in the middle of our town!" Everybody in "Caxton" showed up to mingle in the badlands, and nobody seemed to care whether they were standing next to a white or a black in the crowd. It was carnival time (the cameras picked up a knifing on film but it wasn't serious and the injured woman recovered).

The cross burning went off without a hitch, and when they blew the false front off the church I dutifully shoveled a wheelbarrow of debris over the front. In the spirit of good fellowship I asked the local kid helping why he'd signed up for the movie.

He shrugged. "I just wanted to see what you nigger lovers from up North were like."

Everybody packed in a hurry the next morning and left town before the locals could put two and two together and figure out just what the movie had been all about. Big George and I picked up Charles Barnes, the black kid who was the hero of the film, and drove him back to Chicago with us. He would stay with his grandmother and major in engineering at a nearby university. He had had enough of the movies.

His mother had fried up a huge vat of chicken, and we nibbled on that and compared notes about our Big Adventure. It never showed on film, but Barnes had been frightened all the way through. If he had stayed in town, he was convinced that sooner or later somebody would have taken a shot at him.

The locals cast in bit parts did a great job (the sheriff was played by a man who could put his thumb on the aluminum top of a salt shaker and punch through it). I heard later that a few of the locals had actually traveled to Hollywood to see what it was like and maybe find work.

It had been a three-week shoot of dodging the sheriff, of doing our best to delude the townspeople, of being kicked off the grounds of one high school and driving to another a few miles down the road to finish a scene.

Shatner was a wonder. His most inflammatory scene was actually silent for the first take. He realized there could be a real riot if the crowd heard what he was going to say. He explained in a hoarse voice that he had laryngitis and had to save his voice for later. The crowd followed the orders of the camera crew and moved this way and that, shouting and hollering as they watched the silent Shatner wave his arms.

After it was dark and almost everybody had gone home, the cameras dollied in to get a close-up of Shatner actually shouting the words that could have caused a genuine riot. One spectator in the crowd who hadn't left with the others frowned and asked Shatner if he believed what he'd just said. Shatner shrugged and said, "Hey, it's just a movie, fella."

The Intruder was the only film the Cormans made that lost money. There was no way it was going to play in any theater down South. Distributors up North boycotted the film—they felt the unvarnished use of the "n-word" would be too much for their audience.

The film can be had only on DVD, and while crude and amateurish in spots, it is the only film ever made that gave an honest portrayal of what desegregation was really like, or what the people involved actually believed.

≼ XI ≽

ROGUE MADE A little money, added eight more pages, and doubled the staff. We now had a circulation department (which didn't do much to increase the circulation) and an ad department (which didn't do much to bring in ads). Understandable, I suppose. We were playing Jack the Giant Killer but no way were we going to slay the giant.

I worked for *Playboy* much later on, a well-staffed, very professional organization where the going was sometimes rough. Working at *Rogue*, on the other hand, was frequently a hoot. Looking back, it was one of the most enjoyable times of my life. Hamling stayed down in San Diego most of the time, masterminding the stroke books and visiting Evanston maybe once a month to see how his overworked mice were doing. A lot of our slack attitudes were due to Bruce Elliott, a recent hire from New York, who introduced us to the three-hour lunch. It would start at the "dark place," a bar on Howard Street—which cut dry Evanston off from Chicago—and end at the office with most of us carrying the remains of our liquid lunch in a takeout coffee cup.

(I never did find out what Elliott did in his position as executive editor. I think he spent most of his time trying to subvert the entire staff, and he probably came close.)

Second in popularity were the occasional office fights with Ping-Pong-ball rifles. One day Bruce Glassner—another recent hire—was hit in the eye with a ball and we hustled him over to the eye doctor. The doctor examined him carefully, then called his assistant to come in and take a look. "You won't believe what did this."

Bruce's eyes remained intact and still blue.

Our two new employees, David Stevens and Bruce Glassner, had taken an apartment together on Chicago's near North Side. Bruce had escaped from the Illinois Institute of Technology, and David was a star graduate (so he said) from Syracuse University, a top journalism school. Bruce was a straight arrow, more or a lot less, and David was a would-be world adventurer who later became a life member of the Chicago chapter of the Adventurers' Club. To David the Sahara eventually became as familiar as somebody else's front yard. David and Bruce had the second floor in their apartment building, and the third was perennially occupied by airline stewardesses who considered David and Bruce horny godsends. I stayed over one night and the next morning all three of us jammed ourselves into Dave's Morgan for the ride back up to Evanston. It was winter and the Outer Drive was covered with snow and black ice (invisible to the naked eye). We hit a patch, did a 360, and ended up on the shoulder, still pointing in the right direction.

The Morgan was a British car with a wooden chassis. If anybody had hit us, they would have had to dig us out from under a pile of toothpicks. We finished the drive in absolute silence. Once safely in the office, I raced to the john and wrung out my shorts.

After hours we frequently had dinner at The Bear, a small club run by some of the actors from Chicago's Second City troupe. It didn't last long, but while it did they had a chef who was easily one of the best in the city. They also had a cigarette machine that sold Wings and Spuds, brands that hadn't been carried in the States for years. Where The Bear got them, I never knew.

No club is without its entertainment, and The Bear frequently showcased new talent. One night after dinner the stage was taken over by a performer named Bob Dylan, complete with guitar and harmonica. We listened to his set and all agreed the young man couldn't sing.

Six months later Dylan was featured at Chicago's Arie Crown Theater—capacity five thousand, and it was packed. His first albums had been released and were sensations. I kept wishing I had listened more closely to him at The Bear.

Those of us on the editorial end of the magazine didn't mingle much with the production people, the salesmen, or the art department. We were a little, closely knit group, and we were younger and more adventuresome than the staffers at *Playboy*. At one time we were going to do a piece on a small porno film outfit in Chicago. It would be an inside job, telling the reader what it was like to be in the porn business.

The problem was we didn't know anybody working there. A young and enthusiastic staffer volunteered to infiltrate the organization and get the inside scoop. When he came back that day he was very quiet and didn't want to talk about it. Another staffer suggested that we go down and watch some of the outtakes and write it as an exposé.

Our volunteer refused to go, insisting he had something better to do. The rest of us trooped on down and crowded into the little screening room to take notes. For once we were shocked. Our embarrassed staffer was the third one up, in the buff, and trying valiantly to perform. But it's one thing to have sex in the privacy of your bedroom and quite another to try to do it on a soundstage with a director and a cameraman watching.

Our undercover (no pun intended) staffer flunked, but the rest of us were kind enough not to say anything about it.

The magazine was doing very well by now. The staff numbered twenty-nine, counting the salesmen, the additions to the art staff (we had a very good one), etc. Some of us even got small raises.

None of us realized how soon the gravy train would end.

❧ XII ❧

MY LIFE WORKING at *Rogue* was a lot of fun. My private life was anything but. I had to be constantly aware of what I said and what I did, what jokes I laughed at, my response to various comments regarding "faggots" and "queers"—used mostly in a descriptive sense more than a pejorative one. What would have been the response if I'd come out? I wasn't willing to risk it. Maybe nobody would have given a damn.

Maybe.

When I finally couldn't stand the strain of living a nonsexual life, I called Max. It was a little like ordering a pizza—in an hour or so the product would arrive.

Usually there was no social intercourse at all, very little talking. Ten minutes later they left and the sexual pressure was off for another two weeks.

I was envious of everybody else on staff who had girlfriends, boyfriends, husbands, or wives, and all of whom led a presumably normal sexual life.

Sometimes the rent boy was surprisingly friendly. Business was business, but one time the hustler suggested we visit the yacht basin on Lake Michigan, where he worked. We went to the yacht basin more than once, and the last time I saw him he gave me a large envelope, saying it was for me.

I opened it later, and inside was a photograph of a four-year-old boy smiling at the camera. Written on the side was his name, "Frank," and his age. I hadn't known his father long enough, but it was the thought that counted. His father was straight; sex on a Sunday was a hobby that paid well. And if you were lucky, you had a friendly and interesting john who treated you as something more than a male prostitute.

Another time there was a hasty knock on the door, and a kid I had been with several times ran in, scared to death. The skin was broken between two fingers and he was bleeding. Apparently he had been in a bar when a fight had broken out, there were shots, and a bullet had—luckily for him—passed through his fingers and broken the skin but it was nothing serious.

I cleaned it and stopped the bleeding and bandaged it. He was calmer now and automatically started to take off his pants, ready to thank me the only way he knew how.

I waved him off. He'd had enough trauma for the evening and so had I.

My other good deed involved a kid I'd met through Max but afterward would meet at a coffee shop near my apartment. He was a chess player and a good one. This time when we went to my apartment I asked him what he wanted to be in life. He said "an artist," and I asked him what he was going to do about it. The Art Institute of Chicago had night classes, he said, but tuition was a hundred bucks.

I wrote him a check for a hundred, and when he started to take off his clothes I held up my hand and said, "That's a gift." He looked embarrassed, said "Thanks," and apparently quit the hustling business. I never saw him again but thought of him a lot, wondering if he ever got to art school.

(He never forgot me, either. One time Dave Stevens, now a *Playboy* employee, was drinking in a near North Side bar, and my name came up when he was talking to the bartender. The bartender brightened and was suddenly all over him—did he know St. Frank? He wouldn't tell David how he knew me, and I wasn't about to tell David how I knew his bartender.)

The star of Max's show was easily the most handsome hustler in Chicago. He was also the secretary of his junior class at an eastern university. Why he was putting in time as a rent boy, I never knew. Jeff Hensley didn't need the money, but I think, to him, it wasn't money but power. Every john in town wanted him. He was smart, well educated, in his very early twenties, and I think was proud of his fame. He was good in bed and I could easily understand his popularity. Of all the rent boys in Chicago, he was the class act.

As to be expected, there were also legends about him. The most popular was that he had spent a summer in the Bahamas and seduced a man working for Barclays Bank who embezzled money to prolong the relationship.

Jeff came back to Chicago—so the story went—hired a Rolls-Royce and driver, and one by one took each of his johns (I wasn't one of them) out to dinner. I never quite believed it, but it was a great story and only enhanced his reputation.

All of us wondered what the vintner bought one half so precious as the stuff he sold, and one night we found out. Jeff's boyfriend came up from the Caribbean for a visit. He was a light-skinned mulatto who made even Jeff look homely. A few years later I left the city to visit Haight-Ashbury and stayed longer than I had planned. When I returned I ran into Jeff again when I visited one of Herb's longtime friends.

Jeff was much different from the rent boy I'd once known. He had put on some weight and lost some of his looks along with most of his charm. In the years I had been away he'd gone to law school and picked up a degree.

Sometime after that I bought a copy of a newsmagazine and read about Roy Cohn's yacht being blown up on its way from Miami to New York. The reporter got most of his information from a young spokesman in Roy Cohn's office.

Jeff.

It wasn't six degrees of separation between myself and Roy Cohn—it was only one.

Hanging out with Herb from time to time was an education all its own. He liked to go to the occasional *concours d'élégance*, and once I went along. I didn't even know how to drive but I could appreciate the beauty of the old cars. One time Herb had another young friend along besides his usual driver. The young man's name was René, a French Canadian. We became something of a number, and then one time I asked him why he hustled.

"It's my body," he said defiantly. "I'll do what I want with it."

Herb and I tried to get him a work permit so he could stay in the United States, but no luck, and eventually he went back to Canada. It was the wrong move. He stole something or got into a street fight—I never did get the full story—and was sent to jail. He was a cute kid and within a few weeks one of the regular convicts tried to rape him. René had apparently foreseen this possibility and fashioned himself a knife from a bedspring or some other metal. He knifed the would-be molester and killed him.

The rest of the story I'm sure was embroidered. René, so the story went, was hanged for murder. I checked, and the death penalty had been outlawed in Canada a year or two before his return.

The first part of the story I believed. The rest of the story I didn't. But I doubt that René ever saw the light of day again.

Another time Herb and his blond lover drove down to Mississippi. I went along as a travel companion. I knew that Herb was an expert on old southern mansions dating from the Civil War, and I was curious. Herb knew them all—he had been down there several times before. The aging houses looked like something out of *Gone with the Wind*. The winding dirt road leading through the backwoods to a mansion with the white front pillars peeling paint.

The slave quarters were in back, crumbling and broken down, with blank eyes where the windows had once been—if there had ever been any windows.

The next day we drove to New Orleans, where Herb met an old friend for dinner. "Old" was not the word. Our dinner companion was maybe eighteen, a handsome kid who looked a little older than he actually was and slightly worn around the edges. Dinner talk consisted primarily of him reminiscing when he was the belle of the ball in New Orleans at age sixteen. He was very proud that he had been the most popular rent boy in the city. It was the high point of his life and I had the feeling that when he was thirty or forty it would still be the high point of his life.

Herb and his chauffeur drove on to Los Angeles, and I caught a plane back to Chicago. Shortly afterward the world shifted for gays. The Chicago Police Department had become increasingly corrupt, especially when it came to shaking down gays. The shakedowns were an important part of their monthly income.

It had gotten to the point where the mayor and the governor of the state were faced with disbanding the Chicago Police Department, calling in the state National Guard to police the city, and restaffing the police department all over again.

There was, of course, a more practical way: change the criminal code of justice.

Changing the code could be done, but to get it passed would

require the cooperation of institutions that normally would not be cooperating. The newspapers volunteered to downplay the story. The archbishop of Chicago agreed not to allow mention of the code in Catholic churches.

The complaints of the police department were effectively muffled. They still had their house organ, but the only people who saw it were the police themselves.

When the revised code passed the state legislature the story was relegated to the back pages of the newspapers with an innocent headline. I was thumbing through the newspaper and almost missed it.

It was now legal for consenting adults over the age of eighteen to sleep together.

This was two years before 1969's Stonewall, and Illinois was the first state to amend its legal code to allow consensual sex.

Adlai Stevenson was the governor of Illinois at the time and was primarily responsible for pushing through the changes. (He was now known as "St. Adlai" to the gay community.)

But there was a small catch that somehow Herb had missed. The age of consent was still eighteen. One time Herb picked up a runaway from the bus terminal who was underage. The police got suspicious about the kid, checked his phony ID, then sweated him for a list of the people he'd spent the night with.

A few days later two neatly dressed plainclothesmen showed up at Herb's front door and wanted to talk to him. They said they recognized that he was a pillar of the community and the incident with the young boy was really unfortunate. But there was a way to make it go away. For a small donation of $3,500. I heard later it was split among the arresting officers, the bailiff of the court, and the judge. (I don't know whether this was true, but considering the police corruption at the time, it probably was.)

For myself, the new code meant that my calls to Max were drastically diminished. I was now on my own.

With freedom came a desire to experiment. We had a new hire in the office, Carla. She was trim, probably in her early thirties, and all the straight men in the office gave her the eye. So did I. There were two sexes in the world, and I only knew one. With Carla there was no real desire or affection—it would be another experiment. When it came to sex, Carla liked to take in stray cats, and I certainly qualified.

She wasn't interested in the theater or dinner beforehand, none of the preliminaries. I got undressed, but undressing her presented problems. I had never taken the clothes off a woman before, I didn't know where the snaps were on her bra nor much of anything else. I wasn't very good, but she helped. There was very little kissing, very little affection, a great deal of doubt and dislike on my part for the whole procedure.

Much to my surprise, I could function. I felt a lot different getting out of bed. For all practical purposes, I now felt like a straight man and had the experience to prove it.

It carried over to the next day, and I came back that night. It wasn't any better, but my badge of straight manhood was now a bit brighter. The next afternoon I celebrated and got thoroughly drunk on gin—the worst kind of drunk in the world. I went back again the third night, but this time hid behind a tree to see if she were entertaining anybody else. My experience with heterosexuality had been brief, and now I had gone full circle. I was jealous.

Her visitor was a kid nicknamed "Superman" for what I figured were all the right reasons. Then it hit me and I sobered up. My three-day course as a practicing heterosexual was over. What the hell was I doing? If nothing else, my experiment proved that while I might be many things in the world, a heterosexual wasn't one of them. I wasn't physically attracted to her, by my lights she wasn't very good (more teeth than Jaws), my badge of manhood meant no more to me than it did to a hundred million other men who were capable of enjoying what I found, in the last analysis, to be difficult and traumatic.

We got along all right at work, though both of us were very formal. When she left, we corresponded briefly. I found out later that she had left my letters lying around so her new husband would find them. They helped in the divorce she subsequently got.

Years later a mutual friend told me she had kept a diary and let him read the page she'd written about me. Remembering "Superman," I had a pretty good idea of what she wrote.

Shortly afterward—this was at a time when sex between consenting adults was now legal—I realized once again that I was on my own. I had gone the distance, I had spent time on both sides of the sexual fence.

This time it was much more logical, no experiment. I teamed up with Joseph, a young man who had been dumped by a visitor to Herb's house who in turn had dumped me.

We rejects had something in common. We shacked up for a month of nights in Joseph's apartment on the North Side. The only furniture were two chairs, a table, and two sleeping bags. Plus a stereo along with a stack of records.

There were no curtains—we just pulled down the shades.

For a month we curled up with each other, had simple sex, and fell asleep in each other's arms listening to Janis Joplin.

It was as close to paradise as I ever got.

❧ XIII ❧

AFTER A YEAR or two at *Rogue*, my social life—as opposed to my sexual—began to pick up. Charlie Beaumont came to town to see friends and editors at *Playboy* and one night took me out to dinner at Palmer House, an old-time Chicago hotel with a classy dining room. Halfway through the salad, the waiter came over with a telephone, plugged it into an outlet near the table, and handed the phone to Charlie.

"Hollywood, Mr. Beaumont."

I don't remember what the deal was, but I do recall turning a vivid green on the inside. The call probably had something to do with *The Twilight Zone*, for which Charlie had written a number of scripts, or maybe *The Wonderful World of the Brothers Grimm*, being directed by George Pal at the time and for which Charlie had written the screenplay.

Charlie had gotten to Hollywood, I thought, and here I was working on a second-rate skin book and buying articles for a nickel a word.

Another time when he was in town, Charlie took me over to Hefner's mansion on the near North Side. The vast living room was crowded with people I didn't know scattered among the ferns. Charlie introduced me to all of them—some I knew by reputation—and then ordered hamburgers from Hefner's "man." Another time I turned green as grass.

Some months later I was invited to the mansion once again and this time I threatened to punch somebody out for the first time in my life.

At *Rogue* we wanted to run some photographs of The Gate of Horn, Chicago's hippest nightclub, featuring pictures of folk singers such as the Clancy Brothers and Odetta, and comics such as Lenny Bruce. Along with the photographs we needed some super captioning as to who was who, plus a short history of the club.

The question was who we could get to write it. I don't remember who suggested that Shel Silverstein, one of the leading visual humorists at *Playboy*, would be great for the piece. We knew he was friends with the performers and could write a nice, nostalgic article.

Great idea, obviously, but it would never work. Silverstein wasn't about to write for us. "Besides," I added, "we'd need him to sign a release."

Ann, a relatively new girl on the staff, pretty and red-haired, said quietly, "I can get us one."

"Sure, sure," I said, "you do that" and forgot about it.

A few days later she showed up with a signed release. We ran the article with Shel's name as the byline on the piece and were very proud of ourselves. A few weeks later Beaumont was in town again and it was over to the mansion for a beer and hamburgers. I was halfway through mine when Shel came in and Charlie, with a smile on his face, hastened to introduce me.

"Shel, I'd like you to meet Frank Robinson—he's the editor of *Rogue*."

In a split second Shel was in my face, screaming, "You son of a bitch, you almost cost me my job! I have an exclusive contract with *Playboy*, you prick!"

I was all apologies. "I had no idea," I said—I really hadn't. "If I'd known, we never would have run it."

It was beginning to occur to me just how Ann had gotten the signed release.

Shel continued to erupt, I continued to apologize, and finally I couldn't stand it any longer. In my best steely tone of voice I said, "Would you like to step out into the hall, Shel?"

I knew perfectly well that the other guests wouldn't allow us to throw a punch, but if we had, all Shel had to do was exhale and I would probably have collapsed. As it was, Shel turned and stalked away and I glared at Charlie, who knew damned well what would happen.

"Thanks a lot, Charlie."

Years later I met Shel in Haight-Ashbury—he had a houseboat anchored off Sausalito—and we became friends. One day we walked past a man standing before the Straight Theater and Shel said, "Would you like to meet him, Frank? That's Herb Gardner."

Gardner had written *A Thousand Clowns*, my favorite film— I must have seen it half a dozen times.

I shook my head, embarrassed.

Shel was surprised. "Don't you like it when somebody comes up to you and says they read your latest story and loved it?"

So I dug my toes into the cement, walked over to Gardner, and mumbled, "Gee, Mr. Gardner, I saw *A Thousand Clowns*, and it's one of my favorite movies."

He shook my hand, grinned, and said, "Hey, thanks!"

Unsolicited praise from a total stranger who loved what you did is the best kind.

I finally caught up with Beaumont filmwise when one day our tough-as-nails receptionist—Patty—called from the front reception area, "Frank, there's a Mr. Paul on the phone—wants to talk to you."

"I don't know any Mr. Paul," I grumbled.

"He says it's important."

I took the call and a heavily accented voice said, "Mr. Robinson, I am your greatest fan."

It was George Pal, calling from Hollywood. He had talked MGM into signing for a film based on *The Power*. He asked if I wanted to write the screenplay, and like an idiot, I turned him down—I still had hopes of catching up with *Playboy*. I recommended Charlie Beaumont, who had recommended the book to Pal in the first place. Pal hesitated, then said that Charlie was up to his neck in assignments.

Beaumont couldn't have done it, I found out later. He was in the early stages of premature Alzheimer's, and his writing days were over.

Making the movie wasn't easy. MGM was in a stock option battle with Kirk Kerkorian, a big-time movie mogul, and needed money to fight him. *The Power* starred George Hamilton, who was dating one of LBJ's daughters. MGM hoped to tap Texas money through him. Whatever George wanted when it came to the film, naturally George got.

What he wanted was a new script and a new ending. He got both. It was the second script for the film by John Gay, writer of *Separate Tables* and *Run Silent, Run Deep*. His first effort followed the book almost exactly, and he was happy with it. His second draft was a butcher job.

The film was produced by Pal but directed by Byron Haskin, a friend of Pal's. I had moved to San Francisco's Haight-Ashbury during the shooting and finally saw it at the bottom of a double bill. I walked out in the middle.

Suzanne Pleshette, the heroine, later interviewed for a book about Pal, admitted she had no idea what the new ending was about. (Leonard Maltin gave the movie an undeserved three stars.)

At this time the enormous MGM lot was almost silent. *The Power* was being shot, as was *Dr. Kildare*, a television series starring Richard Chamberlain. The only other item on MGM's agenda was *2001*, being filmed by Kubrick in London. Rushes of *2001* were sent daily to the suits at MGM, but nobody had a clue as to what it was about.

Years later, Tom Scortia, my writing partner, and I were pitching a property in Hollywood and ran into Pal at the Beverly Hilton. The first thing he said to me was, "Mr. Robinson, how can you ever forgive me?"

George Pal was a class act.

AT *ROGUE* WE were putting together the next issue and were looking around for the packet of cartoons by Interlandi. (The artist was Hamling's discovery.)

Every week the one thing we dreaded was going through the slush pile of two hundred or more cartoon submissions, trying to find some worth printing. Interlandi was a real find—a natural funnyman with a pen who had a variety of different styles and could come close to imitating some of the cartoonists on *Playboy*'s staff.

We finally gave up plowing through the slush pile and turned everything over to Interlandi—we gave him an assignment to draw every cartoon in the book.

One Saturday we realized we hadn't received any cartoons from our ace cartoonist. Hamling called him and asked what was going on. When he hung up he was white with anger. Hefner liked Interlandi, too, and had sent a representative to see him. The upshot was *Playboy* signed him to an exclusive contract. What *Playboy* got was every cartoon in Interlandi's office, including the packet ready to send to us.

I don't remember who thought of it first, Hamling or myself, but one of us remembered all the years that Hamling had spent working with Hefner at PDC and buying the occasional cartoon from him for *Imagination*. (Five bucks each? Probably.) He never intended to print any of them—it was a favor.

But that was then and this was now.

If Hamling could resurrect the Hefner cartoons from his garage the next issue of *Rogue* would have "Cartoons by Hugh M. Hefner" in big type on the cover.

I was the one who decided to add insult to injury and sent a note to "Hugh M. Hefner, HMH Publishing Company"—I didn't mention *Playboy*—asking for a photograph and short biography to run on our author's page (standard practice for new contributors). I mailed the note off that same Saturday.

I didn't have to wait long for a reply.

If you don't appreciate that printing these cartoons at this time would be a source of embarrassment to me, you can hardly expect me to cooperate.

A day later, Hefner's personal secretary called (I had met her through Beaumont).

"Frank, what the hell is going on up there?"

I then had one of the few epiphanies I've ever had in my life.

"If I find them," I assured her, "consider them not found. I'll burn them. Mr. Hefner has nothing to worry about."

Someday, I thought, I might be asking Hefner for a job. But

if we had found them that Saturday, the next issue of *Rogue* would have printed on its front cover, "Cartoons by Hugh M. Hefner."

Years later, I was indeed working for Hugh Hefner and occasionally met him in the hallway at *Playboy*. He never recognized me as the kid who'd poured him a beer at one of Hamling's parties or who had interviewed him for his master's thesis.

Shortly after that, *Rogue* almost gave up its ghost. The distributor had run into some trouble.

The regional distributors saw no point in sending their money to a guy who might not be able to publish. The withheld funds included all the monies owed on the sales of *Rogue*. Hamling was left with about thirty grand in the bank, barely enough to cover the editorial costs of the next issue.

One of the first things Bill did was slash half the staff. (He wanted to can Dave Stevens, my right-hand man, and I threatened to quit. The compromise was that David would be assigned to spend half his time helping the handyman burn the stroke book returns. It was a long time before David forgave me for his reduction in rank.) In addition to David, we also kept Bruce Glassner, the editor of *Bruce's Bag*. Bruce stuck with us almost to the end.

We now had a new printer. Dick Thompson, the art director, and I went out to Commerce, California, to scout the scene. The printing plant was small, with its main press an offset unit. While we were watching, flames suddenly shot out from the drying oven (the printed web of paper went through it to dry the still-wet ink.) One of the pressmen grabbed the web and ripped it out—the web had stalled in the oven and caught fire.

Great, I thought. The local fire department probably hated the company.

With a new printing plant I thought it would be a great idea if one of the staff went with me when I traveled to Commerce to watch the magazine come off the press. The first one up was Bruce, who was fascinated by the equipment. The owner of the company was a real entertainer, hauling us around to various restaurants and bars. I'm not so sure how much of the trip Bruce actually remembered. (When we got back to Chicago Bruce quit and found a job with an advertising company.)

David and I went to Commerce for the next issue. We got the same entertainment that Bruce had, got piss-ass drunk, pushed each other around a little in our room, and the next thing I remember we were wrestling on the floor in our underwear. I always claimed I'd won, but David was younger and stronger than I was and it suddenly occurred to me that David's gay boss wrestling on the floor with his very straight employee was not such a good idea. I gave up quickly and David never let me forget it. The next Christmas he gave me a leather-covered brick with "Robinson Sucks" printed in gold on the side. I didn't take it personally.

Along with firing half the staff and finding a new printer, Hamling also found a new distributor, Kable News, an outfit that had taken over—and buried—most of the skin magazines that had failed to dethrone *Playboy*. Hamling moved very fast at this time—as a fellow employee at Ziff-Davis once described him, "all that engine and no steering wheel."

Our very last issue—the one to carry our names on the masthead—almost never made it out. The owner of the plant was more than willing to show me the town, to take me to various shows and fancy restaurants.

We finally made it to the plant about midnight and I found myself looking at the end of *Rogue.* There was almost no paper in the plant—a few rolls stored along a wall plus the remnants of rolls—"butt ends"—scattered around. I was told what few rolls of paper there were had been scheduled for another publication—a West Coast skin magazine titled *Adam*.

The plant had failed to pay its paper bills and had been cut off. They were negotiating for a new paper contract, but that would take a while. In the meantime, *Adam* wouldn't be out for another month. They finally printed *Rogue* on the paper reserved for *Adam*, plus the butt ends of paper on the floor. Some of it was eighty-pound paper, which gave the best reproduction I'd ever seen on a magazine. Unfortunately we couldn't use it—it was too heavy to go through the folder.

Sometime before this, word had gotten around Chicago that *Rogue* was on its last legs. Once home I received a call from A. C. Spectorsky, chief honcho at *Playboy*, who suggested we have lunch.

Lunch with "Spec" meant lunch at a very high-class restaurant, in this case one with marble floors. I spotted Spec half a dozen tables away and walked over, squeaking with every step as my new leather-soled shoes hit the marble.

Spec's first word of greeting was, "What the hell are you wearing?"

Once we got over that hump he offered me a job with *Playboy*, the court of last resort for a number of editors who had worked for other skin books and wouldn't blanch at the shots of naked women.

I thanked him—and said, "No, thanks."

I'd had enough of working in the skin trade, and even though *Playboy* was the best of the lot, working at *Rogue* had worn me out.

Spec looked as surprised as Spec ever allowed himself to look and asked about my assistant editors.

By this time, there was only one.

I casually mentioned David, our in-house adventurer, who was ready to go anyplace and do anything, pith helmet in hand.

David was approached and got the job. I'd like to think I had something to do with it, but I'm quite sure David got the job on the basis of the columns he had written for *Rogue* and because he had "eager beaver" written all over his face.

(Once hired, David stayed at *Playboy* for more than thirty years. He was far more than a diamond in the rough; he was a whole Tiffany's. He wrote articles about hot-air ballooning, raced in the Mexican 1,000 with another driver, and finished 85th out of 247 entries. He did the bobsled course at Lake Placid and went on a five-week, 3,100-mile trek across the Sahara, photographed baby harp seals off Newfoundland and helicoptered out to the ice floes, went down the Colorado River for a week on a raft, visited Finland for the Arctic Circle Polar Rally in the dead of winter, and tested all the cars that came *Playboy*'s way—he claimed he was partial to Porsches and Bentleys, though I'm sure they couldn't match his love for his old Morgan. He'll reluctantly admit his favorite escapade was the night he got sloshed with Prince Andrew.)

More than any other member of the staff, David *was* the real McCoy when it came to being a playboy.

The next day "Uncle Bunky" (David's nickname for Hamling) showed up to ring down the curtain. The last issue from Commerce would be our last issue, period. We had another issue set to go, but the pasteups, artwork, etc., were to be sent to the Douglas Publishing Company in Hollywood, the new publisher. (I'm sure that was at the request of Kable, our distributor and obviously the distributor for Douglas.) I could stay on as the editor with a budget of fifteen grand, half the editorial cost of the issues we were putting out.

I declined.

The *Rogue* indicia were not on the issue sent to Douglas;

neither was the masthead listing the staff, etc. As far as Douglas was concerned, the issue was anonymous.

Hamling's last act was to make out my severance check—two weeks at my present salary. And oh, yeah—would I please sell off the office furniture?

It was 1966, and my golden parachute for busting my butt for six years had turned to lead. When Hamling was out of sight, I tore up the check and spent the afternoon sending out copyright reversion letters to every author I thought of.

The last issue was a damned good one. Frederik Pohl's "Day Million" won a Hugo, and George Bamber's "The Man Who Could Not Feel" was the best story he ever wrote. (He deserved a Hugo, too.) The column by Alfred Bester hung on to the very last, and the final *Rogue About Town* column by Dave Stevens— titled "Hippity Hobbit"—was a love letter to J. R. R. Tolkien and *The Lord of the Rings* trilogy, David's favorite books.

I cleaned out my desk, locked the door, and threw my keys down a nearby sewer. Most of the night I spent looking for a friend who might have some Valium, and when I found one, I dropped two tabs and slept until noon.

I spent the rest of the day sitting on my friend's front doorsteps trying to accept that six years of my life were now over. For six years I had been the air in somebody else's balloon.

≪ XIV ≫

I WASN'T THE only editor suddenly out of work. *Playboy* had discontinued their book division, and A. J. Budrys, formerly of Regency Books at Greenleaf and who had defected to *Playboy* a few years earlier, was also on the street.

We met at his house one night and he told me about an idea he had: instructional paperbacks to be packed with sporting equipment—one to be packed with a box of skin-diving equipment showing the novice how it should be used, another showing the care and use of a kayak, etc.

It sounded like a good idea. AJ had experience with paperbacks, having worked at Regency. I was a writer and had some money saved up that could tide AJ over, since he was flat broke. The first project would be a box for an air ventilator for a skin diver who would find an instructional paperback tucked into the side of the box. We would make up a dummy or two and sell the idea to manufacturers. In the meantime, AJ needed something like two grand a month for his family to live on. I could cover that for a few months.

I left AJ alone for a month and a half—my mistake—then contacted him again and suggested getting together to go over what he was doing.

For once in my life I was speechless. AJ had spent his time constructing a handmade shoe box (that's what it looked like) complete with cover and a little pocket in the side of the box for the book to fit in.

That was it. You could have gone to any box store and bought it for a couple of bucks. What I was looking at was the most expensive box in the world. No printing on the box, no sample book tucked in, nothing.

It would have been a great box for a pair of Nikes.

I walked out without a word. I had either been scammed, or AJ was the dumbest would-be publisher in the world. What the hell had he done over at *Playboy?* Or Regency Books, for that matter? (Unfair, I admit. Regency had once bought a book— *Truman and the Pendergasts*—that had been plagiarized. AJ rewrote it completely in one weekend. What had happened to that, AJ?)

I was now nearly broke (both of us had been living on my savings). I was saved from poverty—so I thought—by the most unlikely man in the world.

William H. Hamling.

He and his stroke book empire were now in San Diego. The stroke books were doing great, and Hamling said he was thinking once more of a legitimate line, like Regency Books. He wanted me to be the editor.

I hesitated for a long moment and decided there had to be a catch. But I was also nearly broke. I'd fly out and see just how serious he was.

Greenleaf was a string of connected offices in a suburb of San Diego. Mine was to be one of those at the end. I unpacked my books and shoved my suitcase in a corner. A few minutes later Hamling dropped by to invite me along on a golf game with a projected partner in the Regency-type enterprise.

When Hamling was out of earshot I queried his golfing partner about what he thought of the projected enterprise and what part he would play in it.

He really didn't have any plans and really didn't know much about the Regency-type enterprise. I didn't think he had even heard of Regency Books.

After the game and Hamling and I were alone, he filled me in a little more on what my duties would be. There would be a Regency-type book once or twice a month and in my downtime maybe I could help Earl Kemp with the stroke books. Earl was the engine that had made Nightstand Books and Midnight Readers run for the past few years. He chose the books, okayed the covers, and every now and then snuck in a title that was a reprint of an old pulp magazine novel that Hamling had resurrected from his garage.

Hamling had lost all direct contact with the stroke books. He made out the checks while Earl was the engine that pulled the train.

Hamling wanted more of a contact with the stroke books and I was the man he had chosen. (Presumably he didn't trust Kemp completely. I, loyal soul that I was, he thought he could.) He knew—how, I didn't know—that I was nearly broke and for a little money I could be his man in Havana, reporting regularly to him on what Earl had done or was planning to do. Not that Earl was a bad editor or production man—far from it. Without him, Nightstand and Midnight Reader would have ceased to exist. (Both imprints are now collector's items among paperback collectors.)

I was to be Hamling's spy.

The first morning of my employment I left my resignation rolled up in my typewriter and left San Diego for Los Angeles.

(Hamling wasn't that much dismayed—he found further use for me in another year or two.)

The Regency-type line of paperbacks, predictably, never appeared.

In Los Angeles, I bunked in with old-time friend Walt Liebscher from Slan Shack days. I had the upstairs, he had the down. (Walt didn't socialize much. After having been outed by another science fiction fan he became pretty much of a hermit and avoided his old friends. Gay liberation was years in the future.)

I bummed around Los Angeles for a week, getting as used to it as I ever would be—an enormous, sprawling city that was more flat than up, like New York or even Chicago. Its one saving grace was that it had the best fast-food restaurants in the country. I was wondering what I was going to do when a friend back in Chicago wrote and told me there was an opening at a skin book publisher out of L.A. titled Cavalier.

I applied, and it was like old home week. The editor was an amiable man named Bob Shea, the publisher a stocky man named Lou Kimzey. Lou's background was in the motorcycle field, where his major claim to fame was draping a half-dressed model over the handlebars of the latest bike. At least for a while, it was something of a publishing sensation. (How Lou ended up as publisher of Cavalier, I never knew.)

I worked my way up from consulting editor to managing editor. I wasn't top dog, but it was a nice place to work at and perhaps the biggest asset was that I no longer had to act as go-between between Uncle Bunky and the staff at *Rogue*.

There was only one fly in the ointment that bothered me. At *Rogue* I worked with a group of people who became personal friends. The staff at Cavalier were friendly enough, but there was none of the after-hours esprit de corps that had existed among the staffers at *Rogue*. No dinners or movies or plays after work. When people said "good night" it was obvious they had no desire to see you until morning.

The one exception was Bob Shea; he and I became close friends. We went together to a party at the *L.A. Free Press*, one of the first "underground" newspapers, where I got smashed on vodka gimlets and gobbled a hash brownie or two. What happened then was that I suddenly became painfully aware of just how drunk I was and had to call Walt Liebscher to take me home. I was very wary of any drug afterward that would fuck with my brain—pot didn't screw up your head, it just made you feel better.

I asked Walt why the staff at Cavalier was relatively standoffish and said I was perfectly willing to change my toothpaste or underarm deodorant if that would help.

He looked surprised. "What can you do for them, Frank? Do you know anybody in the industry? Can you do anything for anybody?"

There was only one industry of note in Los Angeles at the time, and that was the film industry.

Could I do anything for anybody in it?

No.

I made friends elsewhere in Southern California, and it didn't take long to discover that the state had a soft moral underbelly.

Maybe every state had one. New York certainly did, and Chicago had its Herb and company.

Walt introduced me to Mel Kells, who lived in a somewhat ramshackle house in Beverly Glen. Mel may have been house poor but he was certainly land rich—the land behind the house stretched up the sides of a hill for hundreds of feet. He had built a small cabin on it, which he rented out.

Mel's house was never empty. He usually had a renter in the

cabin, a boy or two living with him in the house, and at least three or four dogs of uncertain ancestry running around the house. Mel was a good cook and fed everybody who stopped by—mostly boys and young men. Mel's house was a magnet for every young kid in the neighborhood.

Mel was a photographer who took the occasional male fashion photograph along with nude or nearly nude shots of young men—his "models." The models were nice-looking, bare-assed in the photos, and Mel sold packets of them. He eventually turned his model photography into a magazine titled *Mel Roberts' Boys*, a selection of photographs from his files—naked young men climbing out of swimming pools or lounging against wooden fences in the woods.

Not an unusual occupation—the L.A. newsstands were crowded with collections of naked men and women. Mel's print run was about four thousand copies, most of which he mailed himself.

It was a nice, prosperous little business until Mel made a mistake. A centerfold in his latest issue showed a young man in his early twenties, with a much younger naked boy kneeling in front of him. The photograph was cropped at the critical point but you had a pretty good idea of what was going on.

At least the L.A. police did. They confiscated all four thousand copies, called Mel down to the office, and had him tear out the centerfold from each issue. They also confiscated his cameras, effectively putting Mel out of the magazine business.

What they did not confiscate was the extensive library of nude male photographs in Mel's basement. Mel's mail business tripled. I had no idea how "far" some of the photographs went, but most of those I saw were strictly nude shots.

Well . . . not quite. In a number of the shots, the young men showed erections. I had no idea how young some of the models were, but most seemed of age. A year or so after the closure of his magazine, Mel put out a hardbound book of some of his photographs.

The first book of "tasteful" nude shots was very successful, and the local bookstores sold hundreds of copies. The following book was guaranteed to sell many more—most of the models had erections.

Eventually even this offshoot of Mel's publishing activities struck Mel and his bookstores as potentially dangerous.

Mel then hit upon the best idea of all. He did all of his own printing and turned out gorgeous twenty-by-twenty four-color prints of his better photographs for display in local art galleries. The photographs were tasteful nudes—a young boy climbing naked out of a swimming pool (his parents in the background) with the model showing plenty of bare butt. The photographs were attractive, legitimate in every way, and Mel sold them for thousands of dollars each in the art galleries in town. (Elton John was reputed to be a big purchaser.)

Mel had finally struck it rich by turning completely legitimate.

Mel and I became good friends and had the occasional lunch at the Apple Pan (best hamburgers and apple pie in town). I was never that friendly with his models, who were usually polite but standoffish. I was fond of one of the young men in Mel's center gatefold—the oldest one, Alec, who was much older than the young man kneeling in front of him. He was a decent artist, had a motorcycle, and made most of his living (when he wasn't posing for Mel) "detailing" some of the expensive cars in Glen and Beverly Hills that belonged to movie stars.

The relationship was polite but went no place at all. I was a little old for Alec—he preferred twelve- and thirteen-year-old boys. (Pedophiles aren't always middle-aged men offering kids football tickets or used jerseys or priests who have a fondness for altar boys.) Alec was, of course, the idol of all the young boys in the neighborhood—he gave them rides on his bike and an occasional toke of pot. Both Mel and I warned Alec about playing around with the kids, and his answer was the same as that of every pedophile, including the occasional football coach or local priest: "But I really love them!" It never occurs to them that they may be hurting the child physically or leaving psychological scars that would haunt the kid for most of his life. (Ask me.)

Or maybe they just don't give a damn.

Alec was a hero to the kids, but one of them reportedly told his sister about the relationship who in turn told her parents. Alec was arrested, but I understand that few of the boys would testify against him. The way I remember it, the police finally threw the book at him for the small pot garden behind his cabin.

He was released to a halfway house years later. With the current feeling toward pedophiles, I don't know if he'll ever go completely free.

In his twenties, Alec became friends with Rusty Mason. She had two kids, one of whom was the subject of the movie *Mask*, with Cher playing Rusty and Eric Stoltz playing the part of Rocky, a "lion-faced" boy with a face badly distorted by a rare disease. Rusty raised him right, never making allowances for him or treating him any different from any of the other kids in the neighborhood.

Rocky's younger brother also became a close friend of Alec, who once gave him a week-long tour of the West on his motorcycle. When the kid grew older, he moved to San Francisco and became a member of BAGL, Bay Area Gay Liberation. (He eventually died of AIDS.) Rocky had died some years before, and my own feelings were that Rusty hadn't deserved this.

Rusty eventually moved to San Francisco, and my agent

convinced me there was a story there. After several months of taking notes, I realized there wasn't one. Rusty was a "skimmed property," and the only really interesting thing about this hippie woman from Brooklyn was her son with the lion face and the relationship between them. From a writer's viewpoint that's all there was, but it was pure gold. (A year before writing this, Rusty was killed in an accident while riding her trike.)

One of my most memorable images of Mel before I moved to San Francisco some months later was when one of his dogs developed a disease that made it impossible for him to use his hind legs. Mel didn't put him down. He lifted the dog's hind legs and guided him into the backyard so he could take a pee.

You could excuse a lot for a man who was willing to do that.

❧ XV ❧

I DIDN'T SPEND all my evenings and weekends in Los Angeles, a city I was gradually beginning to hate. A city of few really decent restaurants, little transportation—buses were a rarity—and four million strangers.

On the weekends I usually grabbed a flight to San Diego and spent a few days with Earl Kemp (Hamling's right-hand man) and his family. His backyard was one huge swimming pool with a twelve-foot fence so none of the neighbors could see in. The pool was usually filled with naked teenagers and young men in their early twenties. Earl's wife, Nancy, cooked for the mob—she eventually tired of it but not for years, when she remarried.

Occasionally Earl and I, along with a couple of kids, would grab sleeping bags and go down to Baja California.

On one such trip, we found a stream and followed it for a few miles, slipping on an occasional rock. One of the kids, Robbie, had shed his cutoffs, and an occasional flash of moonlight would catch his bare butt.

We finally found what Earl considered a suitable campsite and spread out our sleeping bags, all in utter darkness, since Earl's flashlight had burned out its batteries days before.

Morning was a shock. We had camped in the middle of a

garbage dump. The days were hot enough so leftover footstuffs had long since baked away. Other campers had thoughtfully left their tin cans in little mounds, which we had luckily avoided.

We trudged over some sand dunes to the ocean and met a German couple and their kids who were skinny-dipping. They invited us in, and Earl and Robbie shed what little clothing they had on and ran into the water. So did I—but I kept on my Cooper-Jockeys, much to everybody's amusement. (I was much too shy—a lifelong handicap.)

Sometimes I, Earl, and a young friend named Steve would go down to Tijuana. At that time it was a run-down, poverty-stricken town stitched together with dirt roads. Nevertheless, it had some great restaurants. (The cheaper joints, crowded with American sailors, had floor shows that left nothing to anybody's imagination. When they brought out the donkey, I left.)

Back at Cavalier, a new hire, Peter Martin, had taken a weekend trip to San Francisco and came back wildly enthusiastic about a "Human Be-In" that had taken place—twenty-five thousand hippies making music, dancing, dropping tabs of acid, and smoking pot in one of the meadows in Golden Gate Park.

"It was the biggest block party in the world!" Martin enthused.

According to Peter, people on Haight Street, the center of it all, were long-haired, friendly, quick to offer you a toke, and were devoted fans of the various rock groups in the city—the Grateful Dead, the Jefferson Airplane, Big Brother and the Holding Company, etc.

A party, I thought. Free food, rock bands. And most of all, twenty-five thousand people in one place having a great time. It was something brand new for the country; it hit the media like a boulder thrown in a pond of water, and the waves soon flooded the country. First the underground press—the *Los Angeles Free Press*, the *Oracle*, and the *Berkeley Barb* enthused about it, and then the major media joined in. The San Francisco hippies were the new Christians.

Another "be-in" was held in Los Angeles, and I think it was then that Lou had his Big Idea. He was not one to let a new cultural craze pass unnoticed, and soon we came out with a few issues of a magazine titled *Paperbag*. It was printed on a form of rough kraft paper and carried articles by us fraudulent hippies on staff such as "The Death of Haight," "Playing It Cool About Pot," and a homage to the death of "Chocolate George," a friendly Hell's Angel whose nickname came from his taste for chocolate milk. One of the meadows in the park filled up with mourners, the Grateful Dead played, joints were passed around, and everybody had a great time.

I think our circulation could have been counted in the hundreds. The hippies could smell a fake a mile away, and nobody had gone out there to read magazines anyway. If they read anything it was the *Oracle*, a colorful underground paper that reached a circulation of a hundred thousand, and Robert Heinlein's *Stranger in a Strange Land*, which quickly became a bible for the crowds of adventure seekers and runaways who soon came to the Haight.

In my free time, I went back to writing fiction. I'd found four pages of a story in the bottom of my trunk and decided to finish it. The story had been intended for *Astounding*, which paid three cents a word. At twenty thousand words that came to $600, which I could really use.

My agent didn't send it to *Astounding*—she sent it to *Playboy*. They said cut it by five thousand words and they'd run it. As a lead.

For three grand.

After all those years at a penny or two a word, I'd finally hit the big time.

Cavalier was going down the tubes by this time, and the end came quickly. Bob Shea joined Arthur Kretchmer (Bob had become editor of Cavalier when Kretchmer had departed for *Playboy*), and Peter Martin, our new hire, decided to become an investigative reporter and followed a story down on Union Street.

Aside from Peter, the first time I heard about the Haight was at a party in Los Angeles. I was with a group of Hollywood hippies—beads, bells, Jesus hair, and $100 worth of the latest mod clothing—who were counseling a young navy deserter on what he should do next. When we were alone I asked him if there was any difference between Hollywood hippies and the San Francisco type.

"They're a lot more real, man—they took good care of me. Look up Emmett Grogan when you get there. He'll tell you what it's like."

I had a little money now and decided to go to San Francisco to see what the noise was all about.

On the trip to Frisco with a friend, we picked up a Mexican whore. She was dumpy and weathered, midforties, and said she'd once knifed a Hell's Angel who had beaten her up. She rhapsodized about the early Diggers. "They feed me, they give me clothes, they real nice to me."

We let her out at the Embarcadero, bought her a cup of coffee, and then she blew our minds by giving us an Indian head penny "from my coin collection."

That night I spent at a hole-in-the-wall in North Beach, trying to ignore the cries of the barkers below and the noise of the tourists leaving Carol Doda's topless club.

I didn't know much about the Haight, but decided I'd like to live close to it but not in it.

For $70 a month I found a small basement apartment—1492

Sixth Avenue (easy number to remember). I had made myself comfortable when there was a scratching at the door. I opened it and a skinny cat stalked in, looked around, and then at me. We had a staring contest for a moment, then he settled down in a corner and ignored me. (I found out later on that raccoons would come around late at night, and if they found a cat, they'd take it apart.)

The cat looked perfectly comfortable in the corner and I decided the apartment belonged to it. The previous tenants had obviously left it behind. My duty was to feed it and give it water and then it would tolerate me.

I said, "Hey, cat," and it turned and looked at me and I guessed that was what the previous tenants had called it.

That afternoon I walked down Haight Street past Ashbury, where the Grateful Dead were supposed to be living—there was a guitar nailed to the front door—and somebody waved at me. I waved back, thinking it was probably Bob Weir, a member of the band.

Lou had given me the address of Mouse and Kelly, the two most prominent artists of rock posters. I think it was Mouse who opened the door and asked me what I wanted. There were about a dozen people in the living room, and the smoke was fairly heavy.

"Lou Kimzey said I should drop by and say hello."

I had everybody's attention then. "That son of a bitch!" Mouse screamed. "He still owes us money!"

It seemed Lou had bought cartoons from them for some of his magazines and forgot about payment. He was thousands of miles away, and what was their hurry anyway?

"What the hell do you do?" I think it was Kelly, but they were all curious—it was obvious I'd just come to town. "You a friend of the bastard?"

I got smart very fast. "He published an article or two of mine," I said. "I usually write science fiction."

The tension in the room immediately simmered down, and I was waved to a spot in the circle. When the joint came around, I took a huge puff and fought like mad to keep from coughing. (I couldn't help thinking of the time at *Rogue* when I had warned the staff that anybody caught smoking weed would automatically be canned.) Apparently most of my new friends were science fiction buffs, and if writing it was what I did, I must be okay.

I left and wandered down Haight Street to Golden Gate Park. Most of the apartment windows were open, and "Sgt. Pepper's Lonely Hearts Club Band" was blasting out. The people on the street frowned at me—I was out of place, a stranger from another world they'd left a few months ago or maybe only a few weeks.

Just past the entrance to the park was a lagoon and a hill that had been nicknamed "Hippie Hill." It was dotted with a few dozen guys sunning themselves, passing a joint around, and watching the parade on the sidewalk below.

"Hey, Frank!" somebody shouted. "Come on up!"

I glanced up the hill—it took me a moment to place him. A photographer whom we had given a few assignments to at *Rogue*. He was sitting next to another contributor who had been briefly on our masthead, Jim Sagebiel.

I stretched out on what was left of the grass, unbuttoned my shirt, and let the sun shine through. Strange world, I thought—a lot different from L.A. I had a hunch I'd be there for a few months.

I had no idea it would be two years.

"You're out of uniform," the photographer said.

"I didn't know you had one."

"Jesus, look down there." A few black kids were playing bongo drums at the foot of the hill, and a girl in a multicolored ankle-length dress was walking past followed by a young man in torn Levi's and a bell around his neck.

"You're a little late," Jim said. "It's changed a lot and it's still changing." He was sunburned and thinner than I remembered, and his eyes looked very bright.

"I've got an idea for a magazine," he said. "*San Francisco Arts.* You want to work with me on it?"

I shrugged. "Sure—why not?"

We would get as far as the cover, a good one—a promising start. But that was it. Jim disappeared and I decided I'd had enough of working on magazines.

I spent the next month exploring, finding out where the bank was, the grocery store, the coffee shops, and getting a history of the area from the few old-timers who'd hung on while the district changed—radically.

The original Haight-Ashbury was a middle-class section of the city, most famous primarily because it was the entrance to Golden Gate Park. It was a mixture of blue-collars and blacks slowly slipping toward a middle-aged gentility. Old Victorians made up the bulk of the housing.

The area was ready for a makeover—and it got one it had least expected. Students from San Francisco State started to sift in, attracted by the low rents. So did some of the beats, forced out of North Beach by higher rents and plunging necklines. Added to the mix were the nascent rock groups who would rent an inexpensive Victorian where they could live and practice together. It was the bands that created the concept of sharing—if one hit it, they shared their good fortune with others who weren't so lucky.

Leavening the mix were the Diggers and the Mime Troupe

and a few beats who had gotten to the area early. There were also some of the middle-class types who had a little money and wanted to buy a Victorian and remodel it. Few of them held on to the bitter end.

Drugs were common, and some of the users went overboard. (Later, almost all did.) Pot was illegal, though Timothy Leary's development of LSD was gradually becoming popular. Leary insisted that taking it was a religious sacrament, a way to find the soul within. As a sign you had taken the "trip," a friend who had taken it previously gave you a string of beads to wear around your neck.

It didn't take long for newcomers to turn the beads into costume jewelry.

In the winter of 1967 the exiled beats from North Beach, the Mime Troupe, the Diggers, the rock groups, and the displaced hippies held a party in one of the meadows of Golden Gate Park. It turned out to be popular beyond anybody's expectations. Twenty-five thousand showed up to listen to the bands, have a picnic with the free food, smoke some pot, and a few of the more adventurous took "acid" trips. A number of couples made love in the bushes (having sex was one of the first things to be liberated— saying "yes" was far more prevalent than saying "no").

It was one terrific party. The motto was DO YOUR THING, and those in the meadow certainly did.

The underground press—the *Los Angeles Free Press*, the *Oracle*, the *Berkeley Barb*—gave it extensive coverage. The mass media wasn't far behind. This was something to write about besides war and politics.

The white middle class was already registering a massive opposition to the "good life" and especially the war. Younger people had become aware of the vast gap between who they were and who they thought they were, between the lives they were actually leading and the lives they were pretending to lead.

Haight-Ashbury was where an optimistic reality existed, and soon cars and buses, trains and planes were headed for the coast. Things were better out there, and far from least, THINGS WERE FREE!

The sources for things that were free had always been their parents—but then something was expected in return. In Haight-Ashbury the only thing that was expected in return was for you to show up. It was flower power—"I love you, man!" It didn't take too many months for the mantra to become "Any spare change?"

Nothing was really free, and some of the kids who flooded in had nothing but the clothes they wore and no talents or skills and resorted to selling the one thing they did have: themselves.

The churches tried to help, but the law prevented that— churches weren't allowed to house you after 10:00 P.M. without permission from your parents. And most of those who had departed home without saying good-bye or were runaways weren't about to call home for help.

By the time most of the original Haight-Ashbury had folded its tent and stolen away, sex had become a medium of exchange, the same as pot. A few of the kids saw what things were really like and called home for an airline ticket back. For the others, if they were hungry and needed food or were cold and needed shelter and couldn't find a crash pad that wasn't already crowded with twenty to a room, the answer was simple. There was always somebody willing to feed them and let them bunk in for the night.

There was no real structure to the Haight; a city of seven hundred thousand hadn't been prepared for the influx of a hundred thousand of the soon-to-be-disillusioned; there were few city organizations designed to cope with it. It was a case of no mama, no poppa, no Uncle Sam.

The Haight became *Lord of the Flies* a generation later.

For the rest of the country, it was entertainment.

There was enterprise, of course. The empty storefronts began to sport new signs—the Garuda and the I/Thou coffeehouses, the Insomnia Bookstore, the Krishna Temple, the God's Eye Ice Cream Parlor, the Print Mint, the Drugstore Café, the Bead Freak, the San Francisco Earthquake Pillow Company, and a month or two later, Love's Hamburger Stand (Love helped a lot of kids stave off starvation).

Some of the more enterprising kids sold copies of the local underground press—*The Haight-Ashbury Tribune*, *Love Street*, and others. These were cluttered with photographs of nudes and ads for young men who wanted to be models. The nude photos were a big help in peddling the papers to the tourists, who came through the area in tour buses or in cars with the windows carefully rolled up. The kids paid a quarter per paper and sold them for a dollar.

(The publisher actually had another business—selling nude photos of boys in his mail-order business. Some of the boys were young, very young.)

Confession: I was a star reporter for both the *Berkeley Barb* and especially *The Haight-Ashbury Tribune* (under the pen name of "Harry Happening"). The *Barb* paid its writers with bananas and sandwiches. It took me a long time before I lost my idealism writing for the *Tribune*. I thought I was doing a public service telling it like it was when in reality I was merely filler around the nude shots.

There came a time, after a few months, when I seriously questioned what the hell I was doing there.

And then I met Jesus.

It was late one night and I'd just bought some old art nouveau postcards from one of the shops.

Suddenly a kid stepped out of the shadows and handed me a sack of greasy french fries.

"Have one, man—they're pretty good."

He looked like the Jesus you saw in Sunday school—soft brown eyes and brown hair falling to his shoulders; thin, handsome face; and a knowing expression in his eyes.

I took one—he'd been right, they were pretty good. Not to be outdone, I held out my postcards. "Take one," I offered, "any one." Then I changed my mind and held back on a miniature of Sarah Bernhardt that I really liked and said, "But not that one." I suddenly realized I'd reneged and said, "Hell, take any one."

He put his hand on the Bernhardt card and for a moment Haight Street fell away and his eyes held mine like a pin holds a butterfly. "Any one?"

"Sure," I said stoutly, "any one."

"Then I'll take this one," he said—and took a different card.

He was playing Jesus and probably putting me on, but for a moment I had been caught up in a biblical parable on the honesty of generosity. I was either generous or I wasn't. Which was it?

I glanced at the remaining cards for a moment, and when I looked up, he was gone. I hadn't even heard his footsteps when he disappeared into the shadows.

A parable on generosity was the last thing I'd expected in the Haight. I wanted to see him again but I was pretty sure that I wouldn't.

❦ XVI ❧

AFTER THE FEW weeks it took to get settled I regularly walked over to the Haight to look up friends who weren't space cases.

I developed a routine where I'd take the scenic route to Haight Street and either the Garuda or the I/Thou coffeehouses for coffee and doughnuts, depending on who was there.

I walked over to Fifth Avenue and took a sharp left past the flat where a dope dealer named Carter had been dismembered by an angry meth head. Then it was down to Golden Gate Park—on chilly mornings the paths through the park were not very crowded, but sometimes you'd meet hippies who smiled and said "hello," and on gray days a smile helped a lot.

Once in the park I would keep to the right until I came to the children's playground, where there was a carousel and a little petting zoo for the kids with goats and rabbits and a weather-beaten old cable car up on blocks in which the kids played on warm days.

The park was almost deserted, and there was nobody sitting on Hippie Hill, but a couple of older teenagers were stretched out on a bench at the front of it. One of them was a deserter from the marines who had asked if he could crash the night before but had never shown up. He apologized, mumbling, "Gee, man, I'm sorry I didn't show. I got all fucked up." His pupils were so large there was no irises left. There was no sense rapping when there was nobody home, so I said, "It's cool, man," and continued walking up Haight Street.

New stores were popping up even in the past month. The most significant was the Psychedelic Shop, the focal point for newcomers looking for friends or wanting to leave notes for those who'd come before or would come later.

Fat Maxey was already in residence at Garuda with a cup of coffee and a plate of chocolate doughnuts in front of him. Maxey was a good friend and my favorite hippie—though he really wasn't a hippie. He was a bystander, an observer, a historian of sorts who could tell me what I had missed in the Haight, especially what it had been like if I had only arrived a few months earlier.

"I used to hang out around State and when I drifted over here a few months ago, there was a lot of kids acting out. Some of them did everything but wear a halo." Two bites of doughnut disappeared. "It's going downhill fast. I understand the Dead have already pulled up stakes and went to live in Big Sur. Don't know where the Jefferson Airplane went but they left here about the same time. Probably Sausalito or someplace else in Marin."

"I wondered about Janis Joplin," I said.

Maxey looked surprised. "Pushing a baby carriage down Haight Street with a bottle of Southern Comfort in it? Pure bullshit—if you don't have a story to tell, make one up." He grinned. "Maybe the kid you saw that night was the real McCoy. Came back to see how God had fucked up his world."

The first chocolate doughnut had disappeared.

"Some of the other old-timers are leaving—the Diggers for

one. They set up a 'free' store—they called it the 'Free Frame of Reference'—and it's falling apart."

I looked blank and Maxey said, "They got a garage on Page Street where they handed out free clothing—you leave what you don't need, take what you do need. Everybody needed, what they left were pretty much rags."

I remembered passing by it and thinking it was just a junk shop. I glanced at my watch and got up.

Maxey looked surprised. "So soon?"

"Got an interview with Father Harris."

Haight Street in the morning was at its best. The shopkeepers were opening up, people on the street smiled at you, and nobody was tripping. It was too early for the dealers to swarm the streets, and the flood of tourists had yet to arrive.

Father Harris ran the All Saints Episcopal Church on Waller, a block up from Haight. It was a quiet Sunday morning, and he was ticked off by the latest indignities suffered by one of his parishioners that morning. She was eighty years old and had her purse snatched on her way to church.

"I tried to help them during the summer," Father Harris said. "It cost the church a lot of support—many of them moved away because they didn't want to raise their kids here." He sighed. "The parish used to be noted as one that had a lot of children. I miss the children."

What did he think would happen to the parish, to which he had devoted his life?

He shrugged. "The bishop knows what we've done here. He won't let the parish sink."

In a letter to the members of his parish, Father Harris later wrote: "If the church is to be true to itself, it won't confine its ministrations to those who support it financially. The church is not a private club for like-minded individuals."

In the basement of the Hamilton Methodist Church, the vibes weren't good. A girl was saying to her friend, "It used to be so nice here—now it's uptight all the time."

At a table in the corner, the manager was talking to five punks sprawled out in the chairs around it. "I've run this place for nine months and never had any trouble. Then you guys come in. You look like hoods, you act like hoods."

Outside, the street was beginning to wake up. A kid who'd lived in the area for two years screamed angrily at the world, "Goddamnit, they walk up to you in broad daylight and steal your guitar right out of your hands!" In the Garuda coffee shop, a kid was talking of being mugged on Ashbury, just up from the Panhandle.

The area also had its martyrs. In late spring, Ernest Beatty, a young professor of English at San Francisco State, came to work at the All Saints community affairs office—at his own expense. He had visited the church several times during the spring, admired the work that was being done, and offered to contribute his summer. By this time the Diggers had more or less fallen apart as an organization, and it was Beatty who built up the office. In a few weeks he was heading the entire operation.

On July 11, he was found dead in bed of a massive stroke.

Most of the kids on the street had never heard of Ernest Beatty, or if they had, never remembered his name. For them, the only martyrs on the scene were their fellow dealers who had been busted.

None of them showed up for his services. None of them posted notes or signs regretting his passing.

It wasn't all bad—not quite. The Straight Theater started opening its doors at night for free happenings. For the people who performed there, the audiences were startling. Margaret Fabrizio gave a harpsichord concert one night, and the theater was packed with teenage hippies who were deathly quiet during the performance and gave her a standing ovation when it was over. Another time the Jane Lapiner Dance Company performed a modern ballet titled *Bodies*, where five performers (three girls, two men) were nude. Again, rapt attention—no snickers, no catcalls. (The cops tried to bust the performers but the hippie audience crowded in toward the stage and the dancers got away.)

Not every performer got a standing ovation. One night in the I/Thou a kid borrowed a guitar and sang and played and was quietly applauded (he was passably good at both). He thanked the crowd and played again . . . and again. The crowd got edgy—the kid sounded like he was drunk or on speed—and somebody reclaimed their borrowed guitar, and when the kid started to sing a cappella, the crowd booed him down. There was the general I/Thou hubbub for a few minutes, and then a loud voice said, "Christ, kid, be a *man*."

But a man was the one thing the kid couldn't be, and the I/Thou sat in shocked silence except for the crying of a little queer kid lost in his loneliness.

A week later a photographer and myself trekked over to Berkeley to see what was happening in a protest at People's Park. At a similar protest some days before, Alameda County sheriff's deputies had used shotguns to break up a demonstration. A student, James Rector, was killed and carpenter Alan Blanchard permanently blinded. The deputies claimed they had only used birdshot. They had actually used 00 buckshot, which can kill—and did. Buckshot was also used to fire at the backs of fleeing demonstrators.

The buckshot was used, according to the sheriff, because he was undermanned and he didn't want to abandon Berkeley "to the mob." He also admitted that some of his deputies were

Vietnam War veterans and treated the protesters as if they were Vietcong.

Today was going to be the biggest protest of all. The police were there, and so was the National Guard. The park itself was fenced off with barbed wire. I couldn't believe it and touched it, pulling back some bloodied fingers.

I thought that some of the protesters would get clubbed, and several killed—maybe a lot of them killed.

Governor Reagan was dead set against "Communist sympathizers, protesters, and sex deviates" taking over the Berkeley campus. (He was obviously in total ignorance of the Haight.) For this demonstration, he had sent in twenty-seven hundred National Guardsmen, and there were also the police and the sheriff's deputies.

I wondered just where the Vietcong were hiding.

Nobody knew for sure what was going to happen, but I was certain there would be casualties. So was the photographer. The crowd started to gather at about noon. I estimated about five thousand people or more—much more. There were crowds of students, women in flat heels and not too much makeup, medical students with Red Cross armbands, and radicals passing out proclamations or charging a nickel or a dime for them as souvenirs of the occasion.

It kept occurring to me that if Reagan wanted a bloodbath, he just might get one.

I wandered over to People's Park No. 2 and wasn't much impressed—it didn't look much like a park to me. It didn't compare with empty lots back in Chicago where neighbors got together and turned the lots into vegetable gardens. There were several plants trying to grow in hard-packed dirt, withered flowers, broken green things that the crowd had mashed flat. I wondered if grass could scream.

I ran into a reporter for *Look* and asked him what he thought. "It's a lot of bullshit, man, it's just a lot of bullshit."

I asked him how many people he thought would be there and he shrugged and said, "Maybe ten thousand—and I'm being generous."

Final estimates were about thirty-five thousand.

They were starting to make speeches now and I figured that would go on for a while, so I started to check what would be waiting for people along the line of march. I squeezed up to the head of the crowd and noted that the Highway Patrol was closing off the side streets.

I couldn't put my finger on it at first, but there was the faint air of carnival in the air. The photographer and I ran up the side streets to Shattuck and University to see what was up.

The California Highway Patrol was in single file in front of the university grounds. The National Guard was at the intersection, waiting. The marchers were still a few blocks away, but one guy was already setting up a lemonade stand.

Not much hostility—just the CHP and the National Guard and Berkeley cops waiting for the unexpected. Then we were on Telegraph and hurrying up the street to the original People's Park. We couldn't go any farther.

Barbed wire on the residential streets of a quiet American city! And behind the wire the unsmiling faces of more National Guard. What struck me was that the guardsmen were not big men but kids, like most of the marchers.

We went down a side street to get a good view of People's Park No. 1. Not much to see—some playground equipment, dying plants, tents for the guardsmen. It wasn't much of a park, really, and I felt surprised. This was what the fuss was all about? And James Rector dead and Alan Blanchard sightless. Behind my disbelief was a growing horror.

The rest of the afternoon was an anticlimax. The marchers came up and circled the park, and the atmosphere of carnival deepened. A few of the marchers chopped holes in the asphalt street and planted some small trees and some assholes showed their hippie patriotism by sitting in the middle of the street.

The barbed wire was soon decorated with flowers and a few of the girls yoo-hooed at the Guard and stuffed flowers down the muzzles of their rifles. Some of the braver ones went topless and the guardsmen immediately snapped to an alert. The cops on the side streets lounged against their cars, bored, and some old ladies served iced tea to the kids and everybody had a fine time.

What a lovely way to fight a war!

That night there was a party in People's Park No. 2. There was a lot of pot, some of the musically inclined were beating bongo drums, and gallons of Red Mountain were passed around. A lot of people were shouting "Jesus, we won!" There must have been more than thirty-five thousand people there.

Some of the chicks were balling strangers in the tents, and many of the guardsmen were thanking God for the assignment.

People's Park was thrown together without much thought, and at least one ecologist said that the plants would never have grown. "It was a grand gesture designed to fail." Mayor Johnson was horrified to discover that lots of pot had been planted, and I thought that confrontation would have come sooner or later. The cops would eventually have had to bust the park, and once again it would have been the cops against the kids.

I've got nothing good to say about Reagan (governor at the time) or the asshole who ordered the gassing of Sproul Plaza or the sheriff who was scared witless and ordered one of his men to murder.

The thing that bugged me all day about the People's Park march in Berkeley was that it was great theater.

And not much else.

But it did predict the shape of things to come.

In May 1970 nervous members of the National Guard fired on a group of students at Kent State, Ohio, who were protesting the Vietnam War. They killed four and wounded nine.

The student strikes that followed resulted in hundreds of universities and colleges closing in protest.

The reasons for the protests against the Vietnam War (and those that were to follow) were—in my opinion—simple:

The government had failed to sell its various wars to the people they expected to fight them.

⤛ XVII ⤜

I HAD SPENT almost a year in the Haight, far longer than I had expected, and I was running out of money. In the early days, I had dealt—once. Pressured by a friend in Chicago, I scored two kilos of pot, wrapped them carefully in tinfoil, and shipped them to Chicago in a Random House dictionary box (the box for the unabridged dictionary), giving the return address as the English Department at San Francisco State.

The box never made it to Chicago. I suspected the hippies in the post office who were more familiar with drug shipments than any pot-sniffing dog. Or, possibly, the box was returned to S.F. State and some astonished (and delighted) students in the English Department opened it.

Much to my surprise, the man who would come to my rescue moneywise was Hamling. Stanley Fleishman, his lawyer (and the lawyer for most of the porn publishers in California), wanted to put out a digest-size magazine titled *Censorship Today*. It would be a ninety-page summary of the censorship activities in the United States and around the world. The magazine was intended for librarians in the United States.

Hamling suggested me as a cheap one-man staff. I edited the copy, pasted up the pages, inserted photographs and captions, and sent the results to a printer in Southern California, who printed three or four thousand copies and sent them to various librarians in the country.

I flattered myself that the printers were glad to get something "decent" instead of the usual publications they handled, even if it was pro bono.

The seventh issue was the last—and it was all my fault. I thought the librarians should see some of the crap that *should* be censored and reprinted a typical Tijuana cartoon. The circulation dropped to zero overnight. I should have checked with Stanley beforehand but hadn't.

My sincere apologies to the shade of Stanley Fleishman for killing the magazine of which he was justly proud.

In an effort to become more a part of the community, I'd bought a fifteen-gallon iron cooking pot to make spaghetti. Once a week I'd buy a gallon of Red Mountain, make spaghetti, and invite the hungriest-looking hippies on the street. On Sundays I usually lugged the pot up to the free medical clinic and made spaghetti for the staff.

Holidays were tough—the make-believe hippies were all home opening presents and eating turkey. (The weekend panhandlers usually came from good families, dressed in the appropriate rags, but you could tell who they were by their blank looks and the new shoes they wore.)

This day was Thanksgiving, and the tourists were anyplace but in the Haight. There was nobody around but the poor and hungry street kids. Love would usually roast a turkey, but this Thanksgiving she was broke. She confided it to Norm Fitzgerald of F&S Distributing (the poster shop), who tapped the till for twenty bucks and ran down to the butcher shop for the biggest turkey they had.

He didn't bother to have it wrapped, but holding it by its legs ran back to the hamburger stand, gave it to Love, and told her to do her thing.

The ovens in the back of the hamburger stand could handle a turkey, and pretty soon the street kids started to gather around. One of them went to the grocery store and liberated half a dozen cans of cranberry sauce, while others found stale bread and spices for the dressing. Love boiled up some rice as a side dish with turkey gravy. By five o'clock she was carving up turkey until her arms were ready to drop. Everybody showed up, both blacks and whites. A cop from Park Station came over to check up on the whooping and hollering and assured Love she was golden for the day.

There was pathos on the street but also comedy. One spaced-out kid tried to hold up the Bank of America with a bag of dirty laundry he claimed was dynamite. He got six months but he and his girlfriend exchanged letters that were posted on the bulletin board at the Psych Shop and followed avidly by the street kids—they now had their own Romeo and Juliet.

For most of the kids, life was pretty grim. I put up one French-Canadian kid who was on a really bad trip. He considered himself a poet and wrote poetry all over the photographs and type in an issue of *Time* magazine. He could read the poems but nobody else could.

He ended up in the bathtub with a pillow and blanket, staring at the ceiling.

I asked him if it was okay if I turned off the light. He nodded "Yes," and when I did, he sceamed.

The Haight was still big news in the eyes of the media, and it was the rare Digger who wasn't willing to talk about the philosophy underlying the community, though most of it had evaporated. The media would always talk about the prevalent dope business but seldom asked questions about the people doing it.

LSD had lost much of its religious overtones but was readily available at parties and concerts, where tabs were frequently given away free. Pot was illegal, which meant it was the big-ticket item. Bad trips frequently resulted from acid—or what was passed off as acid. Pot was generally regarded as a safe drug.

It was the first anniversary of the Haight, and the media swarmed around it like flies. One rumor had it that a reporter had balled a couple of kids before interviewing them. I didn't know the truth of it, but I knew that of all the things that were impor-tant to the hippies, sex was usually at the bottom of the list.

Money was at the top.

The Haight-Ashbury was where the real fabric of American life was being unraveled, and many of the kids discovered too late that some of the threads of that fabric were stitched right through their bellies.

There was a certain uneasiness about some of the new kids coming in. As one older hippie put it, "They never cry and they seldom laugh and if they're bright, they're witty and brilliant and cynical—and essentially empty."

Many of the kids came to San Francisco with no money and no plans for a place to stay—they were *counting* on everything to be free. It always had been so at home, and from what they had heard, it was the same here. They didn't think the generos-ity of the original hippies was unusual at all. Even as they mouthed the standard thank-you—"Wow, man, thanks, you're really beautiful!"—their eyes were curiously blank of gratitude.

Rick was a thin, blond-haired kid whom I met on Hippie Hill. His father and mother had separated just before they put Rick in an outpatient psychiatric clinic. He was turned on to grass by the other kids in the clinic. "It was great, man—I could see the bag that I was in but I could also look at other people and see the bags that they were in." It was dope that gave Rick confidence, dope that gave him what insight he had into other people, and dope that gave him status among his contemporaries.

David looked like a runaway, one of the hundreds who came into the Haight with nothing because they figured everything was already there. I told him I was serving spaghetti that night and that he was welcome. He showed up early, complete with sleeping bag and suitcase, and asked to crash. He wasn't a runaway, and he wasn't the usual crasher—he had $400 in traveler's checks and had been bumming his way across the country as a lark. His father was a bank executive, and David had thousands waiting for him at the other end of a phone call. He wasn't interested in the hippie culture and only mildly interested in drugs. He had a tab of white lightning hidden in the end of a ballpoint pen and finally dropped it while in Golden Gate Park.

It was a good "beauty trip," but he doubted he would ever trip again. He had now "done" drugs—what else did the world have to offer? He was good-looking, and bright as far as attitude went to get along in the straight world.

"I play a lot of games," he said casually. "I'm good at playing games. I usually win them."

David and the original hippies would have had little to say to each other.

Dick was from Oklahoma City, a quiet kid with thick glasses and a scraggly beard who was a natural attraction for highway cops. Hitchhiking to San Francisco had been a series of short hops and overnight stays in various small-town jails. He was from a good family, got along well with his classmates, but was remote from his father and hated his mother. Unlike David, Dick was not good at society's games. For a handsome eighteen-year-old he hadn't been successful with the girls. His first try was traumatic and he was properly outraged by it. "She was a lesbian and when it came right down to it, she didn't like it at all!"

Life since then had been futile attempts to recoup his lost pride and self-confidence.

Harold had come to the Haight as a rebellion against his father—a wealthy, gun-collecting Bircher type. What Harold wanted was to prove that he was independent of his father's money (at least until school started in the fall). He sold hippie newspapers and worked in the local hot dog stand. After a month Harold's father ransomed him from the Haight by paying him $4 an hour to work in his uncle's auto repair shop.

Jimmy was a real pothead—a small, thin kid from Massachusetts, he had come to the Haight primarily for cheap dope. He had never tried smack or speed but was familiar with everything else in the Haight pharamacopoeia—acid, pot, mescaline, hashish—you name it, Jimmy had either smoked it or swallowed it. "I want to get high and stay there," he said with a smile an ad agency would have paid a fortune for. He came from middle-class, intensely religious parents, and back east had been a capable apprentice machinist—but for him that had been strictly a drag. He was a master of the Haight teenybopper vocabulary— *"Wow! Outtasight! Blow your mind! Groovy!"* The Haight for him was not so much love but free dope on Hippie Hill. He could work through the better part of a lid in a day. He crashed at various pads until his welcome was thoroughly worn out. Money was a hang-up. Working was out of the question, and selling hippie newspapers was a bore. Dealing was the logical way of getting money, but Jimmy was very righteous about it. "I'll never deal—it's too much of a paranoid trip." But later on he became a dealer—after burning a crippled shopkeeper for the money to buy his first kilo.

Allen was hung up on drugs and philosophy and for him the Haight was a mystical magic trip except for brief spells of reality when he came down with clap.

Peter, with the piercing eyes and wide cheekbones of a Native American, was a man for whom the Haight was also a trip, but on his last day there, sober and cool, said he was returning to New York because he had some lectures to give.

One of the last crashers I let stay over was Mark. He wasn't handsome—he was what my mother would have called "nice-looking." What gave me pause was that he seemed a little slow. I had a spare sleeping bag and made him up a bed, then turned in, dead tired. It was all of an hour before he climbed into bed with me.

The next morning I fed him breakfast, told him to take care of himself, and turned him loose on a world that would eat him up in nothing flat.

I worried about him and told the story to Fat Maxey next time I ran into him at Garuda's some days later. It was Maxey who suggested the obvious.

I went down to the city jail the next morning and bailed Mark out. He had been languishing in the lockup for fifteen days and, oddly, seemed reluctant to leave. Once home, he told me what had happened—everybody else had been smoking pot in the open, so he did, too, only a new cop had spotted him.

He had liked jail, he said. Everybody had been nice to him, they had taught him a lot. He grinned. He could hardly wait until bedtime to show me. I gave him a $10 bill and turned him out. The first time had been a mistake; there would be no second time. I hoped that some nice gay guy would let him crash, maybe let Mark stay until such time that he was smart enough to take care of himself.

Which, I suspected, would be never.

The crashers could usually take care of themselves; the runaways had a tougher time of it. They could go to Huckleberry's for Runaways and get food and sound advice during the day, but they couldn't crash there at night unless they had permission from their parents. So fourteen-year-old Skippy spent the days at Huckleberry's and the nights wandering the streets.

Stephen was fifteen, a gaunt kid who looked much older than he was and who had run away to the Haight with no money and only the T-shirt and the pair of pants he was wearing. He slept in the back of a laundry until discovered by the owner and then crashed with me for a night. I impressed upon him the virtues of Huckleberry's and convinced him he should go there and have them contact his folks and maybe help iron out their differences. He arrived at Huckleberry's the next night just in time to walk into the arms of the police, who had chosen that particular night to bust the place.

They were the raggle-taggle gypsies of the Children's Crusade who had come to the Haight because the Haight promised dope, excitement, and an affectional society. What the straight world never really wanted to understand was that their kids who fled to the Haight went there for all three.

Haight-Ashbury was not an all-white enclave of San Francisco—it hadn't been for decades. A large number of blacks had been living there in peace and harmony with whites for years. With the largely white invasion, the balance was upset. The streets had been taken over by young strangers who had come from God knew where, rents were going up, familiar grocery stores and hardware stores had disappeared, and in their stead were stores whose signs didn't make much sense.

It was a cultural invasion, and they didn't like it. As one young black spokesman said from the stage of the Straight Theater: "I represent the 70 percent of the Haight that's black—we're the cats you never see, the ones you never look at."

The blacks in the Haight were middle class—muni drivers, postmen, government workers, etc. Some of them had brought food to the hill and given it away to the white hippie kids. Others sat on their doorsteps and watched the hippies wandering by; they were as baffled as any middle-class whites watching the scene. Compared to their own recent struggles, what were the hippies bitching about? They had it made.

There were fights and thefts, but then there were fights and thefts among the hippies themselves. Granted, it was still smart to watch yourself at night, but sometimes the violence was provoked. One time I was sitting on Hippie Hill and noticed a group of four blacks walking along the pathway below. They were being followed by a spaced-out kid intent on doing his bit for race relations.

"You can't make me not love you! I mean it—you can't refuse my love!"

The group's repeated demands that he go someplace else soon changed to a discussion of whether they should beat him up right on the sidewalk or drag him into the bushes and do it. He was finally pulled away by some friends who had no intentions of letting him start a riot.

Toward the end of the summer some whites and blacks had teamed up. Many of the hippies really couldn't go home again—their poverty was very real, and the blacks sensed it. Not all of the hippies had been raised in nice suburban homes— some of them were street types, handy with their fists and who found the trip from hostility to respect to friendship a relatively short one. The more intellectual types sorted each other out over chess games, and finally, some were just friendly, period.

One day I was playing guard at the Free Frame of Reference shop, trying to keep several young black kids from barging in and grabbing everything in sight. A young girl among them was a spitter, and her aim was perfect.

My tolerance level quickly sank to zero. It was hard to remind myself that the same thing sometimes happened in Chicago—with gangs of young white kids.

And sometimes white adults in the Haight were to blame. There was no denying the thefts, the violence, the mutual distrust, but it wasn't just on one side. I remember going to a meeting of the Communications Company—they handed out leaflets warning hippies against everything it was possible to warn them about. Be careful who you hang with, don't go out late at night, etc. A lot of it made sense—and a lot of it was pure paranoia.

The meeting was in an apartment on Masonic, and there was no mistaking that it was sponsored by the Communications Company, which prided itself on being hipper than thou. An open parachute hung from the ceiling, and all of us huddled beneath it.

The warning for the day was that on good authority (always unnamed, of course) the Black Panthers were going to take over the Haight and hold it for ransom until the government stopped the Vietnam War. It made no practical sense at all, but anything that might bring the war to a halt was worth considering.

For a minute or two.

Another time, I was sitting on Hippie Hill watching a muscular black guy in the meadow below playing with a knife. A white friend with me said, "I know the cat—I've rapped with him a lot—he's a good rapper, one of the brightest I've ever met. He's got a degree, but he's black—Christ, it's tough enough for us."

In the meadow the black guy got into a friendly argument with a younger kid that quickly turned sour. The black rapper suddenly started running after him, waving the knife. He couldn't run very fast—he was crippled. I sat and watched him for a long time.

Suzanne and Jean were two blacks who lived together in the

Haight. Both wore their hair native style, but Suzanne was statuesque and regal-looking, while Jean was a thin, nervous type, an ex-actress. Both had been married and were now divorced. Suzanne had two kids—one, a little girl named Angel, who was impossible not to love, and five-year-old Johnny, who was a young version of the "hostile spade" stereotype. He would fight, kick, spit, and swear (if his mother wasn't around).

Suzanne and Jean had teamed up to share their meager resources—they both wanted to go to Mexico and get their kids away from the hostility and filth of Haight Street.

One day I went with them to Berkeley to have a picnic. Going home, we decided to visit Johnny's father, who lived in a small house with his new white wife.

When they came out to say their good-byes, Johnny was holding onto his father's trouser leg and bawling—no longer hostile but a pathetic little boy crying for his daddy.

Of all the groups I both sympathized with and hated, at the head of the list were the police. They had an impossible job and quickly realized they were in a war—the hippies against the cops.

The drug laws were being violated on a massive scale, the district was filling up with runaways, Park Station was being flooded with parents demanding that their kids be found and returned, and the "good" people in town wanted their city cleaned up—which meant the Haight. Nobody had invited the hippies to come to town, and worst of all, they had arrived hungry and broke. The city was indignant.

The cop who was so nice to the tourist in North Beach was King Kong in blue when he was assigned to the Haight. If the hippie was young, he was probably a runaway. If he was in his twenties, he was probably a dealer. If you were older than that—well, you should have had the good sense not to be there in the first place. And don't give the cop all that crap about hippies being nonviolent—if he had drawn duty there the previous summer, he knew better.

The political activists—San Francisco always had more than its share—saw opportunity in the unmotivated kids. Their job, of course, was to motivate them. The same activists who had urged both sides to "cool it" during the Hunters Point riots now started working for a confrontation between the kids and the cops.

It wasn't hard to do. The biggest crime implicating the hippies was dealing or using pot. *Everybody* used grass, and there was no end to culprits being dragged away. When a skinny eighteen-year-old was dragged off in a pot bust by a cop who looked like Bull Connor, onlookers sympathized 100 percent with the kid. Somebody threw a pop bottle, somebody yelled "Fascist bastard!," and quicker than you could say Allen Ginsberg, riot squads would show up to haul away more protesting kids.

The usual flyers would show up on the street urging mass meetings to get together and sue the cops but that was the most empty threat a transient society could make. One time we met, a jug of Red Mountain was passed around, and one witness testified that a girl had been hit by a bottle thrown from the crowd. He was immediately jeered down. Everybody there knew she'd been hit by a cop.

The agents provocateurs were also quick to appear. As reported in *The Haight-Ashbury Tribune*, the writer was grabbed and handcuffed by the cops and thrown in the paddy wagon. One of the cops said, "We're going to show you what fascism is all about," and the reporter said all he could think about were concentration camps. "One guy was tossed in with a bloody head, and blood was gushing out. Then a girl named Louise was thrown in and I could see her jaw was broken. One of the cops even said 'You know what? The next thing we're going to do is turn you into soap.'"

It all sounded very practiced, but few people doubted the truth of what was said. Few people in the Haight *ever* doubted what was said against the cops.

There were some comic overtones. Ballet stars Nureyev and Fonteyn were busted at a pot party, and when the word spread, the upper crust in 'Frisco panicked. Every top lawyer in town was contacted, and the two were hastily released when a comma was found misplaced in the warrant.

Another time it didn't concern hippies, it concerned Cat. I had let a couple crash for the night, and since they had a collie with them, I exiled Cat to the backyard. The next morning, when the crashers had left, I opened the window and whistled for Cat. There was no response. I immediately went out, afraid the raccoons had gotten him. I found him in a little nest he'd dug in the dirt. I picked him up and he went limp. I carried him into the house, put out some water and a dish of food, but he wouldn't eat. Finally I went to the butcher, bought some liver, took it home, fried it up, and cut it into small bits. I then fed Cat by hand. He sniffed it, tasted it, had a mouthful, then dug in, all the time staring at me. I was never to give his home to a dog again, did I understand that?

Another time there was a free dance at the Fillmore, and leaflets were passed all over the city in hopes that the disgruntled kids who couldn't get in would tangle with the police. But only one cop showed up, and he jollied the kids, and the show on the outside soon became as good as the show on the inside.

The case of Randy Buckner wasn't funny. Late one evening

a crowd had gathered a hundred feet from the Straight Theater to listen to a sidewalk guitar player. The cops showed up, Buckner cracked wise, nightsticks flew, and so did blood.

Buckner's dried blood could still be seen on the sidewalk the next day. A kid built a shrine of bottles and candles and created a sign saying, "This is where your brother fell." A cop kicked over the bottles and candles, then leaned against a parking meter a few feet away and stared blandly at this hippie kid Jay, waiting. Jay stared blandly back. The kids grew quiet and watched. Jay outstared the cop, and when he left, rebuilt the shrine. The next day the shrine was enormous. This time the cops left it alone. One of them asked Jay bitterly, "Whatever happened to the good hippies?" "They're all in jail," Jay said, just as bitter.

The cops were pushed to their limit. Once, while booking a kid in Park Station, a cop said, "I've got a son just like you in Vietnam." "*I hope he gets killed,*" the kid said with a snarl. "If I had been a civilian," the cop said later, "I think I would have killed him."

It was public policy, of course, to harass the hippies. You could be arrested for sleeping in Golden Gate Park, for possession of narcotics (almost all of them carried pot), for assaulting an officer. (What constituted assault? Complaining when arrested?) Once booked, a prisoner could be released on bail or on his own recognizance if he had a job or owned a home, etc. But few hippies had jobs or money or even friends when it came to bail money. It was a pretty stupid hippie who didn't realize he had fewer rights than a whore.

The city had finally found a group other than blacks to occupy the bottom rung of the ladder of justice. Maybe the city was even aware of it. But whether the cops were vicious or overworked or just misunderstood didn't matter to the hippie who drew a heart on the wall next to the Psych Shop and wrote in it a bit of wisdom that nobody could argue with:

"I love the cops—I'm from L.A. and you don't know how good you've got it!"

The one group that had a tougher time than the cops were the FBI men trying to track down draft dodgers.

Joe was a kid who had been institutionalized all of his life. His parents had died when he was five and he became a rent-a-kid—the state paid various families to take care of him, for which his foster families were paid for his food, shelter, and clothing. Affection and love were not included.

At age nineteen Joe neglected to register for the draft and headed for the Haight. He wanted to meet the beautiful people he had read so much about. After a week or so of crashing, he wasn't welcome anymore. He was expected to clean up his room, do the dishes, and other tasks that had never occurred to him—he had to be told.

He adjusted, moving in with some friends and getting a job as a messenger boy downtown. He wasn't handsome and had difficulty relating to girls. Then things began to go even more sour. He had a frail personality, but the loungers on Hippie Hill didn't know that—or if they did, didn't care. One day in Buena Vista Park a black pulled a knife on him and forced him to give a blow job. Joe had a thing about "queers," and this didn't help much.

The next night he burgled a gun shop and the cops caught him within five minutes. He was given two months in the county jail, and the worst thing that could happen to him, happened. He was gangbanged by a group of blacks. Aside from having a sore butt, he thrived in jail. It was a structured situation of the type he had known most of his life. Some speed freak chicks worked him over once he was out, and his personality structure really started to crumble.

Then there was the draft. Joe couldn't handle the rest of his life, and handling the draft was out of the question. The FBI man looking for him said if the army had given him a decent psychiatric examination he would never be taken. Joe couldn't manage to turn himself in and take his chances, so he split and the last anybody heard of him he was selling himself in the Tenderloin.

"Fuck me, mister, and make me feel wanted for once."

The FBI man who picked him up shook his head. "I'm not doing police work down here, I'm doing social work. Christ, the kid wasn't even good at hustling."

IN EARLY 1967 the Human Be-In attracted twenty-five-thousand people. It resulted in the Summer of Love, and a city of seven hundred thousand found itself playing host to a hundred thousand young runaways, throwaways, and those who wanted a more adventurous life than the one they were leading. Hardly any of the new arrivals had any money, few had more than the clothes they wore, and even fewer had marketable skills. The only thing they brought with them were great expectations. And almost all of them wanted to live in Haight-Ashbury.

The city had been warned—the mass media had greeted the Be-In as if it were a modern version of Disney's "Pleasure Island" from *Pinocchio*. It was a relief from writing about wars and depressions—it was fun, it was free, and somehow everybody would be taken care of. The hippies were reincarations of Jesus Christ, and dropping LSD was a sacrament (according to its experimenter and popularizer, Dr. Timothy Leary). The media didn't feel any responsibility for what it was writing about—after all, there were no Disney monsters hiding behind doors waiting to change the newcomers into donkeys.

The newcomers managed to do that themselves.

Some of the more enterprising hippies bought copies of the underground papers for a quarter and sold then to tourists for a dollar. The less enterprising held out their hands and asked for "any spare change?," then rewarded the giver with a smile and a version of the mantra "Outta sight, man!," "You're really beautiful!," or simply, "Love ya, man!"

That slowly changed when the professional hippies moved in—the ones from Hollywood High or UC at Sacramento. If you gave them any money, there would be no "thank you." The well-dressed hippie with the carefully torn dress or pants and the new shoes and blank face would move on to the next potential customer and repeat the request. No smile, no thank you, no benediction involving the word "love."

A friend once figured if he gave a dime for every "spare change" artist from Stanyan to Masonic, he would have coughed up ten bucks.

One night I had a visitor—a middle-aged, overwrought man who showed me a picture of his daughter and asked if I'd seen her. I had expected him to be angry, even to be accusatory, but he was none of those. He was a father looking for his daughter who'd run away to the Haight. It would have been like looking for needle in a haystack, but he was too distraught to realize that. I had no idea what the trouble may have been between him and his daughter, but it was obvious he loved her very much and would spend days in the Haight looking for her.

Another time, drinking coffee in the I/Thou with Fat Maxey, we were approached by Sheriff Richard Hongisto, who showed me a picture of a girl and asked if I'd seen her.

I took a long look, shook my head, then frowned. "She looks strange."

"She's dead," the sheriff said, and moved along to another coffee drinker.

This was the first time in my life that I realized people seldom die with their eyes closed. It was like somebody had opened a door and you were looking into a room that was totally empty.

"The scene's changing," Maxey said, "and not for the better. There's always been a hundred street kids dealing pot, but now the heavy hitters have moved in." I looked blank and he said, "You can pick up a key for a hundred bucks. And a key will give you about fifty lids you can sell for twenty-five bucks a lid. You do the math. That's why all the college kids are showing up—a couple of keys they can break up and sell to their friends back home and they've paid their tuition."

I watched the passing parade for a long moment.

"Why do you stay here, Maxey?"

He shrugged.

"I wanted to go to State and maybe get a degree in English. I didn't have the money or the dedication so I came here. I wanted to be a part of State, and it hurt when I couldn't." He shrugged. "There's not much to hurt you down here. What about you? And don't give me any 'writer' crap—you could have gotten everything you wanted to know in two weeks."

I didn't have an answer.

That Sunday I lugged my pot to the free medical clinic to cook up a batch of spaghetti for the staff—doing my bit. Maybe Joan Baez would come in again.

This night, something was wrong. I went through the spaghetti pot, which usually would have been enough, and half the staff were still going hungry. I hid behind a door to watch the substitute cook stirring the pot. He was selling it out the back to a line of hippies for twenty-five cents a plate.

I was more than pissed. When I confronted him he looked blank for a moment, then got angry. "They're hungry, too, man. The doctors can afford to buy a meal downtown."

I picked up a few cans of spaghetti sauce and a couple pounds of meat and finished my obligation to the staff. The volunteer staffer had disappeared into the grumbling crowd at the bottom of the steps.

It was a difficult life for all concerned, including the kids who had believed what they'd read in the magazines and now felt shortchanged. They'd been promised a paradise and found themselves in a city that didn't have the foggiest idea of how to cope with the situation outside of jailing those who smoked or were selling pot.

Why didn't the city allow the churches to house some of the kids overnight? I never found an answer to that.

The hippie powers that be finally thought of a solution— they'd hold a funeral for "hippie," tell the kids the party was over and they should all go home. The Psychedelic Shop closed its doors and put a sign in the window that said "Nebraska needs you more."

Somebody built a large coffin, and a small crowd carried it to the Panhandle, filled it with some tattered rock posters, old clothes, half-empty packs of Zig-Zag cigarette papers (indispensable for the pot smoker), and strings of beads and other symbols of hippie culture. Then they set fire to the coffin and leaped through the flames until the Fire Department arrived and rang down the curtain.

It was all over. The hippie kids would go home, and the few that remained would become "Free Americans."

The only problem was that while the original be-in had attracted twenty-five thousand, only a few hundred had showed up for the funeral. And with every bus that disgorged its expectant passengers, the party was only getting bigger.

Fat Maxey wasn't my only friend in the Haight. I was getting closer to a Romanian immigant named Mike, who I was teaching English. He had an even-keel personality not liable to be upset by much of anything. Maybe this made me realize I really didn't know all that much about Mike. Granted, the disparity in language was one of the reasons why. But I met as often with him for coffee at the I/Thou as I did Maxey, and occasionally the three of us would hit it off, though Maxey was considerably more withdrawn and cautious with Mike.

I found out why one day when Mike came over to visit. He didn't come over often, though I had made it plain he was welcome anytime.

This time after I buzzed him in, he stood at the top of the stairs, his hands deep in his pockets, and he didn't come farther into the room.

He smiled slightly and said, "Gimme all your money."

I could feel the sweat suddenly pop in my armpits. Everything I didn't know about him came into sharp focus. A refugee from Romania who had heard about the Haight and came out of curiosity, not because he had any particular political leanings or was fond of drugs.

I stared at him and he moved the hand in his right pocket suggestively.

"Gimme all your money," he repeated.

There was a pot of boiling water on the nearby stove, and if I could reach it I could catch him in the face with the scalding water.

I hesitated one more second, decided I wasn't Sean Connery after all, took my wallet out of my pocket, and tossed it to him. He couldn't use the credit cards, and there wasn't much cash in it.

He held it for a moment, a quizzical expression on his face, then dropped it on the nearby table.

"You think a friend would do this to you?" he asked.

"It was a lousy joke," I said, though I wasn't sure it was a joke at all.

He shrugged and raised an eyebrow. "Have coffee?" he said. "I have questions about words."

I was quiet all the way over to the I/Thou. When we sat at a table and I had caught my breath I repeated, "That was a lousy joke."

He stood up and emptied out his pockets: a wadded-up handkerchief, some small change, and two keys on a chain.

"A joke," he said. "I sorry." He sounded the ultimate of sincere.

All I could think of then was, what if I had reached the pot of boiling water? Would I have blinded him? Burned his face? Even if I'd had a lot of money in the wallet, it wouldn't have been worth the consequences. I really didn't think that Mike had had a gun or that he would have shot me. Did I?

I told the story to Maxey a few days later and he laughed.

"So you would have reported it to the police and made their day. For the first time in weeks they would have had an actual criminal to chase."

I didn't see Mike for a few days, and when I did, I heard about him through Maxey, who gave me a note.

"He said he was in a hurry and I should give this to you."

I read it, then shoved it across the table to Maxey. "He's going to be a houseman in Walnut Creek, wherever that is."

Maxey looked disgusted. "Houseboy is more like it. He'll clean the house, fix the meals, and ball the owner in the evening. He lucked out."

"He's not the type," I said. "So where the hell is Walnut Creek?"

"East Bay—a really wealthy suburb."

My image of Mike was fading fast.

"He wouldn't sell himself."

Maxey held up a finger for the waiter to bring him another doughnut. "Can be bought. All depends on the money."

A few days later I bought a gallon of Red Mountain and had a group of kids over for spaghetti. The usual "You're great, man, love ya," and after they had left, I tumbled into bed.

At my usual breakfast with Maxey the next morning he told me that the Real Estate Board had redlined the Haight— any more sales or rentals weren't recommended. In addition, according to Maxey, the murder rate for the Haight had hit one per square block, by far the highest in the city.

Disney's Paradise Island had finally sunk into the sea.

When I got home, I was surprised when I went to open the door. It was unlocked, and I swore at myself for being so foolish as not to throw the latch.

Inside, the apartment was a mess. My small FM radio—my one nod to the good life—was missing. So was the Jefferson Airplane poster on the wall. So was the small dish of pot I'd kept for visitors.

Shit. Whoever it was, I'd served spaghetti to him the night before. "*Love ya, man . . .*" I called for Cat and found him hiding underneath the bed, scared out of his wits. He'd pissed on the floor.

I went to the park and flaked out on the hill, watching a red-haired preacher baptize a naked kid in the filthy pond. A girl sitting next to me turned to her friend and pointed. "Did you see that? He wasn't even circumcised."

Home that night to my now empty apartment, then a quick meal for Cat, who curled up in the bed with me.

The next morning, I made my trip to the I/Thou for doughnuts

with Maxey and a little sympathy. I didn't expect much—
Maxey had warned me about a wave of robberies the week
before.

I was crossing Haight Street when somebody beeped at me
from their car and hollered, "Hey, Frank!"

I walked over, puzzled, then recognized Nat Lehrman—I'd
once met him at a party in Hefner's mansion.

"You want a job?"

I couldn't believe the coincidence.

"Doing what?"

"Writing the '*Playboy* Advisor.'"

It was a column in the front of the magazine that gave sexual advice and some general living suggestions to the *Playboy*
readers.

"You're puting me on. What brings you to town?"

"Conference. Then they told me to find you."

I couldn't think of a less likely candidate for the job. I didn't
know at the time that it was Masters and Johnson, two doctors, who gave out the sexual advice, and I would be the guy
who would tell the reader what kind of wine to serve with the
fish.

"How much?"

"Fifteen grand a year."

I stared at him for a moment. He was serious. Jesus . . .

"When do they want me?"

"As soon as you can get there."

"I'm not good at walking," I said. "I'm busted."

He fished an envelope out of his pocket and gave it to me.

"This is an advance on your first assignmnent."

The catch.

"Which is?"

"Interview Robert Heinlein and get his reaction to the moon

landing. A photographer will meet you this afternoon—give you a couple of hours to pack." He glanced around the street. "Where do you want him to meet you?"

I pointed at the I/Thou.

"Right there—two o'clock." Then: "You took a lot for granted."

He stared at me for a moment. "Look at yourself, Frank." He started the car, and turned to watch out for traffic. "See you in Chicago—Bob Shea's found an apartment for you."

In the I/Thou I found a chair opposite Maxey and opened the envelope. A credit card for me, name and everything.

"Heinlein's my favorite author," I said to Maxey.

He looked uneasy.

"What the hell's wrong? Who were you talking to?"

"God," I said.

I got some money from the bank, went to the apartment, and gave some to the landlord to ship my typewriter and my spaghetti pot to me c/o *Playboy*.

Then I went to the john and flushed my love beads down the toilet. I found the suit I'd worn when I'd first come to the Haight. It still fit.

I looked in the mirror. The image looking back at me was too old and out of place to be a hippie.

I'd get plane tickets when I came back to 'Frisco, grab a cab, and go straight to the airport.

I lifted Cat to say good-bye and he licked my nose. When I put him down, he went to the corner and sat facing the door, ready to tutor the next tenant.

I ended up at the I/Thou to wait for the photographer. I didn't say good-bye to Maxey—he'd already left.

In my mind, so had I. I'd drop him a note.

The Haight had started with great optimism and ideals, where a tab of acid really had been meant as a sacrament. I remembered

Love's Thanksgiving party and the night the Straight Theater opened a rear window and projected a movie on the side of the building next door. And the occasional street party where people really were friendly and shared a joint or a bag of fries, and Father Harris, who had busted his butt doing his best for the street kids and was seldom thanked for it.

And then it had deteriorated into a slum where rich kids dressed up and played at being poor and begged strangers for a nickel or a dime when they had hundreds of dollars at home.

I might return to San Francisco someday.

But I'd never go back to Haight-Ashbury.

Bonny Doon was a little suburb south of San Francisco; the Heinleins lived out in the boonies in a nice-looking, comfortable house with a wire fence around it. I found out later they built it to keep the hippies away so Bob could work. *Stranger in a Strange Land* was the favorite novel of the hippies, and I think many of them wanted to adopt him as their guru.

I stayed at the house for three days asking questions, the photographer taking an occasional picture of Heinlein. He never complained. He had been at NASA when the first men landed on the moon and he reportedly had burst into tears. If any man had a right to, it was Robert Heinlein—the man who actually "sold the moon." I knew what it had meant to most people, but I wanted to know more about what it had meant to him.

The days I spent with Heinlein and his wife, Ginny, were among the happiest days of my life. Dinner was always formal, and the Heinleins dressed for it. I was still a latter-day hippie, my suit uncomfortable and scratchy. I was ill at ease at first—the Heinleins were more than friendly but frighteningly formal, and I felt like a country bumpkin with wisps of straw coming out of my ears.

There was a bottle of fine wine at every meal, and it took an effort to remember that I was there on business—not as a fan, which in actuality I was. Ginny filled me in on the ground rules when we were alone. Bob never talked about his own novels—not in a specific sense, though I thought I might be able to tease out the thoughts behind them. But that was one of the provisos of the contract he had signed with *Playboy*. The magazine had paid Bob two grand for the interview, one of the very few interviews they'd ever paid for.

I had a quick tour of the house, the library, and the office where he worked. His typewriter was an old Remington standard with a homemade box built around it to deaden the sound.

After supper, relaxed in his study, I turned on my small tape recorder and asked him how he felt at launchtime.

He described the incredible noise and the feeling of pride when the rocket took off for the moon.

"Somebody in the crowd shouted, 'They're on their way to the moon!' It was then I realized that for the first time in history I was seeing a spaceship—and it really was a spaceship—lift off on a journey to another celestial body. There was absolute dead silence at liftoff, then a spontaneous cheer that could be heard for miles. At separation, the same thing—silence, then the thunder of cheering. That first day of actual space travel to another heavenly body marked the most important thing the human race has ever done."

The actual lunar landing made him tear up again. "'That's one small step for man, and one giant leap for mankind.'"

I was pretty sure the words had been engraved in his heart as well as in his head.

Heinlein suddenly got bitter.

"I'd waited fifty years for this. Half a century of being treated like a madman for believing what has been perfectly evident since the days of Newton."

178 · Frank M. Robinson

"What about the cost?" I said. "The space program has cost billions."

He looked disappointed—I hadn't understood the real worth of NASA.

"When they've finished the accounting we'll discover we got space travel for free—and with a profit thrown in. How many lives have been saved when weather satellites can forecast the path of hurricanes? Freeze-dried coffee, sensors to measure blood pressure, new fuel cells, filament-wound plastics as strong as steel and ten times lighter. . . . NASA has listed more than three thousand spin-offs."

He knew the subject well—he had spent a lifetime writing about the possibilities. I asked him why he had started writing science fiction books for kids. "Because I wanted them to become interested in real science. . . . The books paid well, but that's not the real reason."

Heinlein's books for kids had been immensely popular, and not just among children. In a survey of NASA scientists, it turned out the vast majority of them had read Heinlein, either as kids or young adults.

"Do you think we'll ever go to Mars?" I already knew his answer.

"Of course. It's easier to go to Mars from the moon than it is from the Earth. The gravity of the moon is so much lighter than that of Earth, liftoff would take far less fuel."

"The supplies," I objected. "Food, water . . ."

He shrugged. "We have nuclear submarines that can stay underwater for longer than six months at a time. Waste products will simply be recycled."

For the next two days, Heinlein's imagination soared. We would visit every planet in the solar system. Someday we would go to the stars.

In his imagination, Heinlein visualized the human race conquering the universe. I did not remind him that light travels 186,000 miles per second—eight minutes for the light from the sun to reach Earth. Other planetary systems would be centuries away. If we ever developed anything that could go as fast as light, it would still take years.

Heinlein didn't talk about one of his most famous stories—"Universe"—in which spaceships are doing just that kind of travel with crews who lived out their lives on board, breeding the crews that would replace them when they died. Don Wilcox in the old *Amazing* had used the same theme in his story "The Voyage That Lasted Six Hundred Years." And decades later, I would as well in "The Dark Beyond the Stars."

I asked Heinlein about his best-known book—the first of a number to hit the bestseller lists. The hero was a human boy who was born on Mars and comes to Earth and in effect starts a new religion. (It introduced the word "grokking"—to grok somebody was to understand completely what they were saying. The hippies picked up on that right away: "I grok you.")

Another of Heinlein's books (later turned into a successful movie) got him booed at a science fiction convention. In *Starship Troopers*, a book with a militaristic background where spaceships of troopers—the marines of the future—go to a planet to battle insect-like creatures that posed a threat to man.

In the eyes of the audience, Heinlein had become a fascist because of the military aspects. (If anything, Heinlein was a libertarian.) Heinlein had been a military man for a time, four years in the navy to be discharged as a lieutenant for medical reasons. He had stayed in touch with old friends in the navy and had lost neither the bearing nor the outlook of a naval officer.

The highest calling for a human being, Heinlein said, was to give up his life for his fellow man. It sounded cold when he said it, but in real life, in Iraq and Afghanistan and earlier wars, it happened many times. I had trouble accepting that, but I couldn't argue with the reality. Men would get medals for saving the lives of their companions—or rather their near and dear would.

The catch, which came as a shock to many science fiction fans, was that *Starship Troopers* and *Stranger in a Strange Land* had been written at the same time. After writing so many pages of the one, Heinlein would switch over to the other. Different characters, of course, but Heinlein maintained that the philosophy was the same in each. In one a man gave up his life to save his fellow men. In the other a man was about to.

Starting with *Stranger*, Heinlein abandoned ordinary science fiction to write more philosophical books. Most of them were also bestsellers, though he left the bulk of his science fiction readers behind.

By the third day my head was spinning, and when I transcribed my tapes later, I came up with close to 150 pages.

I left as much in awe of him as I had been at the start. He had made me painfully aware that human beings were insignificant creatures on a minor planet circling a small star in a galaxy that was only one of billions in the universe.

I hoped to hell I didn't come down with what was called "island fever"—where I had once visited Maui, for example, and suddenly realized I was on this tiny bit of land in the middle of the gigantic Pacific Ocean and all I wanted to do was go home, where my existence might mean something.

Would future astronauts ever feel like that someday? I wondered. The desire to leave this tiny ball of dust and explore the vastness just beyond?

Heinlein didn't wonder; he *knew*.

My three days were up, we had a going-away dinner with

several bottles of the best, and the next day the photographer and I were dropped off at the I/Thou, where we had started. I hailed a cab and went directly to the airport.

I had been a stranger in a strange land . . . but it had taken me two years to realize it.

❧ XIX ❧

I SQUIRMED IN my first-class seat, took a pass on the meal, and closed my eyes to try to sleep. Bob Shea would meet me at the airport and drive me to my apartment on the lakefront, not that far down from Northwestern. I understood the apartment was furnished, complete with both bedding and kitchen supplies.

I'd miss Cat. I should have thought of some way I could take him along, but I had a hunch he was more attached to the apartment than to me.

Good luck, Cat. . . . I hope your new master loves you as much as I did even if I didn't always show it.

And then the memories started to slide back in. Fat Maxey, a fixture at the I/Thou, who had the most handsome boy in the Haight as his lover. Nobody knew how he did it, least of all me, though I was properly jealous. . . . Then the one Haight hanger-on who had connections down the peninsula and took me on a guided tour through the locker room at Stanford. I was supposed to be impressed, but I had spent too many years working out at the Evanston Y to do more than glance at the athletes changing into their uniforms.

What I remembered most was my first night in 'Frisco, when "Jesus" had stepped out of the shadows and offered me a french fry.

Then most of my San Francisco memories started to slide away. It was dark out and I fell asleep. The next thing I knew the stewardess was shaking me gently to say we'd arrived at O'Hare.

Shea met me at baggage claim, told me it would be a short ride, and threw my bags into the backseat. I was out of it and saw little of the city. It was a windy night and I could hear the waves of Lake Michigan sweeping over the beach.

There were lights on in some of the windows of the apartments, but I couldn't make out the whole building. Bob gave the apartment keys to me and told me they didn't expect me at *Playboy* until noon.

I fumbled for the light switch and glanced around. I had lucked out. Wall-to-wall carpeting, big living room, large windows overlooking the lake, medium-size bedroom, and what looked like a fully equipped kitchen.

There were two huge floor pillows in the living room and I collapsed on one of them, too tired to go into the bedroom and strip to my shorts.

It was a very bright morning when I woke up, wondered where the hell Cat was, then jerked fully awake. An hour to brush my teeth and make it down to the Palmolive Building, renamed the Playboy Building. They had really come up in the world since the last time I'd been in their offices. *Playboy* was now the biggest-selling newsstand magazine in the country, with a circulation of seven million. It usually ran to three hundred pages, half of which carried ads. *Playboy* now paid the rent of many of the magazine outlets that carried it.

The receiving line to greet me included Nat Lehrman, the head of the department; Bob Shea; Robert Anton Wilson—he and Shea later collaborated on the popular *Illuminatus* books; Toba Cohen; and a black woman, Estella. If I ever had any questions about who to see for what, I went to Estella.

My office was small but okay, equipped with a filing cabinet and a large electric typewriter. I'd never used one before—I'd rest my fingers on the keys and find I'd typed a whole line. It was a week before I stopped swearing.

The Advisor division was larger than I thought. A battery of three girls kept large file folders of copies of all the letters that came in. The answers were canned and the girls would choose one to fit the letter. Every single letter was answered, but the same writer was never repeated twice—we didn't want to start a correspondence with any of them.

The letters asking sexual questions were referred to our sex experts, Drs. Masters and Johnson—but I would edit whatever they wrote, rewriting their answers into *Playboy*ese.

I tried only once to run a sexy letter and answer it. The writer said he liked to go to the local theater and sit in the balcony. Some of the other patrons would hit on him, which he didn't mind but which gave him such a huge headache he had to go home. What should he do?

My answer was simple:

"Take two aspirin and go back to the balcony."

My three assistants, the watchdogs for the column, told me college students frequently wrote in with "humorous" questions, thinking the Advisor would fall for them. This was obviously one of them.

I'd lived in Los Angeles and San Francisco for three years, but Chicago was still my hometown—and always would be.

When I worked on *Rogue*, I used to hang out at "The Gate of Horn," along with others of the staff—we even ran a short pictorial on them. The Horn was a great hangout and featured Peter, Paul, and Mary; Gibson and Camp; Odetta; the Clancy Brothers; Joan Baez; Jo Mapes; Hamilton Camp; Judy Bright, and others. It was the middle of the folk music boom and at least one member of the staff took up the guitar.

I was similarly inspired and spent a couple of hundred on a banjo. I enrolled at the Old Town School of Folk Music and did my best to learn the simplest of folk songs about running to Cripple Creek. After several months of picking at the strings, I realized I'd never be able to do more than hobble to Cripple Creek and consigned the banjo to a corner of the closet.

A previous favorite spot in Chicago when I worked on *Rogue* was Second City. It had started as the Compass Players—originated and run by Mike Nichols and Elaine May—then in 1959 it moved to Old Town and renamed itself Second City. It specialized in improvisational comedy (make it up as you go along). In later years it was the chief supplier of actors for *Saturday Night Live*.

The editorial staff of *Rogue* became ardent fans, and from 1961 to 1963 we ran full-page house ads featuring some of the players (Severn Darden, Paul Sand, and Melinda Dillon). Second City moved several times and for a while it had a small courtyard in back. I remember snooping back there once and ran into Alan Arkin, practicing on his guitar. (No reason he should remember me but I never forgot him.)

When I came back to Chicago in 1969 to work for *Playboy*, I became a fan of Second City once again when John Belushi (later a star in *Animal House*) had been added to the cast, along with Joe Flaherty and Harold Ramis. Ramis moonlighted writing jokes for *Playboy*'s joke column and later became the director of hit movies such as *Ghostbusters* and *Groundhog Day*.

Another asset of the city was community theater—probably more popular in Chicago than in New York. The most popular theaters were the Organic Theater and the Kingston Mines, along with more than a dozen others.

The hit of the Organic Theater was a three-part science fiction play—complete with special effects—titled *Warp*. The play died when it moved to New York. The Organic was a small theater, and *Warp* didn't do well in a larger Big Apple venue. Its last show in Chicago was a sensation—all three episodes of *Warp* played on the same night and the intermission was catered by the high-class restaurant next door.

The Kingston Mines specialized in really offbeat plays, especially those put on by the Theater of the Ridiculous, directed by "Eleven." Probably the most successful of Eleven's plays was *The Whores of Babylon*. I loved it and saw it a dozen times. The three whores (two guys in drag, one woman) were something of a Greek chorus. The major actors played various characters from comic books, movies, and mythology. Probably the most impressive was Frankenstein's monster. The actor entered from the back of the theater and clumped his way to the stage, arms outstretched. Once onstage, he broke into a smooth waltz, then froze for a moment while one of the whores delivered a soliloquy. (I paraphrase here.)

"What do we really know about the monster? What was his favorite song? Did he dream? What did he like for breakfast?"

The "whore" cocked his head, became more serious and the audience grew absolutely still. In one way or another, we were all outcasts playing a role for the people we met. It especially hit home to me. What did people—my friends, my relatives—really know about me?

Not very damn much.

I covered a drag show at a club named Sparrows—drag was not my favorite thing, but I knew it would appeal to a lot of readers. A lot of talent went into the show, including one of the performers who did a "triple"—he did a drag as the MC from *Cabaret* doing a drag.

I watched him put on his makeup for a photo shoot and he explained the process. "First you take off the face"—he powdered his entire face—"then you put on the face." Rouge, lipstick, eyebrows, etc. When he put on his wig, the transformation was complete. I would have opened the door for him, helped him into his chair at dinner, etc.

The wardrobe "mistress" was a thin black man who came up from the South Side in complete drag. I asked him why he worked in the club and he said, "I want to be onstage someday, God willing."

That was his ambition, and he was deadly serious about it.

A few months after I came on staff, Spectorsky asked his troops to submit any ideas on how the HMH company could expand. It had the magazine, a book division, and published several one-shots each year. The company was very rich (I think by this time Hefner had bought his own 737—*The Big Bunny*). The magazine was now worth $1 billion, and apparently expansion was on Hefner's mind.

I wrote a memo suggesting he invest in—at the time—a relatively little-known magazine published in San Francisco titled *Rolling Stone*. Baron Wolman, the magazine's top photographer and a friend, had taken me to the offices, which struck me as fairly primitive. A newsprint tabloid folded in two so it could be sold on the newsstand with the same size as the regular magazines. With one exception the staff struck me as very young, but that was one of its appeals.

By comparison, the staff of *Playboy* was middle-aged.

Stone's best cover—a real grabber at the newsstand—was a nude shot of Yoko Ono and John Lennon. *Playboy* had nothing to match it—the airbrushed covers of *Playboy* featured anonymous nudes, but who the hell were they? And who really cared?

Yoko Ono and John Lennon were real people.

In one sense, the stats were discouraging. A print run of a hundred thousand with estimated sales of eighty thousand (a statement of ownership in the magazine scaled that down to sixty thousand).

Advertising rates were $1,600 and almost all of the ads were record company ads (what else?).

The company had no book division, but World Publishing, Bantam, and Holt, Rinehart and Winston were all doing books on the rock scene "by the editors of Rolling Stone."

In general, *Stone* published a combination of news and feature articles—Bob Dylan, the Beatles, and other rock groups were frequent subjects. The young staff were eager beavers; the oldest member/part owner was Ralph Gleason, who held down the post of music editor of the *San Francisco Chronicle*.

Stone was definitely not a "fan" magazine like most of the youth-oriented publications. It was serious, it was honest, and it had the respect of its readers. What I caught was an attitude of yes, it would always be a "rock" magazine, but the staff wanted to branch out into other areas and eventually did. The magazine "made" Hunter S. Thompson.

Jann Wenner, the major owner/editor was as young as his staff—early twenties—but had a very good idea of what he wanted the magazine to be and had the reputation of being a hard driver.

The thrust of my long (two pages, single-spaced) memo was not what the magazine currently was but what it could be—and would be—in the future. The ground floor was there if anybody wanted to invest in it.

So much for my memo. Hefner was mildly interested, but he wanted a 51 percent interest in *Stone*—ownership. What he was going to do with it, I had no idea—a teenage version of *Playboy*? He knew everything about "sophisticated men's magazines" but absolutely nothing about the sort of magazine that *Stone* wanted to be.

I'm pretty sure that Wenner could have used the money—later, he moved the magazine to New York, and that must have been expensive—but no way was he going to sell a controlling interest to the king of the "sophisticated men's magazines."

I had written the memo, I had pointed out the possibilities. I was also glad when Hefner decided to consign it to the circular file. It would have been a good investment for Hefner, but he would have made a lousy owner.

Hefner's next decision hurt not only me but Bob and Ginny Heinlein as well. The interview with Bob was finally edited, set in print, and announced in the magazine for the following issue.

It was suddenly pulled, with no explanation.

A reporter for the *San Francisco Examiner* had claimed he interviewed Charles Manson—the leader of the notorious Manson murderers—who stated (according to the reporter) that he had modeled his career after the character of Michael Valentine Smith, the lead in *Stranger in a Strange Land*.

Hefner sensed a scoop for the magazine and asked Bob to comment on Manson's statement. Bob refused—it wasn't in the contract that he'd signed with *Playboy* for the interview. Heinlein was one of the very few subjects that *Playboy* had paid for an interview—the magnificent sum of two grand.

I probably could have covered it in my introduction to the interview, saying that Bob never discussed his own stories, but if he did, he certainly wouldn't have had anything to say directly about Manson.

Nobody would buy that, and Hefner shelved the interview and substituted something else. Bob returned *Playboy*'s check, but Spectorsky wouldn't accept it. Spectorsky stated that as far as he was concerned Bob had fulfilled the terms of the contract.

Heinlein then donated the two grand to the charity for the three astronauts who had been burned alive while testing their capsule.

Bob himself had never sent back *Playboy*'s check. Ginny had. Bob was much too sick to do anything, least of all rework any part of the interview. Ginny did what she knew Bob himself would have done.

I was pissed, but the man behind the curtain had spoken, and there was nothing I could do. I apologized profusely, but neither Ginny nor Bob blamed me. I was merely a cog that had been caught in the gears—nobody blamed me, and the Heinleins remained friendly.

The interview finally surfaced when Hefner decided there were so many imitators of *Playboy* on the market, he might as well start one of his own and dilute the competition. The title was *Oui*, a knockoff that looked very much like *Playboy* itself, complete with centerfold, cartoons, and various departments. The nudes showed a little hair (the magazine did not go "pink," as *Hustler* did, but it came close). The Heinlein interview, shortened and cut up with several full-page cartoons, appeared in the third issue. I figured later that the original interview had run close to twelve thousand words and that three thousand of them had been chopped out.

Hefner was in charge of the cartoons for both the magazines, and they were much closer to his heart than a science fiction author he was probably totally unfamiliar with.

I never read the shortened version until years later, and to give the devil his due, the new introduction was good and the interview itself hadn't suffered that much.

Oui was eventually discontinued, the feeling being that rather than taking circulation from competitors, *Oui* was taking it from *Playboy*. There was also the fear that if they tried to compete with *Penthouse* and other magazines in the field, it would lose its reputation as a "sophisticated men's magazine" and become just another skin book.

Other competitors engaged in what was called the "pubic wars." More hair, more pink showing, and finally one of the magazines printed a photograph of male and female models having simulated intercourse.

Playboy was smart to get out when it did, its reputation and its gloss of sophistication still intact.

When Heinlein recovered from his illness, he hired a private eye to interview Manson. It turned out Manson was illiterate. (Other sources claimed that Manson read good literature. Take your pick.)

There was one more task that *Playboy* assigned me, which was to change my life. They had a roundtable discussion of homosexuality, which they wanted me to bring up to date. Stonewall had happened a few months before, and the powers that be decided it would be a hot topic. Shortly after Stonewall, gay liberation groups had sprung up at most major universities in the country. There was a meeting to be held in Chicago of representatives of gay groups from the Universities of Michigan, Wisconsin, Illinois, and Chicago. *Playboy* decided to send their somewhat suspect (I'm sure by this time) Advisor to cover it.

I went to the hotel where the meeting was, found the room, and walked in.

My life changed in an instant; it was like slamming a door. In the room were all the guys I had wanted to meet in college but who, at the time, were as much in the closet as I was. We had passed each other in hallways, sat next to each other in class. I had lusted after some of them—and hopefully, some of them had lusted after me.

I had been leading two lives for years and now one of them was abruptly dead. I would never see Herb, Ron, and $50-a-trick rent boys again.

I didn't have to.

Self-portrait of author, photo booth, circa 1948.
(Courtesy of the Bancroft Library, University of California, Berkeley)

Frank M. Robinson, a supporter and speechwriter for Harvey Milk,
with city supervisor candidate Milk in his office at Castro Camera, 1976.
(Photograph by Daniel Nicoletta, courtesy of the Bancroft Library,
University of California, Berkeley)

Tom Scortia and Frank M. Robinson at a book signing event for
The Nightmare Factor at Books Plus, February 26, 1978.
(Photograph by Daniel Nicoletta, courtesy of the Bancroft Library,
University of California, Berkeley)

Frank M. Robinson looking through the etched glass in the front door of his San Francisco home, which he purchased and remodeled with his proceeds from the film *The Towering Inferno*, February 21, 1982. (Photograph by Daniel Nicoletta, courtesy of the Bancroft Library, University of California, Berkeley)

Frank M. Robinson on the red carpet at the San Francisco premiere of the movie *Milk*, October 28, 2008. (Photograph by Robert Moloney, courtesy of the Bancroft Library, University of California, Berkeley)

Frank M. Robinson in his writer's office in his San Francisco home, overlooking the city's Castro District, the northern hills, and San Francisco Bay, which were often the settings for his thrillers, March 3, 2010. (Photograph by Daniel Nicoletta, courtesy of the Bancroft Library, University of California, Berkeley)

Celebration of Dustin Lance Black's Oscar for Best Screenplay for his film *Milk* at the Palace Hotel, March 29, 2009. BACK ROW, LEFT TO RIGHT: Maggie Weiland, Anne Kronenberg, Adam Kamil, Daniel Nicoletta. FRONT ROW, LEFT TO RIGHT: Dustin Lance Black, Frank M. Robinson. (Photograph by Michael Pinatelli, Jr., courtesy of the Bancroft Library, University of California, Berkeley)

Frank M. Robinson at the May 2008 unveiling of the memorial bronze bust of assassinated city supervisor Harvey Milk in the rotunda of San Francisco City Hall. (Photograph by David Moloney)

LEFT TO RIGHT: Brian Kamps, Robert Angell, and Frank M. Robinson celebrate Robinson's 2014 Nebula Lifetime Achievement Award in Science Fiction at their favorite sushi bar in San Francisco. (Courtesy of Brian Kamps)

Frank M. Robinson with his world-class collection of early pulp fiction magazines, photographed for the dust jacket of Robinson's 2004 thriller, *The Donor*.

Frank M. Robinson and coauthor John Levin pose for the dust jacket
of their 1982 political thriller, *The Great Divide*.
(Photograph by Marvin Lichtner)

≪ XX ≫

THE FIRST MEETING place for Chicago Gay Liberation was in the home of one of the members who lived on the North Side. All of us were gung ho. We had a cause—"liberate" Chicago so gays would be accepted by everybody. It was a black member who shook his head and brought us down to earth.

"You'll be lucky if you liberate yourselves."

Tom Biscotto, one of the actors in *The Whores of Babylon*, edited the first few issues of our newsletter; then I took over with help from Marie Kuda and Henry Konkie.

Our first action was to picket a restaurant that had canned one of its employees because he was gay. (To the best of my knowledge, they never hired him back. So much for gay pressure.) Somebody then suggested we picket the local branch of the Chicago Police Department, which had made Lincoln Park off-limits to gays at night.

That idea was dropped when we learned the police were tired of dragging out bleeding gays who had been beat up when they made the mistake of propositioning the wrong man in the park.

The next big affair was a dance in "Wobblies" Hall, which in years past had been the meeting place of the Industrial Workers of the World Union.

A gay dance! My God! I showed up five minutes late, after the phonograph had started and the floor was filling with dancers. I watched for a while, then somebody said, "Hey, you wanna dance?"

It took a moment for me to realize he was talking to me. He was about my height, slender—we all were back then—with bright red hair.

I couldn't believe it and promptly chickened out. "Ah—I'm waiting for a friend."

The friend I was waiting for was standing right in front of me, but it took me a good five minutes to realize it. When I did, I went looking for him, but several people told me he had already left—obviously with somebody else.

What was the sense of gay liberation if you refused to liberate yourelf? Our black member had been right.

Like most political groups, it wasn't long before our little group split in two. Chicago Gay Liberation (the original name) and Chicago Gay Alliance. I went with the Alliance, though I'll be damned if I ever knew what the argument was about.

There was another dance a month or so later that was open not only to our Chicago groups but also to groups from the surrounding universities. It was held at the Aragon Ballroom, one of the largest ballrooms in the city.

Our newsletter had been filled with the details and short articles urging one and all to attend, and the various university groups had done the same.

This time I got there early and watched the floor gradually fill. A thousand gays! Five hundred couples! And a number of singles like myself.

I tried a few steps with those nearby, and nobody walked away like I thought they would. I was having a great time when

I noticed that on one of the small balconies overlooking the dance floor were Herb and five of his rent boys.

I stared at them for a moment, then out of the corner of my eye caught a glimpse of a single dancer in navy travel blues who was easily the best dancer on the floor.

I asked why he was wearing blues when it was close to summer and the uniform of the day was whites. He shrugged and said they liked blues better at the club. It turned out that on the weekends he worked as a male stripper at a gay nightclub in Cicero, a suburb of Chicago.

I pointed at Herb's balcony and asked my new friend if he'd come over there, dance with me, and do a strip. He was all for it.

(I didn't really dance, but when you boogie, it's free-form.)

I soon realized why people would pay to see him perform. Off came the cap, a few steps, then the kerchief, the shoes and socks, a few more steps, then the jumper, and finally his belt and trousers. He wasn't just undressing, he was taking them off like he was a male Gypsy Rose Lee, taking them off with a sexy flair that must have left his customers at the club wanting more. A circle of dancers had gathered around to watch and applauded when he had finished.

He bowed at Herb's balcony, dressed, and then disappeared into the crowd. On the balcony Herb's group were nudging one another and pointing at me.

I understood from friends later the word was that Robinson was obviously on drugs.

I was a lot more relaxed now and danced with several pickups on the floor, then settled down to attempt serious boogeying with a young man who was dressed completely in white—white pants, white shoes, white T-shirt with the sleeves rolled up. It was the only time in my whole short life of dancing that I ended up dancing with somebody who looked like an angel. All he needed were wings.

We switched partners several times, and then he disappeared. I had forgotten rule number one. Get their full name and phone number.

I had no idea who he was.

I put the word out to members of the Alliance, who spread the word that I was hunting for him.

It was a week later when the doorbell rang, and when I opened it, there he was.

"I heard you were looking for me," he said. He sounded a little bashful. "Sorry I lost track of you—I went to Milwaukee at the end of the dance and spent the week up there."

I motioned him in without saying a word. This was my first chance to catch up on a lot of lost years, and I was going to make the most of it.

A few weeks later we decided to hold a "kiss-in" at Civic Center Plaza to call attention to gays. Our little group marched down Michigan Avenue past the Playboy Building, chanting "Two, four, six, eight, gay is just as good as straight!" I wanted to be a member of the group but didn't want anybody at *Playboy* to see me. I compromised and bopped along the side of the small parade with a pad of paper and a pencil, pretending I was taking notes.

One of the younger members of the group watched me for a moment, then suddenly thrust his banner in my hands and said, "Here, you carry it for a while."

The banner read something like "Gay Freedom Now!" I looked the other way, hoping that nobody from the magazine had noticed me.

But if they had been hanging around Civic Center Plaza, there was no way they could have missed me.

The people in the plaza looked at us with absolutely no interest whatsoever. We made a show of smooching for ten minutes (I hugged but never kissed, afraid somebody from *Playboy* would see me), then shrugged and broke for lunch. Chicagoans make a point of never being surprised at anything.

Something more was needed, I thought. The newsletter went only to ourselves, but what about a newspaper? Something we could pass around just before Gay Pride Week. And maybe even a few stores might carry it.

It was then I thought of a tabloid, something that wouldn't be too difficult to make. I already had a title—*Chicago Gay Pride*—and a slogan to go with it:

"The trouble with the world is not that some people make love differently.

The trouble is that most people don't make love at all."

I was proud of it, even more so when Frank Kameny, a prominent gay politician in D.C., stole it. But the more the merrier; that was why I had written it.

Gay Pride Week was three months away, the anniversary of the Stonewall Rebellion in New York. I wasn't kidding myself on how much work would be involved. I started soliciting articles, wrote a few of my own, and typed up all of them after work for an offset press, even justifying the margins. There were no usable computers then, so I knew I was in for three months of pure ditch work. I stayed late in the office to work on it and during the day invented helpful advice for *Playboy*'s readers.

A few weeks later a thousand copies were dropped off in front of my apartment door. I was immensely proud, convinced that I had turned out the first gay tabloid in the country. (San Francisco's *Bay Area Reporter* may have beaten me, but they were a weekly, while I had no idea when I would find the energy to publish another issue of *Chicago Gay Pride*.)

The paper was a huge hit, with photographs from last year's gay celebration on the front cover and a shot of our new Chicago Gay Alliance community center inside. It didn't look like much, but it was where we held meetings, threw parties, and in our own minds established ourselves as a going organization.

Most of the articles were political in nature—at least one mentioned gay marriage, and this more than forty years ago! There was a list of all the activities that would be occurring during Gay Pride Week—workshops, a demonstration in Civic Center Plaza, a picnic in the forest preserves, etc.

A prose poem, "Queer Fear" (reprinted fom *Chicago Seed*), was about a man who doubted his homosexuality and was afraid to break out of his closet when a friend came out of a Gay Pride parade and kissed him. It was too much for the man, who scurried back to the safety of the closet, where nobody would think he was gay. Except himself.

Life went on as usual at *Playboy*, with me trying to slip in the occasional sexual double entendre and my watchdogs catching them all. I think it became a contest.

The next big thing was a party at the mansion (a remodeled nunnery on the near North Side, I was told.) Everybody on staff was expected to come, though I didn't know anybody who would have refused. Most of our more prominent contributors would attend even if *Playboy* had to fly them in.

It was early evening when Bob Shea and I got there. On the door was a bronze plaque that read (in Latin):

If you don't swing, don't ring.

I understood that was Spectorsky's contribution.

Inside there was a hat-check girl, and young men in waiters' uniforms carrying trays of hors d'oeuvres circulated among the guests on the crowded living room floor. At one side of the room were glass portholes, which some of the guests were looking through.

I wandered over and got my first look at the "woo grotto," of which I'd heard so much. A swimming pool sunk one floor lower than the one I was on. Sometimes guests would swim there in the nude; other times I suspected Playboy bunnies were pressed into service.

I helped myself to some of the finger food, and Shea and I played a game of identifying the various celebrities who were there. At one point I spotted a youngish man, probably in his thirties, wearing a few thousand dollars' worth of Italian suit. Handsome for his age, maybe a little too handsome. With my experience with Herb and his tribe I considered myself something of an expert on rent boys. I knew what he was immediately.

"Who let the hustler in?" I asked Shea.

Shea looked at me, surprised.

"Jesus, Frank, that's Rudolf Nureyev."

He was in his early thirties but looked much younger. There was the possibility that Shea was putting me on, but Hefner collected celebrities like they were postage stamps.

Or maybe Shea was simply mistaken. But I really didn't think so.

That spring I got my second never-to-be forgotten assignment. *Playboy*'s interviews had been very popular, and Spectorsky figured wouldn't it be great if we ran a dialog between two celebrities rather than having the *Playboy* reporter constantly butting in with questions.

The first subjects were to be Arthur C. Clarke and Alan Watts. Clarke was one of the most popular science fiction writers of the period (he and Stanley Kubrick had written the script for *2001*) and another of my favorites. Watts was the leader of the popular

Zen movement, about which I knew absolutely nothing. I hastily boned up on an article or two and then realized I'd have to fake it.

There was another problem. I was halfway through organizing the next issue of the club's tabloid, now retitled *The Paper*. In addition to information about Gay Pride Week, it would carry a lot of news about community theater in Chicago and various musical groups in an attempt to broaden the interest of the paper. It was taking up a lot of my time, and with the new assignment, I'd be stretched to my limits. How badly, I didn't know at the time.

I flew in with Watts to the Chelsea Hotel in New York, where Clarke was staying. When Watts and Clarke met, I thought, *oh, Christ*. They hated each other on sight and didn't bother to hide it.

Clarke was a scientist as well as a writer. Watts regarded science with more than a little suspicion, probably because there was little of it that he understood. Clarke regarded Watts as nothing more than the leader of a popular cult. The only thing they had in common was that both were frequent contributors to *Playboy*.

The first evening's supper was a disaster as far as I was concerned. Watts was wearing his Zen robes, and Clarke had on similar Sri Lankan attire. I walked a good three paces behind so nobody would think I was with them.

Our destination was the last (I think) of New York's Automats. Stick a quarter in a slot and you'd get a piece of pie; two quarters would get you a dish of macaroni (or something).

Both picked at their food, and we went glumly back to the Chelsea.

The next morning both Watts and Clarke were similarily attired but took one quick look at each other and both had the same thought. Why the Automat? *Playboy* was paying for all of this!

Clarke knew all the booksellers on Eighth Avenue. Alan, on the other hand, knew all the millionaires and Zen enthusiasts—frequently the same—and the best (and most expensive) places in New York to eat. Alan was immediately appointed our personal restaurateur.

They immediately went back into the Chelsea and came out half an hour later dressed well enough so no maître d' would throw them out.

I don't remember what we had for breakfast, but I was immediately seized with the idea of calling *Playboy* and telling them I needed a few more days.

Clarke loosened up quite a bit and was trading little-known facts of the coming computer age and offering to demonstrate his personal handheld laser when it got dark. Even Watts brightened at that.

Unfortunately I wasn't aware that I was making one of the bigger mistakes of my life. I was no longer a reporter, taking notes and worrying about what I should ask that would get conflicting commentary from both of them.

I was a writer, just like them, and the three of us were having a ball. It had become "Alan" and "Arthur" and "Frank."

Of the two of them, Clarke was the more fascinating. His mind was a storehouse of little-known scientific facts and questions, and he delighted in springing them on us.

When, he asked us, did man first invent the computer? Alan was entirely at sea, not sure of what Clarke was getting at but perfectly willing to go along for the ride. I was thinking something like 1950 or maybe late 1800s.

"It was an ancient Greek," Clarke said, eager to tell us all about it.

Both Alan and I just gaped at him.

"A couple of fishermen discovered this twisted mass of bronze in Pireaus Harbor around the turn of the century. It ended up in the back of the Athens Museum and was discovered again by two American scientists in the fifties who figured out it was an ancient computer, cogs and all. It displayed a degree of complexity not duplicated until we built a grandfather clock centuries later."

I couldn't think of a thing to ask him, and Alan had started to study the menu.

Clarke suddenly shot another one at me.

"Frank, what was the advantage of the horse collar?"

I was born in Chicago, not on a farm, so I had no idea.

"It was the first time beasts of burden could pull more than their weight without strangling themselves."

Well, yes, I could see that.

"How about spectacles?" Clarke went on. "The advantage there?"

I was trying to concentrate on my bread pudding. This was turning into Twenty Questions.

"I haven't the faintest," I murmured.

Clarke was delighted to have found a student.

"They multiplied the lifetime of the scholar. Early scientists ruined their eyesight copying ancient manuscripts. Glasses were a godsend."

His most thoughtful question came while I was paying the bill with *Playboy*'s credit card.

Clarke hesitated before springing his last one, and I stopped computing the tip. Even Watts was suddenly alert.

"What's the one thing a fish could never conceive of?" Clarke asked quietly.

"Air," I said.

Clarke shook his head, and both Alan and I gave up immediately. Both of us thought there were too many possibilities.

"Fire," Clarke said quietly.

It wasn't a science question so much as a philosophical one. Humans were like fish, swimming around in their tight little world and thinking they knew all the answers to the mysteries of the universe when in reality there were so many things of which they couldn't possibly conceive.

That evening Clarke took us to the top of the Chelsea to demonstrate his laser. I was aware that a laser generated coherent light, that the beam would not spread out as in a flashlight. If the lens were a half dollar in diameter, when its beam hit a wall the spot of light would be exactly the same diameter.

Clarke turned on his small laser, and when the beam hit the sidewalk, there was the tiny spot of light the same diameter as the lens of the laser. He moved it around at just the moment a matron came walking her poodle. She glanced at the moving spot, then carefully walked around it and continued on her way.

We got more response from a drunk who spotted it, and when Clarke moved it around, the drunk danced with it. All three of us were fascinated.

The next day it was time to catch a plane to Chicago. Alan and I piled on board, and once seated, I pulled out my notebook to get Watts's response to his meeting with Clarke. Alan was no help. He mumbled a few words, then closed his eyes and slept until Chicago, where he changed planes for San Francisco.

He was profuse in his thanks and I made all the appropriate replies, desperately thinking my notes wouldn't fill a small address book.

It was nice to know that Alan now regarded me as his friend and maybe he would be more forthcoming when I phoned him for his reactions.

He wasn't.

The only thing I had to go on was my memory.

I started putting in seventy-hour weeks, finishing up the issue of *The Paper* and then trying to fill the sheaf of blank pages of the dialog between Watts and Clarke.

The Paper was a harder job to put out than I thought—I had lost one of my chief assistants, Harry, who had been running for the down escalator in the subway, tripped, and broke all the fingers on his left hand.

The estimated cost for putting them back together was $600 (doctors were cheaper then). Harry went to his parents—Mormons—for the money, and they refused. Harry was an out gay, which they detested. They considered him no longer a member of the family and hated his guts.

Harry had known they didn't like his sexual orientation but until then he had no idea they hated him personally as well.

I lent him the money and he got his fingers fixed but I could do nothing for his loss of self-esteem. He got a job as a night clerk in a sleazebag hotel and finally decided to leave town and his family behind. If only he had the money . . .

The hotel kept a gun behind the counter in case of trouble, and Harry took it and went upstairs to a room where there was an old man who had a reputation as a miser. Harry pulled the gun and asked for the money. The old man wasn't going to let a goddamned faggot hold him up and went for him. In the short tussle that followed, the gun went off, and Harry made the six o'clock news.

His parents came to the trial—a little late—and Harry was sent to state prison. A young, white, somewhat pudgy gay kid was an easy target for those in prison who considered "white" as beautiful. Harry had no friends and little ability to defend himself.

A number of the prisoners were heroin abusers at the time when there was no test for HIV. Some years later Harry died of

AIDS in prison. I have no idea whether his parents bothered to go to the brief funeral.

I spent a lot of hours finishing up the second issue of *The Paper* and started putting in more seventy-hour weeks trying to fill the sheaf of blank pages of the dialog betweeen Watts and Clarke.

It wasn't working; it was never going to work. I'd have to make up a lot of the conversations from memory, then invent others, and finally make two copies and send one each to Clarke and Watts and let them fill in the gaps.

The next evening I turned in my copy to Murray Fisher, my boss on the project, and went home dead tired.

When I got in my apartment, I turned on the light, and nature suddenly took its revenge for all those seventy-hour weeks. My heart sped up until I thought it was going to burst. I kept track and I was logging two hundred beats a minute (normal is about sixty to seventy).

I called an ambulance and ten minutes later I was on a gurney in an Evanston hospital. They assured me atrial fibrillation was seldom fatal. Then the nurse striped off my shirt and pants and T-shirt and they put paddles on my bare chest, just like I'd seen in so many TV shows.

The anesthesiologist made various adjustments with his equipment and asked me to count backward from a hundred.

When I got to ninety-seven for all practical purposes I died.

⊰ XXI ⊱

I DON'T REMEMBER how long I was out, maybe just a few minutes, maybe an hour. But the doctors and their apparatus had disappeared, so I figured it was someplace in between. I felt for my pulse and it was a normal sixty or so.

The doctors couldn't tell me how often I'd go into afib. There was no specific medicine for it at the time, unfortunately. I checked in with the head cardiologist at Northwestern and he said if it happened again, just lie down until it went away.

My own doctors were a little more specific. Sit down, put your head between your knees, hold your nose, and blow out. The idea was to put pressure on your diaphragm and bring the heart back into sinus rhythm. It worked—most of the time. In the years that followed one drug after another showed up that was more or less a specific for afib.

Eventually they found one. A dangerous drug—amiodarone—because it reacted too often with other drugs. But it worked for afib.

Back at work, I didn't know whether I had a job. I'd get an occasional sympathetic look in the hallway, and I figured they all thought I'd had a heart attack. Eventually everything was back to normal—except for an occasional head-between-my-knees routine—and I figured at least my job was safe.

The most exciting thing that happened was the appearance of a competitor to *Playboy*, and this one looked like it had legs. Oddly, or maybe not so oddly, it also came out of Chicago. A wealthy man named Ron Fenton had started a "Millionaire's Club" in the style of the "Playboy Club" and—naturally—wanted a magazine to go with it. What he really needed was talent, and one by one he'd take a *Playboy* editor out to lunch and ask them if they wanted to edit his magazine. They all thanked him kindly for the lunch, but no, they were very happy where they were.

Fenton finally got to the bottom of the barrel. A young kid on staff who wrote the record reviews had been canned when he didn't get along with a senior editor.

Eventually Fenton got around to our former record reviewer, James Spurlock, and made him the magnaminous offer of $150 a week for three days of work to put out his magazine. Fenton obviously knew nothing of the small army of editors who worked on *Playboy* every month.

Jim came to us slaveys who worked on the front of the book and asked our opinion. We had all liked Jim, were sorry to see him go, and said, "Take it!" It would be found money, since Fenton was never going to put out a magazine, but by that time maybe Jim would have put away a few bucks.

A few months later a startled *Playboy* editor going to work stopped at the newsstand in the lobby and spotted a new magazine titled *Gallery*, dated November of '72. He thumbed through one, then immediately bought the entire stack and ran upstairs to distribute them to all the editors at *Playboy*.

All of us who knew Jim were totally shocked. Ron Fenton and

Jim Spurlock had finally put out a magazine. The only catch was that Jim had worked on only one magazine in his entire life: *Playboy*. *Gallery* was a fairly thick magazine—as thick as most issues of *Playboy*. Considering Jim's past experience, you couldn't blame him if it looked a little like *Playboy*. In fact, *exactly* like *Playboy* down to the layout and the type sizes.

F. Lee Bailey, lead defense attorney in the O. J. Simpson murder trial, was listed as publisher; Ronald L. Fenton was president (and presumably moneyman); and there, big as brass, was James L. Spurlock, editor.

I had the lead, under the pen name of "James Walsh." It was a reminiscence of Lenny Bruce that I had given to Jim when Fenton had wanted to see something. (All us "Friends of Jim" had scrambled around in our trunks to give something to Spurlock to make him look like a working editor in the eyes of Fenton. Everything was under pseudonyms, of course.)

I didn't realize it at the time but it was probably the best piece about Lenny Bruce ever written. (No bragging here—it's true.)

None of us expected the magazine to last long; neither did Hugh Hefner, who would try to make sure it didn't. A competitor was one thing, a carbon copy from a publisher across the street was another. His first strike was a letter to all our cartoonists saying that if they sold anything to *Gallery* they could forget about *Playboy* as a market.

Within a few days, fleets of lawyers were flocking kitty-corner across Michigan Avenue from *Playboy* to *Gallery* and back. But F. Lee Bailey wasn't titular publisher of *Gallery* for nothing. He was also a friend of Hefner's and within a few days had convinced Hefner that he was acting in restraint of trade.

A second letter to the cartoonists followed the first saying it was all a mistake. But it was a pretty dumb cartoonist who didn't realize that Hefner was not compelled to buy their cartoons.

I don't know how long Jim stayed with *Gallery*, but he surfaced again a while later as the editor/publisher of another "sophisticated magazine for men," titled *In Touch*. The first issue was June of '74, and this time I had the lead fiction under my own name (I'd left *Playboy* by that time).

In Touch didn't see many issues, probably because Jim's main contribution to the skin field had been to add a male lead in the same photo as the girl—all in very soft focus, of course. But it was difficult for the reader to imagine himself in the same photograph as the girl when some other dude was already there.

Gallery was the fourth men's magazine out of Chicago that I was connected with. There was to be still another. (I think Chicago had a corner on the market.)

I used to hang out in a coffee shop on the North Side, and one day the waitress asked me if I would show her boyfriend around *Playboy*, especially where they shot the centerfolds (off-limits to all but the model and the photographer).

Richard Leo struck me as eager as David Stevens once had. He was an hour early and I gave him a cursory look around the offices—offices like any other offices in any other company. I had a luncheon date, so I sent Rick across the street to *Gallery* after calling Spurlock to say he'd have a guest.

Two hours later Rick showed up looking like somebody had taken him out for a liquid lunch.

I asked him what had happened and he said he'd been offered a job—though not at *Gallery*. George Santo Prieto, the fashion editor, had asked him if he knew any writers. Rick's father was a reporter for the *Chicago Sun-Times*, and of course he knew some writers. It turned out that Santo Prieto was starting his own "sophisticated men's magazine"—guaranteed to show a little more skin than the opposition—and would Rick like to be the editor? The new magazine was titled *Coq*—pronounced in French, "cock." (Clever man, Santo Prieto.) *Coq* looked exactly like all the others, except cheaper, and after three issues was history.

Rick became a story in himself. He'd been bit by the publishing bug and went to the South Seas, where he edited the English-language edition of the *Samoa News*.

After a stint of some months there, he came back to the States, went to Harvard—I'm sure they had a quota system, but the months in the South Pacific obviously qualified him. Rick left after two years and worked as an editor in Manhattan, got bored, and convinced his girlfriend that they should go to Alaska.

Not a bad idea if you were an adventurer, and Rick certainly was. Alaska was the first chunk of the United States to be bought by an oil company. Buying it was easy—the oil company split the proceeds (not even-steven, of course) with the people who lived there. Every year every Alaskan would get a check for some thousands of dollars.

Furthermore, land was free. Stake a claim, register it, and it was yours. Except for the bears, the cold, and a few irritated Eskimos, it was a great deal.

Rick married his girlfriend (a hippie-type wedding—she walked out later to have a more legal arrangement with a bush pilot), built a cabin, fathered a son, chopped his own wood, had his own dog team, and was living the life of Richard Halliburton.

There's more to Rick's story—a lot more—but these are my memoirs, not his, and he's perfectly capable of writing his own.

Which is exactly what he did.

Back in the lower forty-eight, things were not going well for

Playboy. In 1972 A. C. Spectorsky had a fatal heart attack. His contribution to the magazine was actually a good deal more than anybody realized until later, when circulation began to sag. The fight was on to see who would succeed him, and Arthur Kretchmer won. It was, naturally, congratulations all around.

Except for me.

At the elevator I gave him my condolences. I figured I was the only one there who knew what was really involved. Granted that Hamling now spent most of his time in San Diego and Hefner spent most of his in his bedroom, so—ultimately—it was *you* who was responsible for the failure or success of the magazine.

I had failed with *Rogue* but I sure knew what the struggle was like.

The final straw—or close to it—was when I was asked to tie a can to Alan Watts. The magazine figured they'd published enough material about Zen and it was time to ride another hobbyhorse. I had never fired anybody who had worked for me and I didn't know how to do it gracefully. This time I hemmed and hawed and made a mess of it, finally telling Alan that we wouldn't be buying any more Zen articles from him. At two grand or more a pop a major fraction of Alan's income had just disappeared. He stared at me for a moment, then looked away and said, "I know what I am—I'm a public entertainer."

He couldn't hide the bitterness, and I had nothing to say to soften the blow. I promised myself I would never, ever do anything like this again.

Now it was the dead of winter and in Chicago that meant the weather was vicious. Strong winds, swirls of snow, temperature about twenty-five. Kitty-corner across the street the Fanny May candy shop had caught fire, and I watched as the firemen turned it into the world's largest ice cube.

I even caught myself thinking—vaguely—about San Francisco, where the worst that usually happened was fog in the early morning.

The phone rang, and when I picked it up I found myself talking to Tom Scortia on the other end of the line. I had bought a few stories from Tom for *Rogue* and thought he was going to pitch me something for *Playboy*. I was the wrong editor, I was about to tell him, but Tom's excited voice made it plain that wasn't what he wanted.

He had this great idea for a novel and wanted help in writing it. About a fire in a high-rise building and people trapped at the top, etc.

Across the street one wall of the candy store caved in and I imagined I could feel the heat.

Fire in a high-rise . . .

I had been in the business long enough to know when an idea smelled of money.

He had pitched it to Doubleday, Tom continued, and they had offered a twenty-grand advance. Now I was all ears—half for me, half for him, that was ten grand for each of us. How long would it take to write the book? A few months?

I took his number and said I'd call him back in an hour. He was now living in San Francisco, which was something of a plus considering the Chicago weather.

I picked the latest issue of *Playboy* off my desk and thumbed through it. It wasn't like any of Spectorsky's issues. I couldn't put my finger on it, but it was like a punctured balloon with the air seeping slowly out of it.

It wasn't fatal, I thought; the magazine would last for years . . . but the touch wasn't there.

I called Tom back and said sure, I'd be out there in a few weeks, but I wanted to do some research first. I didn't know a damn thing about fighting a fire in a high-rise except I guessed it would be tough.

Which meant there would be a lot of visuals, which always made a book—or a movie—sell.

I hired a friend to go through the Hancock Building, the tallest building in Chicago at the time, to see what they had for fire prevention. Myself, I went to the Illinois Institute of Technology and thumbed through their files looking for information on fire fighting. One thing I found out early was that fires are difficult to fight above seven floors—a fireman's ladder doesn't reach much higher than that. (Since then I've never booked a room in a hotel above the seventh floor.)

The last thing I did was read a copy of Arthur Hailey's *Airport*, one of the earlier "tech" thrillers, all about the operation of an airport, complete with interesting characters and more interesting disasters. I divided the book in three, then each third into chapters, and a brief summary of events in each chapter.

It was, admittedly, "monkey see, monkey do."

When I got to San Francisco I rented in the same apartment building as Tom so we'd be close during collaboration. The apartment building on Red Rock Way was nicknamed "Pneumonia Heights" because the fog rolling in from the bay hit there first. But on sunny days you could see the San Francisco–Oakland Bay Bridge and at night the twinkling lights outlining it.

Not bad, I thought. Not bad at all.

The next day Tom slumped in with the bad news.

He'd misunderstood Doubleday. It wasn't twenty grand, it was ten. Half on signing and half on delivery. Deduct 10 percent for the agent, and we were faced with turning out a major book for $2,250 each. I was suddenly glad I had taken a year's leave of absence from the Bunny.

I called up Martha Winston, our agent at Curtis Brown, and

she was encouraging. It was a good idea and she could probably sell it on the basis of three chapters and an outline.

Tough—but doable—and Tom and I set to work blocking out scenes and writing short synopses of the characters.

Every morning I'd walk down the hill for breakfast and through a section of the city called the Castro. There was a camera shop along the way with a dog sniffing around in front, peeing on all the trees, inspecting the passersby, and if he really liked you, showed his affection by humping your leg.

A week of trying to find a restaurant that served decent bacon and eggs and this time the owner of the shop was out in front playing with his dog—"Kid," a black mongrel that would play with anybody who wanted to play with him. This was the Castro, after all, and both of us knew the other was gay. (So was most everybody else I met.)

Harvey was dressed like a hippie and looked like a hippie complete with beard, mustache, and ponytail. But he semed friendly enough and didn't hold a hand out for any spare change.

"What do you do?" he asked.

I told him I was a writer and had moved to San Francisco to write a book. He waved at the camera shop and said it was just temporary. He was running for supervisor.

"My second time. I got more than fifteen thousand votes last time."

In Chicago the best we had done was muster a hundred brave souls for the kiss-in at City Hall Plaza—one that nobody noticed.

"What's it take to win?"

He shrugged. "Fifty thousand."

Never in a hundred years, I thought.

He shooed Kid back into the shop and said, "How would you like to write speeches for me?"

At first I thought I had better things to do. But I had made a lot of good friends in Chicago, *The Paper* (*née Chicago Gay Pride*) had been a hoot. And this was one way of making friends. At heart I was a gay politician, junior grade, and holed up in an apartment thinking up novel ways of frying people was already starting to wear thin.

"How much?" I asked.

He grinned. "You got it all wrong, friend—we don't pay *you*, you pay *us*."

No surprise, I thought. I had never given a dime to the people who worked on *The Paper*. I never had a dime to give and I figure he didn't either.

"So who do I work for?" I asked.

He held out his hand. "The name's Harvey Milk." He spent about five seconds sizing me up. "C'mon, we'll stir some shit."

Jesus Christ—how could you write speeches for a guy with a name like that? The moment he was introduced, the audience would bust out laughing.

He recommended a decent ham-and-egger and an hour later I was back in my apartment trying to think up names for a fire chief, one of our heroes. We hadn't thought of a villain yet.

But we *had* settled on a title.

The Glass Inferno.

Catchy, we thought.

The next week I spent an occasional evening in the camera shop meeting the staff and making a stab at writing a few words for Harvey. He was easy to write for since we both had the same political outlook. The shop had a back room with a long table where we gathered around to stuff envelopes with political flyers. The front of the store was where Harvey and his lover, Scott—a blond who had no right being that handsome—worked. Harvey was the politician, Scott his manager. Danny was a young kid who kept the stock in order, filed the envelopes of photos when they came in, and tried his hand at taking photographs. He was a good student—some years later he was one of the ace photographers in the city when it came to the gay community.

The store itself was a meeting place for Harvey's friends and for people Harvey could convince to vote—for him. Harvey knew perfectly well that power came from the ballot box, and the only way he could get it in San Francisco was if all the gays voted for a gay man as supervisor. There were other gays running for political office, but they all relied on the patronage of "friends of gays"—straight politicians who would bullshit with gays for their votes. When the going got rough—and it wasn't long before it did—they would all fade into the woodwork.

Harvey reasoned that an out-and-out gay man couldn't change his identity for political expediency any more than a black man could change the color of his skin. The game was to get gays to vote for Harvey so they would have one of their own in the office.

The camera shop was ideally suited as a meeting place, with a dental chair and a long, broken-down red couch—a political hangout to shoot the shit with a usually smiling, very funny, and politically astute Harvey. (A biography—*The Mayor of Castro Street*—was later to be written by Randy Shilts, an openly gay reporter for the *San Francisco Chronicle*. Randy was probably the only openly gay newspaper reporter in the country at the time.)

Harvey Milk was the last of the storefront politicians who ran for public office with absolutely no money and whose headquarters was the store where he worked.

Everybody was welcome in the store, and everybody dropped in. One day a young girl asked if she could put her "Save the Whales" poster in the window. We let her put up her poster and immediately pressed her into service in the back room stuffing envelopes with political flyers. The only drawback was that we had to watch our language.

Harvey had absolutely no chance, I thought, but on the other hand I'd meet people and it might be a lot of fun.

There was one evening meeting that wasn't so much fun. Our guest was a middle-aged man who'd run for the BART (Bay Area Rapid Transit) board and won by a sizable majority. We shook hands, then sat around the table and looked attentive. He was going to tell us how to win an election. We edged closer, all eyes on him, to listen to his secrets.

"Speeches," he started. "You have to be prepared to make speeches. Hold meetings in halls or even on the street." He glanced at Harvey. "You could hit the gay bars—you're a natural."

Harvey had already hit the gay bars. He'd been thrown out of a few—a hippie, from out of town at that, wasn't welcome, and they weren't about to vote for him no matter what.

"And mailers," our political oracle continued. He glanced at the boxes of half-stuffed envelopes against the wall. "You just can't send them out scattershot—pick an area of the city where they already know and like you. Lock those up and you can hit other sections of the town. And posters are always good—place them around the walls of buildings close to the BART stations."

I was beginning to squirm. He was telling us things we already knew.

He hesitated. "It worked for me," he continued. "And you might hit the bars with a speech or two on the weekends when they're crowded with those interested in fifty-cent spaghetti and dollar fried chicken." He smirked. "I suspect that might be most of them."

He looked at Harvey closely, moving so he could see Harvey from the sides.

"A lot of the gays in town are Republicans. You might shave, cut your hair, and pick up a suit. Give 'em somebody they can identify with."

The BART man now realized he was talking to a bunch of amateurs and didn't try to hide his contempt.

"Probably the most important single thing you can do is get up early in the morning and hit the houses with small posters you can hang on doorknobs with a big picture of you and a list of other candidates on the ticket. And don't forget the large posters—they're the last thing most voters see before they hit the polling booth."

He nodded at several of his own that he had propped against the wall. In the poster he looked twenty pounds lighter and ten years younger.

"It worked for me."

I couldn't see myself wandering around the city hanging posters on people's doorknobs. There were a lot of houses in San Francisco.

"Who do we get to do it?" somebody asked.

Our guest's smile turned sour. He was wasting his time.

"Pay a little money to some of the early risers in the Haight who want to earn a buck of two before the bars open. Or maybe the guys who deliver the morning papers—stick a hanger in every copy of the *Chronicle*."

I knew from personal experience that nobody in the Haight got up early in the morning. And that included me.

It was Harvey who asked the clutch question.

"What do you think all this would cost?"

Our guest glanced at his watch, probably figuring he'd be late for a meeting of the young Republicans or Democrats or whomever.

"I did it on the cheap—thirty-five grand." He gathered up his posters and managed a smile. "Don't forget me next election."

After he'd left we sat around the table staring at one another and then Jimmy Rivaldo, one of Harvey's ace political advisors, stood up and emptied his pockets on the table.

The rest of us did the same and somebody turned the cash box over on the table. Danny separated the coins from the paper and did the count. A little over a few hundred dollars.

We were beat before we'd even started. Our only ace in the hole was Harvey himself, and he didn't give up.

Within a week or two Harvey had cut his hair and shaved and bought himself a secondhand suit.

Two weeks after that disaster Tom and I got much more of it from the publishing front. Tom showed up with a copy of *Publishers Weekly* announcing that one Richard Martin Stern had just sold a book titled *The Tower*, whose major idea was exactly the same as ours—fire in a high-rise.

A desparate call to Martha Winston, our book agent at Curtis Brown, the parent agency, who advised us to keep working but under no conditions should we read Stern's book. We consoled ourselves with the thought that well, there was always the movies . . .

Our consolation didn't last very long. Two weeks later Tom waved another copy of *PW* in my face and this time the news was that Warner Bros. was going to film Stern's book.

We immediately called Richard Parks, who handled movie rights for Curtis Brown. His advice: take our outline and fill it with as many visuals as we could think of.

Parks assured us we still had possibilities. Irwin Allen, the producer at Twentieth Century Fox, had lost out on the auction of Stern's book. It was Parks's idea to give him another chance. Allen had made a fortune for Twentieth with *The Poseidon Adventure* and had desperately wanted to follow water with fire.

Parks put up our outline of *The Glass Inferno* for an auction that would close in New York on a Friday at 6:00 P.M. (3:00 P.M. in San Francisco).

At 3:05 Parks was on the phone sounding gloomy, and our hearts sank. A moment later he gave us the good news.

Twentieth Century Fox had made a peremptory bid for *The Glass Inferno*, meaning a bid that they knew no other studio would top. The deal was film rights for *The Glass Inferno* at $400,000 and 5 percent of the producer's profits.

Tom went out to get roaring drunk.

I went to the hospital again. For somebody with atrial fibrillation, good news can be as bad as bad news.

Neither of us shouted in the phone to tell Parks that the deal was fine with us.

We didn't have to.

⋘ XXII ⋙

THE FIRST THING that happens when you find yourself sitting on a pot of money is you discover how much you can keep and how much the government will take. Back then federal taxes were unbelievable. (I almost felt sorry for Mitt Romney, but for us the sale was a onetime thing—so we thought—while for Mitt it happened every year.)

The answer presented itself in the form of Harry Margolis, a lawyer who specialized in setting up overseas accounts for the average man who struck it rich—like us. His fee was simple: One half of the money we'd save versus the taxes we'd have to pay the government.

The way it would work was we'd turn over all our assets and future income to this outfit in the Cayman Islands. (Later it would be the British West Indies.) In the United States, technically speaking, we'd be broke. But if we ever needed anything, the people in the Caymans would buy it for us.

It didn't take much urging for us to sign on the dotted line.

Tom and I only had an outline, so we started to work, turning out chapters we'd send to screenwriter Stirling Silliphant, bouncing around in his yacht (so we were told) in the Caribbean trying to make a single script out of two books.

222 • Frank M. Robinson

In the meantime, Allen emptied his bungalow on the Twentieth lot of all its furniture, then called in a group of artists to do paintings of the exciting scenes in the books. When they were through, he called in the honchos from Warner Bros., who took one look and figured that Allen was way ahead of them. When Allen suggested a coproduction deal, they jumped at the chance. (Twentieth got the take in the States, Warner the money from overseas.)

When the *The Glass Inferno* came out as a book, Doubleday, our publisher, threw a luncheon for us. They had their own kitchen, whose specialty was pies—they were great pies, and since I couldn't make up my mind, I had a slice of each.

The biggest party was the one that Perry Knowlton, the head of the agency, threw in his brownstone in the Village. Most of the literati in New York were there (certainly the gay ones were). Perry had a private bar and everybody was more than friendly.

I was awestruck meeting the literary guests, and Tom preoccupied himself trying to make out with the kid working as bartender. At evening's end, the kid fled out the back.

Myself, I left by the front door, reminding a young ballet dancer that my hotel room was big enough for two. He was very nice about it. He had a lover, he said. I complimented both of them on their good taste (money and fame, sadly, don't buy everything), and I left for the hotel tired and lonely.

The next morning I went downstairs for breakfast and noticed Tom in the bar, looking unhappy and remorseful. What he was remorseful about was not losing the barboy but the possiblity of losing me as his collaborator. He knew I would have to apologize for him to everybody at the agency.

For just a moment I wavered. Did I really need him? All collaborations are the same—each partner feels that they've done

60 percent of the work but are getting only 50 percent of the money. Tom swore on a stack of bar napkins that it would never happen again, and I caved. I put my hands on his shoulders and told him that come what may, we were partners. (We really were—we wrote four more books together.)

By this time Allen had hired a cast for the movie, with Paul Newman and Steve McQueen heading it, plus Fred Astaire, Richard Chamberlain, and—ahem—O. J. Simpson. The gag in Hollywood was that if you were out of work and needed a gig, see Allen—he'd hire you.

We met Newman and McQueen in an elevator one day and Newman struck us as a nice guy but McQueen was full of himself and repeated back everything we had researched about fire captains (his role).

A few months later was the premiere. My sister-in-law went to the beauty parlor at nine in the mornng and told them not to let her out until four. Her son, eighteen or so, bought a powder blue tux with white ruffles. I was tempted to ask him what he was going to charge . . .

I walked the red carpet and discovered how fleeting fame can be when somebody on the sidelines said in a loud voice to a friend, "Who the hell is he?"

After the premiere there was a party in a huge ballroom for charity. I recognized Groucho Marx and that was it, but my sister-in-law had a tablet and kept score of all the celebrities she recognized. I wished my mother were still alive and seeing what had become of her son who spent his evenings in the kitchen typing on his old Underwood.

It was great to get back to San Francisco—I had almost forgotten how beautiful the city was. I went back to the camera shop and wrote flyers and a few speeches. It was one thing to write them, and quite another to hear Harvey speak them. He had the ability to make them come alive (Sean Penn studied news clips of Harvey and imitated his voice for *Milk*.)

A month of doing nothing and I began to feel bored. Tom had acquired a lover (a slim, handsome young man nicknamed J.J.) and had come up with a great idea. His tentative title was *The Prometheus Crisis*, about a new, huge nuclear reactor in Southern California that our villain intends to blow up.

I thought it was a terrific idea. We wrote an outline and then let our agent shop it while we went ahead writing the novel itself.

We lucked out once again. Peter Bart (then with Paramount and now editor at large of *Variety*) and his moneyman, Max Palevsky, optioned it for two hundred grand. It was real Hollywood this time. A limo met us at the airport and we ended up at the Beverly Hilton, which had great room service.

After we were settled, we met Bart and Palevsky at Bart's home. Tom talked business with them and I entertained Bart's little girl with origami—paper birds that flap their wings when you pull on the tail. (I was oddly proud when I found out recently that the little girl I had met so long ago was now a registered nurse.)

John Carpenter tried his hand at a script, and even Tom took a turn. Then the project was blown out of the water.

The China Syndrome, starring Jane Fonda and Jack Lemmon, was released to great reviews and tremendous box office. In *The China Syndrome*, the plant almost blows up but Lemmon saves the day. In *Prometheus*, the plant actually does blow up and takes most of Southern California with it. *Prometheus* turned out to be one of the many projects in Hollywood that look great and then sink.

We were vastly disappointed and so were our agents and, of course, Harry Margolis.

Once again back to the camera shop. Tom and his lover bought a house in Sausalito, and I had bought one near the Castro section of San Francisco, a short walk from the shop.

I had just finished remodeling it when Harvey dreamed up a terrific idea—a Castro Street Fair. One of the exhibits was a "dunk it" pool, where you threw a ball, and if you hit the target, the ledge on which the "target" sat would collapse and whoever was sitting on the ledge would get dunked in the pool of water at the bottom.

Harvey was a popular target.

There were tricycle races and art exhbits and booths selling food and beer. It was a huge success, and a lot more people were aware of Harvey afterward than before. In his secondhand suit and a neat haircut he looked like a real candidate. As a politician, Harvey's ace in the hole was his sense of humor, the one thing the other candidates didn't have. Harvey was rapidly becoming a "character" in the race for supervisor—you could always rely on him to provide a spot for the six o'clock news or a dozen lines on the front page. Reporters and photographers were picking up on him.

I still didn't think he would win, but he was certainly doing better than when he started.

Tom and I began still another book, *The Nightmare Factor*, dealing with a tainted blood supply. But I don't think either of us had our hearts in it. In one sense, I think the public had typecast us. "So what happens this time? Who dies? And who cares?"

For myself, I was devoting more and more time to Harvey's campaign. Much to my pleasant surprise, it looked like he had a chance in the supervisorial race.

A few months after the Castro Street Fair was one of the first Gay Pride Parades. Hundreds of thousands of people lined Market Street waiting for the spectacle to follow. You could hear the roar of motorcycles in the distance and then the "dykes on bikes" showed up, a number of them braless.

There were marching bands, various political organizations

marching, and floats of all kinds, the most popular being those sponsored by the bathhouses, with musclemen in Speedos gyrating to music from phonographs. Most of the supervisors got into the act, riding along in open convertibles.

(After he was elected, the most popular politician was Harvey Milk, sitting on the edge of the backseat of a BMW and holding up a sign reading "I'm from Woodmere!" The crowds lining the curbs went wild, and I wondered if Harvey had ever thought of running for mayor.)

When the parade came to an end everybody decamped to a huge mall in front of the city hall to lounge on the grass, eat hot dogs and ice cream bars, and look around to see who else was there also looking around. I noticed one partygoer who looked familiar. When he was much younger, he'd driven me crazy in Chicago, always flirting and always inaccessible. As a kid, he'd loved the power he had over older men. He was paunchy now, his hair receding.

Age levels all of us.

It was the real start of the campaign season, and Harvey was everywhere, giving speeches in bars, meeting people on street corners, and playing host to everybody who came into the camera shop.

It all paid off. There were open slots for six supervisors, and Harvey came in seventh. Not bad, not bad at all.

There was a victory party in a former pot supermarket a few blocks off Castro, and Harvey was surrounded by well-wishers. The surprise of the evening was when Mayor Moscone showed up to congratulate Harvey.

The owner of the restaurant snooped to hear what they were talking about and promptly told everybody what he had overheard. Harvey had mentioned casually that the mayor must now have a number of commissioner positions he could hand out.

The mayor smiled and said why didn't Harvey make an appointment and drop around to see him in city hall when he was free.

Harvey grinned and said he just might do that.

Once the rest of us heard about it, there was a lot of gossip about just what Harvey might wind up being commissioner of. Harvey was very proud and said he was well on his way to becoming "head queen," lording it over every other gay politician in town.

None of us guessed what he was going to do next.

By this time a flood of gays were moving to San Francisco. The number went as high as one out of five (I think that was too high, but then, I never counted). Housing prices went up and many of the older inhabitants took the money and ran. (Who wanted to live in a neighborhood of gays?) The Castro was now a stop for tourist buses, visitors from Dubuque and Harrisburg, their faces pressed against the windows hoping to see two men kissing in a doorway.

The buses dropped the Castro when a young man ran after one of them throwing rocks and screaming, "We're not freaks! We're not freaks!"

What Harvey did next was to run for public office again—this time as state representative from District Five. Harvey had found being a commissioner was a very boring job—he wanted to be elected to a position that really meant something. It finally occurred to me that Harvey enjoyed running more than sitting in an office twiddling his thumbs. Scott had left, and his replacement was John Ryckman, an old-style Democrat who knew most of the old money on the North Side. (I didn't notice any of it coming our way.) Most of us who had worked on Harvey's previous campaign were tired. But there was an aura of excitement around Harvey when he was fighting politicians.

Harvey's decision was a shock to the local Democratic machine. The various warring factions had gotten together and divided up the city and its various official positions like it was a cake—and everybody was given a slice.

Except for Harvey. Mayor Moscone fired him from his post as a commissioner because of his ingratitude. Harvey had held the post for something less than two months. As a politician Harvey was persona non grata to the Democratic machine as well as the entrenched gay political groups.

It was only later that I saw the electoral map that Jim Rivaldo had drawn up and why Harvey had made the decision that he had. In District Five, Harvey's vote for supervisor had swamped the competition. Being elected state representaive should be a walk in the park.

The machine put up a candidate that nobody had ever heard of—Art Agnos. Art was a small cog in the Democratic machine and had been nominated for state rep as part of the spoils. He had a respectable background in social work, but aside from that, nobody had ever heard of him.

The San Francisco Bay Guardian, a local paper, immediately endorsed Harvey, and Harvey had every reason to believe he was on his way. He was—until just before the election, when the *Guardian* double-crossed him and endorsed Agnos (the only time I ever saw Harvey cry in anger). Governor Brown, who had promised to remain neutral, sent a postcard to every voter in the city, plugging Agnos. They arrived the day before the election.

All of us huddled in the camera store watching the returns being posted as they came in. At first, Harvey led (the state Democratic machine must have come close to heart failure), but toward the end of the evening, Agnos edged ahead. Harvey lost by three thousand votes.

By this time, I had other things on my mind. Tom and I ended up in court. MetroMedia had released a "made for TV" film titled *Terror on the 40th Floor*. It was different enough from *The Towering Inferno* that Twentieth Century Fox had no interest in joining our suit. MetroMedia hadn't infringed on the movie; they had stolen the guts of *The Glass Inferno*, our book. Twentieth considered (probably rightly) that the TV film was an ad for their major theatrical production of *The Towering Inferno*.

The trial was before a judge and lasted the better part of the day. In the end, Tom and I won $10,000—"stamp money" for a major Hollywood producer.

After it was over I went to the back of the courtroom and ran into the lawyer for MetroMedia. A man in his sixties, slender, carefully combed gray hair, and several thousand dollars worth of Italian suit. I found out he was from Winnetka, a wealthy suburb of Chicago, and I decided to be hail fellow well met. After all, the case was over, and I was set to reminisce about Chicago and its suburbs.

He wasn't having any.

"Mr. Robinson," he said quietly, "if I had gotten you on the stand, I would have made you look foolish."

He turned on his heel and walked away and I stared after him, crushed.

(I think it was something like eight years before I got even. Hollywood, I was to discover, specialized in two things: movies and lawsuits.)

Tom—always smarter than I was when it came to money—bought something that looked like a hunk of junk but could replace a typewwriter. It had a silly name: Apple. I spent seventeen grand on a dedicated word processor from IBM that had daisy wheels and eight-inch discs and could print a page a minute. My God, what speed! (IBM once sent over several repairmen to fix it and they told me it should be in a museum.)

We both invested in oil wells and I sold mine when oil was $15 a barrel (who knew it would hit a hundred?)

I also bought a time-share in Maui, which was all mine for a few weeks a year. I made the trip to Hana—a small town along the worst road I've ever bumped over, but it was worth it. I had never seen so many small waterfalls in my life. I admired all the natives who didn't much admire us haoles. We drove to the top of the local volcano, Haleakala (ten thousand feet), but the fog had rolled in and there wasn't much to see, and not much air to breathe.

On the fourth day, something strange happened. I came down with "island fever." I was painfully aware that I was on a very small patch of land in the middle of a very big ocean.

We left for the mainland the next day. Various friends and relatives used the rest of my time-shares on Maui, and all were very grateful.

I had always collected old science fiction magazines and one weekend was badgered into attending a pulp mgazine convention in Dayton, Ohio. The convention was held in a local university, home for the weekend of some three hundred pulp magazine nuts. I came into the airport late and there was nobody to meet me. It took an hour for somebody from the convention to get me, and by then I was ready to go home.

The next day in the "huckster" room I changed my mind. It was jammed with tables groaning under piles of old pulp paper magazines I had never heard of: *Adventure*, *Blue Book*, *Spicy Mystery*, *Dime Detective*, etc. As a collector, I fell in love and later made posters of the covers and reconsructed hundreds of pulps from covers and interior pages saved by a local magazine authority and edited several books of the old covers and wrote introductions for several others. *Pulp Culture* got more reviews than any other book I wrote. Newspaper editors had never seen one, and their art departments, like I had, fell in love with the covers (all but my hometown paper, the *San Francisco Chronicle*).

I didn't collect them as an investment but later it turned out they were the best investment I had ever made. The magazines ranged in value from $10 up to the thousands, depending on condition and rarity. I became famous for my "wall of pulps"—bookcases filled with magazines with their covers on display.

When I finally auctioned them off years later—no hobby holds its appeal forever—they brought close to $1 million. I would have made more if I'd bought Apple stock, but that wasn't bad. I left the Dayton convention with two suitcases packed and for twenty years never missed a convention.

In the meantime Tom and I had once again lucked out when it came to writing books. Skip Steloff, a former submarine officer, had a great idea for a story. It was pure thriller, and Skip had connections with Warner, who were interested in the screen rights.

Steloff's idea dealt with a rogue US submarine in which—for reasons of plot—one of the crew slowly loses his mind over the purpose of their mission. The two plot threads were where the hell was our nuclear submarine, fully loaded with armed nuclear missiles, and what did the now unreliable crew intend to do with them. We titled the book *The Gold Crew* (submarine crews, one a blue crew and the other a gold crew, went down for six months at a time).

Warner loved it but the catch was they wanted a book first. Steloff approached Arthur Hailey, author of *Airport*, but he wasn't interested. The next stop among thriller writers were Scortia and Robinson. The book would be published by Warner Books (a new imprint at the time), and Warner Films would make the movie.

The money offered was, for us, mind-boggling: $200,000.

Tom and I knew squat about submarines, so we started to map out our research. We went down to San Diego and interviewed sub crews. We divided them into two groups. One were the submariners themselves, and the other was their wives. A woman who finds herself husbandless for six months out of the year had to have a much different view of things than her husband. I wouldn't have bet money on how long many of the marriages would last.

Next I went to Groton, Connecticut, home of most of the submarine pens, and was cordially welcomed but that was all. The officers were familiar with *The Glass Inferno* and had a pretty good idea of what we had in mind. The closest I got to a submarine was a few hundred yards away, but even then, the sight was chilling.

A number of writers—and artists—had been there before us, and most of the information we got was from them. Few of the captains and admirals they interviewed had seen fit to censor the same things. An article in a *Reader's Digest* told us the maximum depth a nuclear sub could go, and Kelly Freas, a science fiction artist, was kind enough to let us see his sketchbook— what was left of it after an admiral had torn out what he considered to be incriminating pages. But enough were left to give us a pretty good idea of what the interior of a nuclear submarine looked like. Tom and I had lucked out.

Back in San Francisco, Tom and I decided to split the writing of the book in two. Tom would handle all the above-water scenes, and I would handle all the scenes in the interior of the submarine, with its increasingly nutty—and dangerous—crew. We would alternate the chapters for a sense of pacing.

It worked out pretty well, and both Tom and I were convinced we had a bestseller. We became hermits while working on the book. There are always interruptions, but not all of our guests were turned away.

One early evening there was a knock on the door, and when I opened it standing in front was a young man—maybe in his early twenties—in sloppy blue jeans and a big smile. I was not happy. He had interrupted an important chapter.

I asked him what he wanted and he said, "Tom sent me." It took me a moment to make the connection. Tom Youngblood was a tall, handsome Texan (rumored at one time to be a Maplethorpe model—the one with a flower growing out of his butt) that I and a few others usually had breakast with.

The stranger at the door frowned at my blank face and added, "Tom said it was your birthday."

I'm not a slow study and figured that Tom had sent me a birthday present. I took my guest down to the Neon Chicken for a quick supper and then back to the house, still engrossed in the book. Once inside my guest finally introduced himself: Eric Ashworth.

I told him I was working on a book and he took a quick tour of the living room, with two movie posters—one for *The Power* and the other for *The Towering Inferno*—hanging on the wall.

But he still didn't give me any idea of what he was really there for, though it was becoming increasingly easy to figure out. (Later, I found that Tom's gift had cost him $100. The kid probably had a wealthy patron who was sending him to the University of California in Berkeley, but $100 had been enough for him to break his vows. I was only partly right.)

I pointed at the stairs leading to the second floor. "The bedroom is up there." I wanted to get it over with so I could get back to the book.

He gave me an odd look, then climbed the stairs.

"You really don't talk much," he said. It finally occurred to me that he'd come over because I was something more than just a trick.

I followed him up a few minutes later, opened the bedroom door, and then abruptly stopped. The floppy blue jeans had been a disguise.

I was looking at a man who could have given Michelanglo's *David* competition.

I didn't have much to say after that, either. I thought I'd known a lot about sex, but in truth I had known very little besides the old in-and-out. Then it finally occurred to me that Eric had come over to the house for something more than $100.

He was more than friendly in bed and essentially taught me that there was a huge difference between making love and "having sex." I didn't know how many people in the Castro knew this.

I still didn't know why, but for whatever reason, Eric liked me and wanted me to like him. That part wasn't difficult at all.

Downstairs he looked at the posters again, then said, "You're a writer, aren't you?" Tom had probably told him.

"I try to be," I said.

When the truth came out it was more than flattering. "You're the only writer I know," he said. "I want to go to New York and get into publishing and I thought you might give me some contacts."

In a way he was using me, but at least he was honest, and a dozen names quickly came to mind. I scribbled a few names on a sheet of paper—agents I knew, a few publishers, then hesitated a moment and at the head of the list I wrote "Craig Musser."

Craig, a little older than Eric, was working on a series of fantastic kaleidoscopes that he was selling for ten grand each (*Smithsonian* magazine once published an article about Craig). He was the best friend of my friend in Alaska, Rick Leo. Craig had gone to Harvard for several years for a little polish, learned how to dress, worked out in the gym to get biceps and pecs, and finally went to a plastic surgeon to sculpt his face. (Rick was straight as a string but Craig was not, which didn't affect their friendship at all.)

Craig was a self-made man, and to finish his education, he became a rent boy. He didn't need the money; he came from a wealthy family. It was an education that he didn't spend too much time on, and when he tired of it, he went into advertising and ended up handling a camera account.

I was quite sure he and Eric would love to meet each other.

After Eric left—by this time we were good friends—I called Craig and told him I was sending him an 11. A few days later Craig called to tell me he'd watched a young man consult a piece of paper as he looked down the apartment buttons. Craig asked if he could help and Eric said, "I'm looking for a Craig—a Craig Musser."

As Craig put it, "I thought I'd died and gone to heaven."

They were lovers for a while, then drifted apart and Eric got a job working in the Candida Donadio literary agency (its client list included Thomas Pynchon, Bruce Jay Friedman, and Mario Puzo, among others). Eric had been a literature major at Berkeley and had a flair for the business. A few years after working for Donadio, he became a full partner ("The Donadio-Ashworth Agency") and had a respectable client list of his own.

I had dinner with him years later and in one sense it was old home week. He was a somewhat older but very handsome man, and a small part of me kept wondering if he would still go for a hundred.

I was a fool for even thinking about it, but one does not always think with one's head. In one sense, I thought, it was really a compliment. In practical terms, I owed him far more than he owed me.

❦ XXIII ❧

HARVEY MAY HAVE lost the race for state representative, but the election returns had a silver lining. District elections had passed in the city—meaning the supervisors were elected by district; you didn't have to run citywide. If we looked at the map that Jimmy Rivaldo made, it was obvious that Harvey had a lock on District Five.

There were some changes in Harvey's little group. John Ryckman had left and his replacement was a young woman named Anne Kronenberg. Wayne Friday, a political friend of Harvey, was convinced she was too good to be true. In Wayne's mind was the possibility that Anne could be a "plant" by somebody in the competition who would faithfully report back to her boss what Harvey was planning to do. He grilled her for two hours and was finally convinced that if she was too good to be true, Harvey was a lucky man.

There was very little in the way of pay—her salary was usually what was left in the cash drawer at the end of the day. And there was also a good deal of doubt whether she could handle Harvey, who had his mercurial side. Harvey had worn out Scott, Ryckman was good for one term, and the question was: How long would Anne last?

The low and irregular pay didn't seem to bother her, and much to everybody's amazement, she seemed to have no difficulty in "handling" Harvey.

The other addition to Harvey's little group was Jack Lira, a slender, smallish man who had moved in as Harvey's new lover. All of us figured that Jack was trouble. He drank too much, he demanded attention, and if he didn't get his way he threw a tantrum. None of us liked him, and he didn't like any of us.

His appeal to Harvey was that he was great in bed. Harvey was painfully aware that he was in his early forties, not an age that would normally attract younger gay men. He also thought that he could "straighten" Jack out, help him to become much more of a normal human being. Every time Harvey began to doubt his own good intentions, Jack would strip and curl up on the mattress.

His primary asset, we all figured, was that he was a "hot" number and knew it. He resented the attention that Harvey paid to the rest of us and made it obvious to Harvey. He was a political liability, resentful of the time Harvey spent campaigning, and not afraid to show it.

It was a situation that slowly spun itself out and finally ended in tragedy.

Sixteen candidates ran for supervisor from the district. Harvey, of course, won. The gay community was ecstatic.

In 1977 Harvey Milk was the first openly gay man to be elected to a prominent political position in the United States.

When the figures started to come in, all of us gathered around the television set and held our breath. When it was final, that Harvey had won, the camera store quickly filled with well-wishers, all of whom claimed to have played a part in Harvey's victory. Bottles of champagne were passed out as if they were cans of Coke. Outside, the street in front of the camera shop was jammed. The newly elected Sheriff Hongisto rode up to the front door sitting on the back of Anne Kronenberg's motorcycle. There were chants and shouting and huge applause when Harvey appeared in the doorway. When the other candidates and their financial backers showed up to congratulate him, he wouldn't let them into the shop, claiming it was jammed (which it was).

The next day Harvey held a victory march from the camera shop to city hall. There was a parade of his supporters following him, but he walked with his lover, Jack, at his side. Jack didn't mind that at all—once at Harvey's side he was Somebody.

The trouble was that he wanted to be at Harvey's side all the time and resented it when Harvey had to act as a supervisor. That was, in Jack's mind, all Harvey's fault. One night Harvey had to spend some extra time at city hall—he was usually home around six—and made the mistake of not calling Jack and telling him he would be a little late. Jack of course, interpreted this as proof that Harvey cared more about his work than he did about Jack.

When Harvey got home the front door was unlocked and he was surprised to see a trail of campaign flyers and Coors beer cans leading from the front door to the second floor. He followed them up, stopping when the trail ended just outside a curtain strung across the porch. On it was a note reading "How do you like my last act?"

Harvey pushed it aside to see Jack hanging from a rope attached to the ceiling. The half hour that Harvey had been delayed at city hall convinced Lira that he was playing second fiddle to Harvey's job. He might have thought that Harvey would be only five or ten minutes late and would arrive in time to see him kicking and cut him down.

A grief-stricken Harvey found a knife and cut the rope, then called the police and an ambulance for help. It was much too late.

The papers and television stations reflected how Harvey felt. Not all of their readers or viewers felt the same way.

Harvey told me he had gone to work the next day; there was nothing more he could do. The first phone call he received was from an irate elderly woman asking when was he going to fix the pothole in front of her house.

I often wondered why Harvey didn't pick up his briefcase and walk out of city hall for good. For all of Jack's faults Harvey had loved him to the bitter end and thought that somehow he could help him.

The rest of us sympathized, but we knew better.

The one thing that helped was when Harvey went to the funeral and met Jack's family. Their sympathy was more for Harvey than for the deceased. Jack had been an alcoholic, headstrong, and full of self-pity all his life. His family had tried to help him, but everybody had failed. When Jack had started to go with Harvey, they all knew Jack was on a short string, and it was only a matter of tine.

Harvey's win at the polls was a symbol of change. Attitudes toward gays were becoming different. San Francisco, and especially the Castro, was the mecca they traveled to. It was estimated that at one time 150,000 or more gays made up a good part of San Francisco's 750,000 population.

There were a number of gay political groups in the city, but Harvey was now "head queen." He had an enormous audience that he played to at the Castro Street Fair. There were booths selling food and beer and various trinkets. At one end of the two blocks of the fair (it became much larger later) there was a band, and if you were lucky, maybe Sylvester, the favorite singer in the

Castro, would be on stage. And there was always the chance of meeting a friend for the evening. The uniform of the day was Levi's, boots, and a T-shirt if it was warm so you could show your pecs.

The party wasn't just for gays—it was for anybody in the city who dropped by. Whatever else could be said about them, gays knew how to throw a party.

And then there was the Gay Pride Day Parade, held on the anniversary of the Stonewall riots in New York's Greenwich Village. The parade would start at the foot of Market Street and wind up at the mall in front of city hall. There would be politicians waving at the crowd from convertibles, floats for the various political organizations, several bands, and—naturally—floats sponsored by the bathhouses featuring musclemen in Speedos gyrating to phonograph music.

When the parade ended, there was always the grassy mall to sun yourself and eat hot dogs and ethnic food. At the far end would be a platform and usually Harvey giving a speech.

It was a great place to meet and greet strangers who might not be strangers for long. You hadn't come to San Francisco to spend the night by yourself.

The first parade I went to had perhaps a quarter of a million spectators, not counting those stretched out on the mall.

With time the parades grew more serious but they always opened with the "dykes on bikes" roaring up Market to open the parade. In the first parade the riders were braless but became more sedate in later parades. There were stilt walkers, marching bands, baton throwers, political contingents of gays, and in front of city hall, booths peddling hot dogs and Korean dishes, kids selling ice cream bars, and always, booths touting the virtues of this and that political group and handing out flyers.

The Castro was getting to the point where it was overflowing; there were new arrivals every day. You could live a life in the confines of Castro Street and never meet a straight man. There were gay restaurants with gay cooks and waiters, offices for gay doctors and lawyers, and gay bookstores.

On Friday and Saturday nights there were lines of men standing before the bars waiting to get in. Sexual tension was strung across the street like piano wires. And if you were unlucky in finding a partner in the bars, there were always the bathhouses. Strip and wrap a towel around your waist, then wander the hallways looking through open doors at the men on the inside, most of them naked and waiting.

A few years later a friend told me he had had five thousand sexual partners. Do the math and you realize that not a day had gone by for ten or fifteen years when he was not having sex with somebody.

By this time I was thoroughly nonjudgmental no matter what. But I kept thinking that considering the number, he couldn't possibly have remembered what they did or all their names and faces.

There were some upper-class bars as well, the best known being the Corner Grocery Bar. The jukebox featured nothing but operatic arias, and every Sunday there were recitals by talented locals or those singers performing in shows downtown.

One time I picked up a young man at the Corner Grocery Bar, and once in bed he started crying. I didn't know why and he couldn't tell me. I dressed and did my best to cheer him up and then it occurred to me that he was suddenly faced with the prospect of doing something that he wanted to do but in the back of his head were the strictures put there by his parents and his church and the public attitude. If that was so, it was a problem he couldn't handle.

There weren't many like that. The Castro was a sexual candy

store, as Cleve Jones, Harvey's talented rabble-rouser with the bullhorn, once said. But it wasn't without its penalties. If there were lines forming outside the bars on Friday and Saturday night, in a week or two there would be lines at the medical center downtown. It was also a meeting place—a quick shot for clap and in a few days you and your new partner would shack up in his bed or yours.

Two friends of mine used to have breakfast together close to the window on the street. As the men passed the window my friends would count which ones they had slept with, and the one who counted more paid the bill.

There were a few who partnered up and were loyal to each other and some who had "open" relationships—faithfulness to one's partner was not always expected. "Marriage," as such, was usually frowned upon. It was a "straight" practice and not held in high repute. Those who came from broken homes or who had parents who didn't love each other could be forgiven. They had no role models they could look up to or serve as guides through popularly accepted sexual practices. And then there were those who had loving parents but had simply been born that way. (In a family with three or four boys, it was the youngest son who was usually the gay one.)

During the day, especially during the summer, shirtless, well-built men would stand along "Hibernia beach"—the wall of the Hibernia Bank on Castro (now a branch of the Bank of America). They were there to be admired or perhaps to find partners for the night. They usually weren't disappointed.

It was a curious dichotomy. Those who wanted to be "gay" were right at home in the Castro. But once you got beyond the confines of Seventeenth and Market, or caught the bus to go downtown, it was a different story. Harvey Milk was one of the very few citizens of the Castro who was openly gay to the entire world. He hid from nobody. Most of us envied him the ability to be himself no matter what. The teller who waited on you at the bank downtown, the clerk in Macy's, or the waiter on your table at lunch might be living two lives, but they made sure you only knew of one.

At night some might pocket little vials of pills and go to the bathhouse for a night of "unendurable ecstacy, indefinitely prolonged" with one or many partners, but downtown nobody knew it.

In the back of almost every gay's head were the memories of the city or town they had come from. Of being bullied in the schoolyard, hit when nobody was watching, their heads pushed down the toilet by other students anxious to prove how butch they were, who called them names that cut or made fun of them behind their backs.

That life they definitely kept to themselves. This might be San Francisco, where almost anybody could be anything, but past memories were too much to overcome. In a few years they would pay a horrifying price for their silence in a country that would consider them anything but honorable citizens, that would go out of its way to pass laws to punish them, and when they got sick and died it would be because they deserved it. If you were gay, few people held your life very dear.

In a few decades gays would discover once again that they were the last group in the country that suffered permissible prejudice. And depending on the circumstance, it was all right to kill gays. Parents who found out their boy was gay were horrified and did everything possible to "change" him, including sending him to psychiatrists and other doctors who would give him shots of only God knew what to "correct" his hormonal system.

(That wasn't restricted to the United States. In England, Alan

Turing, the man who had broken the Nazi submarine code and saved the British Isles, was caught with a rent boy and given injections of hormones to make him "straight." When Turing started to grow breasts, he committed suicide. The country he had saved had rewarded him by killing him.)

In the eyes of religious conservatives, the Castro was Sodom and Gomorrah. For many gays, it was Camelot.

For a while it seemed like things might change. In January 1977, the Dade County Commission in Florida voted 5 to 3 to ban discrimination in employment, housing, and "public accommodations." It was the first time a southern political entity had passed a gay rights law, joining cities such as St. Paul, Detroit, Seattle, and Minneapolis. By late spring, the total of states and cities that had decriminalized consenting adult sexual acts had grown. Wyoming was the nineteenth state to join the group.

Few people made a fuss about it except a mediocre singer who flacked for Florida orange juice.

Anita Bryant considered the commission's decision as flaunting the Almighty. At first, nobody paid any attention to her. (Gays, of course, stopped drinking orange juice.) If pressed too hard in debates, Anita Bryant would endear herself to her fans by singing "The Battle Hymn of the Republic."

Much to the surprise of most gays, Bryant's campaign caught fire, and on June 7 Dade County voters repealed the new law by two to one. The antigay fervor spread across the country, and fundamentalists filed for repeal of gay rights ordinances in Seattle, Eugene, Wichita, and St. Paul. In Oklahoma teenage gangs beat patrons in gay bars with baseball bats. In Arkansas the legislature considered a bill even more draconian that would ban gays from teaching and revoke their credentials in pediatrics, child psychology, and psychiatry. It you had a license, it would be taken away. If you lied about being gay, you could be sent to prison for five years. (Given their druthers, the voters in Wichita would probably have passed a law authorizing castration for any boy caught masturbating behind the barn.) Not to be outdone, Bryant introduced a bill that would send a man to prison for twenty years if he committed one homosexual act.

All of this was not lost on California state senator John Briggs, who introduced Proposition 6 in the state legislature, which would have prevented gays from teaching in the public schools. It also meant that gay teachers could not drink with a friend in a gay bar or even discuss homosexuality in the teachers' lounge.

This time Briggs had overreached himself, and opposition started to build. The teachers' unions rejected it, and even President Ronald Reagan came out against it.

"Whatever else it is, homosexuality is not contagious," Reagan said.

Most gays—myself included—were frightened by the anti-gay wave sweeping the country. It was Harvey who had the guts to do something about it. He decoyed Briggs into debating his Proposition 6 up and down California. It was a risky thing to do—Harvey was already getting death threats, and they would only increase if he fought against Prop 6, the welcome weapon of the righteous conservatives. His stack of hate mail was growing larger by the day, and he once showed me some. The writer would dismember Harvey and stuff his privates into his mouth. Others were a little less uncouth, but all had the same message: Harvey Milk would be killed.

It was probably this that made Harvey dictate a number of copies of his last will and testament in the event he should be murdered. He gave me a copy, and I threw it in my desk drawer and told him he was being morbid. He expected it, he said. If they could get President Kennedy, they could certainly get a lowly supervisor.

He didn't take me on his tour of the state—he didn't need a writer (I didn't think he ever needed one—he didn't lack the talent, he lacked the time).

His one-liners were priceless.

"How would you teach homosexuality? Like you'd teach French?"

"If little girls copied their teachers, there would certainly be a lot more nuns running around."

Proposition 6, which had started with a sixty-to-forty majority, was now fighting an opposition that had started to build. The teachers' unions had come out against it, and people were impressed by Harvey's courage in debating Briggs, even in the red-hot middle of the Republican bastion of Orange County. If he was going to be shot anyplace, Orange County was the most logical spot. All of us were afraid for him.

The kiss of death for Briggs was when Jimmy Carter came to town campaigning for the presidency. As he was leaving the speakers' platform, Governor Jerry Brown ran up to him and suggested he tell the audience to vote against Proposition 6. (Carter, Brown said, had nothing to lose.) Carter returned to the microphone and said, "And I want everybody here to vote against Proposition 6."

Proposition 6, which had started with a sixty-to-forty margin, lost by the same amount. The frosting on the cake was that on the same night voters in Seattle rejected the even more draconian Proposition 13.

The back of the antigay movement had largely been broken, and gays danced in the street at Castro and Market.

They didn't dance for long.

≪ XXIV ≫

THE GAY PRIDE Parade that year was huge. The year before it had shrunk to something like a quarter of a million (the "friends of gays" and their acolytes had failed to show). The name of the game was to show solidarity against Prop 6. Doctors, lawyers, Teamsters—every group had a contingent in the parade. The count this time was 350,000—almost half the population of San Francisco was strung out along Market Street. It wasn't all gays—this time sympathetic straights had their contingents as well.

But the ten days toward the end of the year were to be more than any city could have taken.

Earlier in the year the Reverend Jim Jones had moved his entire congregation of close to a thousand down to Guyana, a country on the northern coast of South America, to start a small paradise of their own. Most of the city's politicians were sorry to see him go. He was every politician's helper—you needed people to hang doorknob posters early in the morning? Jones could lend you a few hundred from his congregation. It didn't matter what side you were on; Jones played both. That way he couldn't lose no matter who won—they were all beholden to Jones.

Once Jones had left, reporters started snooping around, searching for corruption by Jones. It wasn't hard to find. Later there were notes and letters from some of his parishoners in Guyana saying they wanted to leave but Jones wouldn't let them go.

One week Jones's wife sent Harvey a letter saying she'd seen a photograph of him in the newspapers and he looked worn out. Why didn't he come down for a week or two and rest up? When Harvey told me about it, I warned him not to go, that the papers were digging up a lot of dirt on Jones, and the more space he put between himself and Jones, the better. Jones had helped all the politicians in town, including Harvey, lending him a small offset machine and an operator to work it, printing flyers for Harvey.

Harvey wouldn't have gone anyway; too much to do back here. But the complaint by some of Jones's parishioners that they were being held against their will got to Congressman Leo Ryan, and he decided to go down and have a look, maybe talk to Jones. With him went an NBC photographer and several members of Ryan's staff.

Whether some of the disaffected got to Ryan, I don't know, but I was pretty sure he talked to Jones himself. The group went back to the plane, tailed by a truck with some of Jones's men in it. As Ryan and company were getting into the plane, the men in the truck opened fire, killing Ryan and the photographer and injuring some of the others. Those still alive managed to get into the plane, which promptly flew back to Georgetown, the capital of Guyana. Police were sent to investigate, and what they found was horrifying.

Jones and his parishioners had committed suicide. Jones's wife, who had written Harvey, was found with her throat slit, along with her two children. Some of the others were shot, but most had been forced—or perhaps volunteered—to drink Kool-Aid laced with cyanide. Nobody was spared; babes in arms had had the Kool-Aid forced down their throats.

Jones's church and its parishioners were mostly San Franciscan, and the city made headlines all over the country. Mayor Moscone was appalled, as were the city's officials and inhabitants.

The election results grabbed the headlines in a few days, and relatives of Jones's parishioners, mostly black people plus a scattering of white converts, were left to grieve by themselves.

But Fate wasn't through with San Francisco, and the next disaster to hit it was equally as horrifying.

Dan White, the All-American boy from the conservative section of the city, had been elected to the Board of Supervisors, along with Harvey. What was important to the Police Department, the real estate boards, and business interests was that the presence of White on the board preserved the board's conservative outlook, despite the presence of a liberal mayor and that noisy liberal, Harvey Milk.

There was one major fly in the ointment that would lead to the city's second major headline-grabbing event in something like ten days. San Francisco was not the biggest city in the country but it was the most notorious, dating from the days of the Barbary Coast. What happened next kept it on the front pages.

The fly was that the salary for a supervisor was $9,000 a year. Unless you had an outside job, there was no way you could live on that. Dan White and Harvey Milk were the two poorest members of the board. Harvey eked out a living with the help of his always failing camera store. Dan White and his wife had a "hot potato" stand on the waterfront, which didn't do much better. The major financial difference between the two was that White had two kids while Harvey had lovers who more or less supported themselves (with the exception of Jack Lira).

Harvey was no longer a storefront politician. He had a much bigger stage now and much more influence. He had hit the "big time," or at least a small version of it. I thought that Harvey's election to city hall had made him lose some of his street smarts. There was no more dropping by the camera store to shoot the shit with Harvey. Now you had to make an appointment. The number of drop-ins dropped drastically. He no longer had a public that kept him in touch with the pulse of the city, though he did marvelously well with what he did have.

The difference between him and Dan White was the difference between night and day. White was the type who was the star of the local football team, a war hero, and the darling of the elderly Catholic ladies who made up the bulk of his constituency. He was the son that all the old ladies had wanted to have. White didn't like the influx of gays into *his* city, and neither did they. There was something . . . unclean about them.

White had his flaws, of course, all of which his voters overlooked. He had been a policeman, and failed at that. He tried being a fireman, and that was another failure. Now he was a supervisor, and he was sure that this time he'd make all his voters proud.

One thing he really wished he had: the charisma and the headline-grabbing abilities of Harvey Milk, the ability to connect with the various ethnic groups in the city (no way was that in the portfolio of the All-American boy). But then the little old ladies really didn't care that he wasn't buddy-buddy with the Asians, the blacks, and the various uncouth union members, all of whom were ruining the beautiful city of their youth.

None of us liked White. In a sense, he was a failed snob. And it was more than obvious that he didn't care much for gays.

Harvey, on the other hand, was convinced that he could "educate" White into understanding and accepting the minorities. He had tried that with Jack Lira and failed; now he was aiming higher. None of us understood why he didn't see that White was homophobic to the core.

Once again I was convinced that Harvey had lost his street smarts.

At the start Harvey did his best to befriend White, and the two frequently appeared on talk shows together. It was a mistake on White's part—he was straitlaced and reserved and paled next to Harvey's outgoing personality. On a lot of topics, they disagreed. Once again, White would come out the loser.

We all warned Harvey that White was excessively proud of his conservative outlook and not about to change it. If he had any reaction to Harvey, it was one of contempt.

And envy.

The real split came when White argued passionately against locating a psychiatric center in an empty convent that happened to be in White's district. His cadre of old women were dead set against it, afraid dangerous riffraff would be sent there. The supervisors voted 6 to 5 against it, and that included Harvey's vote, which White was counting on.

Later, looking into the problem of the children who would be sent to the convent, Harvey changed his vote so the final tally was 6 to 5 for.

White had promised his constituents that once he was supervisor, the center would never be located there. He had failed again. He considered Harvey's switch, of course, a betrayal.

A week later, when Harvey's pet project of a gay rights bill came up, White was the only supervisor who voted against it. He admitted that he was getting even.

He was, White decided, a supervisor with very little power. When Prop 6, the Briggs bill, failed by sixty to forty, White turned in his resignation three days later. The reason he gave was that his family couldn't live on the little money the hot potato stand brought in and his meager supervisor's salary. But the Police Department, the Realtors, and the business interests had counted on White's vote when a bill came up that directly affected them. White was the swing vote that they could always rely on.

Representatives of the groups cornered White and promised they would make up the difference between a livable wage and what he was making as supervisor.

A few days after White had submitted his resignation, he told Mayor George Moscone that he wanted it back, that he had changed his mind. Bighearted Moscone handed his resignation back to him, remarking to the press that White was young and new to the political game and was entitled to change his mind.

Apparently the other supervisors greeted it with a shrug except Harvey, who boiled over. He had been delighted with White's resignation and that the board could now break 6 to 5 in favor of the liberals.

Moscone hesitated until Harvey reminded him that he had gotten the gay vote in a very tight race. If he let White back on the board, Harvey would see to it that his gay vote would vanish.

Moscone decided Harvey was right and he would consider White's initial resignation as final.

Unfortunately, somebody in his office leaked the news to a radio reporter, who promptly called White to ask for his reaction. White said he knew nothing about it and hung up.

He didn't talk about it to his wife and ended up lying on the sofa eating junk food and brooding. He guessed the reporter had been right and he had been double-crossed once again. It wasn't hard for him to figure out that Harvey Milk had been behind it.

Harvey had gone to the opera a few nights before and spent time talking with Bidu Sayão, a favorite old-time opera star, and left in high spirits. He wrote a short note to Tom O'Horgan telling him about the evening, ending with "ah—life is worth living."

The next night he spent talking to old friends, who remarked later that it was unlike Harvey, that he had seemed lonely on the phone.

Early the next morning White dressed, then found his police revolver and loaded it with hollow-pointed bullets (dumdums, which explode on impact).

Denise Apcar, White's aide, picked him up at home and drove him to city hall. He did not go through the front doors, which had metal detectors, but went to the side of the building and climbed through an open basement window. A janitor saw him, asked who he was, and White told him and hurried past—he was late, he said.

He got to Moscone's office at about ten thirty. The secretary told him Moscone was busy, but she would let him know. Moscone knew White was there to see him and a few minutes later buzzed the secretary to let him in.

Upstairs, in his office, Harvey was waiting for an aide, Carl Carlson, to show up with a check. Carlson was late, and Harvey started to make his morning phone calls.

Outside Moscone's office, his secretary, heard voices raised in argument. Inside, Moscone had gone into his den to get two drinks and offer one to White to try to molify him. He lit a cigarette and returned to his office to find White pointing a revolver at him.

White fired a shot, hitting Moscone in the arm, and another shot to his chest. Moscone sank to the floor, and White knelt and fired two more shots, directly into Moscone's head. He then stood up and reloaded his revolver.

Outside, his secretary thought she heard a car backfiring. She did not see White leave by a side door and hurry down the corridor to the supervisors' offices. He brushed past the office of supervisor Dianne Feinstein (later a US senator). She saw him and called out to him. He said he didn't have time to talk and hurried to Harvey Milk's office, where Harvey was still on the phone. White asked if he could see him for a moment. Harvey said "Sure," and followed White into his old office, where White closed the door. Once inside, Harvey turned and White shot him twice in the arms, then shot him in the chest with another dumdum bullet. Harvey fell to the floor and White knelt and shot him twice directly in the head, blowing Harvey Milk's brains out.

Harvey died on November 27, 1978.

I didn't know anything about this—I read about it later. I was walking down Castro and somebody stuck his head out of a bar and shouted, "Harvey's been shot!" I thought it would be followed by another announcement that Harvey was in such and such hospital and was being patched up.

I hurried into the bar just in time to see a disheveled Dianne Feinstein—now the de facto mayor of San Francisco—in a close-up on the tube announce:

"As president of the Board of Supervisors, it is my duty to inform you that both Mayor Moscone and Supervisor Harvey Milk have been shot and killed." You could hear gasps from the crowd of reporters and the police behind her. She continued: "Supervisor Dan White is the suspect."

Feinstein had opened the door to White's old office and saw

Harvey in a pool of blood on the floor. She had had some medical training and tried to feel for a pulse. There was none. She hadn't expected that there would be.

Dan White, who had failed at almost everything in life, had finally succeeded at being a Class A assassin.

He left the building and called his wife at the potato stand to ask her to meet him at St. Mary's Cathedral. When they met, he told her what he had done. She replied that she would stand by him no matter what. They then walked to a police station, where White had friends.

The word had spread in the Castro, and crowds started to gather at Castro and Market. It was something that was very hard to believe. Harvey had been close to most of them for years; it was difficult to believe he was dead.

It was starting to grow dark when somebody showed up with lit candles in paper cups and passed them around. Others found more candles and cups, and a rough parade began to form. They automatically started to march to city hall.

It was dusk by the time the march got under way, and by now it had finally hit me and I started to cry. I marched with Jim Rivaldo and Denton Smith, two close friends of Harvey, though all of us were close friends of Harvey.

In some of the apartment buildings that we passed I noticed that people had put candles in their windows. It was a blow not alone to gays—it was a blow to everybody who lived in San Francisco.

There was an underpass before we got to city hall, and I turned and looked behind us. The line of mourners carrying paper cups with candles stretched from where I was all the way back to the Castro. I found out later that there were some forty thousand people in the march—probably the biggest spontaneous funeral march there had ever been in the country. More than any other, it was one of the people, by the people, and for the people.

I don't remember when we got to city hall. There was a bronze bust of Lincoln on the corner, and we doused our candles on it as we walked by. The next morning all you saw was this mountain of wax hiding Lincoln.

At city hall Joan Baez sang "Swing Low, Sweet Chariot." Dianne Feinstein spoke a few words: "Those of us on the board will remember him for his commitment, for his sense of humor, and for his ability to develop a sense of destiny."

It was probably the nicest thing that Feinstein ever said about Harvey.

Harry Britt followed. "He was to us what Dr. King was to his people. . . . How many times have we made that walk down Market Street and known that when we got to city hall, Harvey would be there? Harvey will be in the middle of us, always, always, always."

Then the words were over and everybody went home.

I went to bed that night, still crying.

The coroner decided that Harvey might have survived his body wounds, but then he shaved Harvey's head and found where the coup de grâce shots had hit. Harvey had died instantly. The coroner then removed his eyes to give to the living, as Harvey had requested.

The next day Jim Rivaldo and Scott Smith went through Harvey's closet, searching for clothes to bury him in. Most of his clothes were threadbare; it was difficult to find socks with no holes in them.

Moscone's choice for somebody to replace White was no problem—Moscone had already named him. For Harvey, it was a different story. His will had requested a choice from four successors in case he was killed: Anne Kronenberg; Bob Ross, editor and publisher of *The Bay Area Reporter*; Harry Britt, a close campaign worker; and myself.

Ross was out beause he had once been the emperor of the drag queen court, and Feinstein had no use for drag queens. Anne Kronenberg was the most logical choice, but Feinstein decided she was too young, and in the interview Feinstein had with her, Anne had refused to pledge undying loyalty to Feinstein's political wishes. It was rumored that Feinstein was also afraid Anne would show up at city hall on her motorcycle, wearing leathers.

I was next and very nervous about the possibility of filling Harvey's shoes. Of all those nominated by Harvey, I was the least likely (it was rumored that I had been his number one choice, but I don't know the truth of it; I had never read his last will and testament.)

It was a position I didn't want and knew I could never fill. I told Feinstein I was working on a book and she pooh-poohed it—being a supervisor was a part-time job. I had been too close to Harvey to know that wasn't true. I had no political following and knew little about the politics of the board. Feinstein shrugged; I didn't have to, all I had to do was follow her lead.

I remembered the arguments that Harvey frequently had with her and his generally low opinion of her.

I then pulled what I thought was my trump card. I wasn't in the best of health, I said—I had atrial fibrillation, an irregular heartbeat.

She looked into the distance for a moment and remarked that when she had been on television to announce the deaths of Moscone and Harvey, Police Chief Gain had had to hold her up—her heart had hit two hundred beats per minute (normal would be about sixty).

The next day I sent her a brief letter withdrawing from any

consideration as a supervisor. There was a brief boomlet for Anne that collapsed, and Feinstein settled on Harry Britt. He was the least controversial of all of us, had worked closely with Harvey, and had once been a Methodist minister.

Most importantly, he pledged undying loyalty. It wasn't true, but it took a few votes before Feinstein realized that Britt was reflecting the wishes of the gay community, not hers.

Britt made a good supervisor, but he was no Harvey Milk. Who was? God had made only one Harvey Milk. As mayor, considering all the problems Feinstein had, I thought she made a pretty good one. She was fairly tight with the police, so there was no difficulty there. After two terms as mayor, she ran for the governorship and lost. She then ran for senator. Jumping forward a few decades, she has turned out to be one of the stellar Democratic senators. If she ever leaves office, it will be because she doesn't want the office, not because the voters would reject her. At this writing, I can think of no Republican who could possibly beat her.

Considering Feinstein overall, I would have run her against Maggie Thatcher any day.

Feinstein would have won—she's one tough lady.

I was disappointed that she didn't care for Harvey. He talked too often and talked too long, she said. I would have replied that was because he usually had something important to say.

≪ XXV ≫

WHITE'S TRIAL WAS a farce.

We all thought that White deserved life in prison, where the inmates would have showed the All-American boy what being gay was all about. Or better yet, that he would get the gas chamber.

As Randy Alfred, a local reporter, quoted—*res ipsa loquitur.* In Latin, "the thing speaks for itself." Dan White had murdered two men in cold blood. Period.

The only ones who favored White were, predictably, the police. If you went to Castro and Market you'd find a cop car parked there, the car radio blasting "Danny Boy." There were signs posted around town reading "Free Dan White!" And there were rumors floating around that Moscone had not been the squeaky-clean moral mayor he had been portrayed. He'd had a thing for young, black, female prostitutes, so the story went. It wasn't difficult to figure out who was responsible for that one.

Anybody who watched the O. J. Simpson trial knows that the outcome of jury trials are usually decided when they pick the jury. If you thought Simpson was going to get the gas chamber, you were naive.

We all thought that was what White would get. His was one

of the very first trials of a politician in the country—the second only in California, if memory serves.

Give the devil his due—defense counsel Doug Schmidt was brilliant. There were 250 prospective jurors. Tom Norman, the prosecutor, used only six of his twenty-six peremptory challenges (where you could dismiss a potential juror without a reason).

Schmidt ended with a jury that had seven old ladies from White's home district. There were no blacks, Asians, or gays. There was also one cop-lover who rushed over to Schmidt when it was all over to shake his hand. Schmidt had seen to it that Dan White was indeed being judged by a jury of his peers.

Schmidt's defense hung on what a great All-American boy White was. How could anybody believe that such a lad could shoot somebody in cold blood? The reason, never stated, was that Harvey Milk was gay and the jurors hated the gays who were ruining their fair city.

Homosexuality was on trial, not just Dan White.

White had been the captain of both his baseball and football teams in high school, he was an ex-paratrooper who'd fought for his country. Quoting Schmidt, "Good people, fine people, with fine backgrounds simply don't kill people in cold blood."

Leaving one to wonder just who the hell did it. As for fine people with fine backgrounds killing people, all you had to do was read the morning paper.

Schmidt played White's taped confession, taken by one of his old cop buddies who'd been his coach in high school. White was all choked up on the tape, and some of the jurors cried. White claimed he hadn't planned on going to city hall, didn't know why he was wearing his Smith & Wesson. . . . In Moscone's office, he'd heard a roaring in his ears and his taped voice trailed off. . . . His police interrogator didn't press him on describing either murder.

On Harvey's murder, White played a good guy. He'd wanted to talk to Harvey, to explain things to him, that while they didn't agree on a lot of things, White had always been honest with him. . . .

Then Harvey had smirked at him so White got all hot and bothered and shot him five times, twice in the head.

The real reasons never came up—Norman, the prosecuting attorney, never cross-examined him.

The defense psychiatrists testified that White's consumption of junk food the night before had raised his blood pressure and brought on fits of manic depression. (I'm fond of chocolate cake but no doctor ever warned me to stop eating it because I might have a fit of manic depression.)

After thirty-six hours of deliberation, most of it spent sobbing into their handkerchiefs, the jury returned a verdict of voluntary manslaughter. White was sentenced to seven years and eight months; with time off for good behavior, he'd be out in less than five.

The sentence stunned everybody in the city, excepting the little old ladies who lived in White's district.

One old lady was quoted as saying "It all came together as if God was watching over us, as if God had brought it together."

God would get no medals that day.

A reporter covering the trial called White's defense the "Twinkie" defense, and maybe White should have been convicted of hyperglycemia. Dianne Feinstein, who had found Harvey's body, knew exactly what it was: two murders. Willie Brown (later mayor) said: "You've got to be kidding me. A man executes two men over fifteen minutes and gets voluntary manslaughter? This is like reducing two counts of drunken driving to two counts of double parking."

Another of the jurors crossed her heart and said, "The verdict had to be God's will or it wouldn't have turned out that way." When White died, he would surely go to heaven.

Asked by a reporter his opinion of how the trial went, lawyer Doug Schmidt shrugged and said, "The only opinions that matter are those of the twelve people in the jury box."

Cleve Jones warned a police captain that there might be riots that night, and the captain reassured him, "We'll see you get a bullhorn, march them down to city hall, and give your usual speech."

Tom Norman, the prosecuting attorney, had tried dozens of murder cases. In this case he never introduced the possibility of malice—including White's hatred of gays. Norman was an experienced prosecutor, and the possibility arose that perhaps he had thrown the case. But the dead were dead and the possibility of city officials working with an angry Police Department would be, at best, a difficult one.

It had been, in short, a political trial. Any number of overseas tyrants probably took pointers.

I don't know if defense attorney Doug Schmidt lived in San Francisco. My guess is that if he did, he moved out shortly after the trial.

The entire city was upset. The gay community was mad with rage. The mob predicted by Cleve Jones started to gather at Seventeenth and Market shortly after the verdict was announced and headed for city hall, joined by more furious citizens as it went. By the time it got there, there were perhaps ten thousand angry gays in the crowd. Cleve Jones hastened to the front of the crowd, but nobody was interested in listening to a speech about restraint.

A thin line of moderate gays stood in front of the doors of city hall to protect it from entry—John Ryckman, Dick Pabich, Harry Britt, Scott Smith, and others. For a while they succeeded, fending off demonstrators while rocks were thrown at them and glass windows were shattered behind them.

One of the monitors shouted into a bullhorn, "Harvey Milk lives," and a voice from the crowd answered, "Harvey Milk is dead, you fool."

A phalanx of police showed up and marched through the crowd, ignoring the rocks thrown at them. The monitors on the steps sat down to show they were the good guys, and the cops promptly charged them and started beating them.

Out in the crowd, one of the rioters kicked in the window of a police car, lit a pack of matches, and threw it in, waiting for the upholstery to burst into flames. When it did, he started down the line of parked police cars and eleven of them went up in flames.

Bricks continued to fly, and soon all the first-floor windows of the building had been smashed. When more police showed up the thin line of cops who had been trying to protect the building moved back inside, hastily. One supervisor, Carol Ruth Silver, was hit by a rock and dragged inside, blood streaming from her face.

When another phalanx of police showed up and moved into the crowd, some of the demonstators tore up parking meters and fought back, using garbage can lids as shields.

Police Chief Gain told the cops to hold their ground, not to attack the rioters. Not many paid any attention. Still more cops moved in, beating their batons on the pavement—San Francisco's own Roman legion. Once they were in the crowd, small knots of rioters and police broke off and fought hand to hand. The cops were enraged as rioters broke branches off of trees and tore up asphalt from the streets to use as weapons.

The cops gradually pushed the rioters back, and Feinstein announced, "The city is secure."

It was wishful thinking.

Some of the police took off their badges and drove down to the Castro. They beat gays on the street and broke into the Elephant Walk bar and took it apart, breaking the mirrors behind the bar. Then city hall rioters showed up at the end of the street, ready for another go-around. Cleve Jones said that he had seen several men with rifles on rooftops. He and his roommate had been busy pulling wounded rioters off the street into a storefront.

Chief Gain had never authorized the trashing of the Castro and gradually got his police off the streets. The cops were reluctant to go—they said they had lost at city hall but no way were they going to lose in the Castro.

The diehards gradually left, and the only sirens were those of ambulances taking away the wounded. Something like a hundred rioters and seventy policemen ended up in the ER.

(I wasn't there—I was in Cleveland visiting relatives. But I read the reports and eyewitness accounts when I got back.)

There was one thing the reports missed. The Castro was gay turf—it was OURS. The Castro had been a happy hunting ground for gay-bashers in the past, and whistles had been issued to those who lived there so they could call for help if needed. Some, I knew, weren't satisfied just with whistles and bought more substantial armament.

I don't know how many guns were in the Castro, but there were more than just a few. If the police had continued down the street, breaking up stores and beating gays, if they had refused to obey Chief Gain, shots would have been fired and there would have been a full-fledged revolt—maybe not as large as Watts but large enough for the mayor to call in the state police.

By the next day, things had gotten almost back to normal. It was Harvey's forty-ninth birthday, and they were already building a stage at the corner of Castro and Market for the rock bands and singers who would show up. The city didn't like it, but the permit had already been issued days before, and to revoke it now would, perhaps, once again spur violence.

The police were all set for trouble—perhaps hoping for it. They had assembled in the side streets, ready for any violence. Doctors and nurses had established their own presence in storefronts along Castro. With the help of Cleve Jones, the police had established a command post in the second floor of Cliff's hardware store. What Cleve could have done, I don't know, but he would have done his best to stop any violence. He had coordinated the training of some three hundred monitors to stop any violence by the crowd.

The street itself was ready for it. Volunteers were hoisting a huge portrait of Harvey up the front of the Castro Theater, and on the theater's marquee was the message "Harvey lives!"

There were posters on buildings all around, pleading "PLEASE—No Violence!"

The streets gradually filled with people and Cleve Jones gave an opening speech.

"Last night the lesbian and gay men of San Francisco showed the rest of the city and the rest of the world that gay people are angry and on the move. And tonight we are here to show the world what we are creating out of that anger and that movement."

For anybody who was paying attention, the riot and the violence had changed the public perception of gays as being a collection of hairdressers and sissies. It was as important to changing the public image of gays as the Six-Day War had been in changing the public perception of Jews as weaklings and moneychangers—Shylock had disappeared forever. So had the images of the movie stars who portrayed gays as funny pansies.

Sylvester, a gay favorite, had come onstage and was singing,

and gays on the street began to dance and pass around joints—
nobody worried about violating the pot laws.

The night ended with twenty thousand celebrants singing
"Happy Birthday, Dear Harvey—Happy Birthday to you!"

In New York a small group of gay pickets had gathered in
Sheridan Square, across from the old Stonewall bar.

Their signs read, "We all live in San Francisco."

❧ XXVI ❧

BY THE EARLY 1980s Harvey was still a vivid memory, a memory that seemed to grow with each passing year (a local play, a documentarty, an opera by the Houston Grand Opera, and much, much more to come). I subscribed to the *New York Native* to keep track of the gay scene in New York (as far as gays were concerned, there were only two cities that mattered—San Francisco and New York; Los Angeles was just a suburb).

The paper covered a lot more than just the gay scene, and it was there I first read of a growing disaster, one that would become the greatest health disaster to ever hit the United States. The paper reported a short news item from the "Morbidity and Mortality Weekly Report," the newsletter from the Centers for Disease Control and Prevention (CDC).

Five young gay men in Los Angeles had been diagnosed as having pneumocystis carinii pneumonia (PCP), a disease that commonly affected young infants or the immunosuppressed. Two of them had died.

Faint alarm bells rang in the back of my head. A follow-up article in a CDC item reported twenty-six hemophiliacs with Kaposi's sarcoma (KS), six in California. Eight of the patients had died within two years of diagnosis. And ten more cases of PCP were reported in addition to the five original. Four of the KS patients had both KS and PCP.

The article did not state why only gays were involved.

I was both interested and worried. Gays never came down with anything that a quick trip to the med center and a shot wouldn't cure. You waited in line to get your shot and maybe meet your next bed partner. It was as much a social affair as a medical one.

The previous mystery disease—Legionnaire's disease—had the doctors and medical researchers all over it and was squelched within a few weeks. Everybody apparently thought it would be the same this time.

The technical journals. *The Lancet* and *The New England Journal of Medicine* reported that the victims were young gay men who traveled in the fast lane and were addicted to "sex, drugs, and rock 'n' roll." (Major media such as the daily newspapers had yet to give it much coverage.)

There was no mention of immediate cures or what was causing it. With time, more groups were involved than just gays—hemophiliacs, Haitians, and drug abusers made up the rest of the "4H Club."

I followed it in the *Native*, and coverage became more and more puzzling and gloomy. I didn't know anybody who had it but suspected it that was just a matter of time.

Some months later I met my first KS patient.

One morning Tom Youngblood and I drove over to pick up his friend Reid and take him to the AIDS clinic (the disease had a variety of names before the doctors settled on "AIDS"). Reid's apartment was in the middle of Haight-Ashbury. He was the sole occupant of a second-floor railroad flat (one with all the rooms strung along the side of the main corridor).

Tom asked me to stay in the car while he went up to get Reid, who was sensitive about strangers seeing his lesions.

I had never seen any KS lesions.

Tom was gone a long time and returned looking worried. Reid didn't have the energy to go to the hospital right then. Tom didn't think Reid would make it to Thanksgiving—or even Halloween. He swore to me that he would sit with Reid and read to him "until the end." Nobody should die alone like this. He climbed back into the car and said we should take Reid to the hospital that afternoon.

I had known Reid for a far shorter time than Tom, meeting him during a tour of Ward 5B, the "AIDS" ward at San Francisco General Hospital. He was blond, blue-eyed, and personable despite his illness—he could still crack a joke and wink at the nurses. He was thirty-four years old and before he got sick was considered a "hot number" in San Francisco's gay community.

He was smart—he had a degree in Slavic languages and literature from Princeton. He had been a member of one of Princeton's "eating clubs"—fraternities. Once he and a male friend had danced together all night. Other members thought that was a little much and asked for Reid's resignation. He refused.

He moved to San Francisco and got a job as a bartender— a job that pays handsomely in San Francisco and makes you a minor celebrity, one very much in demand.

He was diagnosed as having AIDS in April of '83. He'd had all the standard symptoms—night sweats, swollen lymph glands, fevers, weight loss, and thrush (whitish patches on the mucous membranes of the mouth). Later, he was diagnosed with a few small, reddish marks on his upper arms.

The diagnosis was KS, usually found in elderly Italian and

Jewish men. It's a slow disease, and they usually died of something else. In gay men, you can die of it in a short length of time.

Later, Reid was admitted to Ward 5B with a case of pneumocystis pneumonia—as final a death sentence as medical science knows, hands down.

Tom and I came back early that afternoon to Reid's flat. He was sleeping again. Tom went to get him out of bed, and I looked over the apartment. It was stripped—Reid's roommates had taken most of what might have been there.

The kitchen was clean—no dirty dishes in the sink. In the fridge was a carton of milk, a few eggs, a plastic bowl of orange Jell-O, a half-eaten sandwich. Reid hadn't been eating; the garbage can was as empty as the sink. I offered to scramble some eggs, but Reid wanted a bowl of dry cereal, nothing really solid.

The change from when I had seen him in the hospital before was appalling. His face was puffy, his left eye swollen shut, and the other a mere slit. His blond hair was sticking out at all angles, the purple bruises of KS scattered randomly across his neck and face. His flannel shirt and Levi's had become far too large for his shrunken frame. We had to help him put on his boots.

He didn't want any help in descending the stairs but wanted us to be close in case he fell. Once outside, he sat on the steps to rest while Tom drove over in his car. A young man with hair to his shoulders was working on his motorcycle on the sidewalk, with two young boys as an audience. None of them looked at Reid. I was sure they had seen him before, and once was enough.

In the car, Tom and I worked hard at making small talk. Reid was animated only when I mentioned some of the volunteers in Ward 5B. "They're beautiful," he said in a fadeaway voice. "They're the most beautiful people I've ever met."

It was old home week on the sixth floor, where the clinic was located. Tracy, a young nurse, hustled over to talk to Reid.

Jeremy, a worker for Shanti, a support group for AIDS patients, kissed him on the cheek and said, "How ya doin', gorgeous?" Reid brightened; he was among friends. A moment later they took him away to weigh him and draw blood and start him through the clinic routine.

It was a shadow show, I thought. There was nothing to be done for Reid. It was psychological—for the few weeks he had left, he could feel that at least somebody gave a shit.

We couldn't locate a social worker. It might be another day before arrangements could be made with Shanti for a volunteer. The only solution was to have Reid readmitted to the hospital.

Dr. Connie Wofsy, one of the doctors on duty, was sympathetic, but Reid hadn't been her patient. She said she didn't know much about him from the clinical aspect. I suspected that the ward was full, that Dr. Wofsy was practicing AIDS triage, and sick as he was, Reid wasn't sick enough.

Half an hour after Reid had disappeared into the treatment room, Dr. Paul Volberding, the young oncologist who had been treating him, came out to talk to us.

Reid was dying. The only treatment for his lesions was more Vinblastine, a chemotherapy drug. If that didn't work—it hadn't so far—there was other experimental chemotherapy they could try, but the side effects were severe. It would be up to Reid if he wanted to try it. In the meantime, we should take him home.

But Reid couldn't go back to his apartment; there was nobody there to take care of him. Dr. Volberding didn't understand. Reid said he didn't want to be admitted to the hospital, he wanted to go home.

Then it was time for Reid to leave. One of us would stay overnight with him until we could make arrangements for a Shanti volunteer.

I stayed with Reid while we waited for an elevator. He suddenly said he had to sit down. Just then the elevator arrived and I helped Reid inside.

As we passed the fourth floor, Reid collapsed, hitting his head against the elevator wall. I had broken his fall, but it had been like catching an armful of sticks. He lay quietly on the floor, exhausted. He had done his share—he had said he wanted to sit down; now it was up to somebody else. I hit the button for the sixth-floor clinic.

When the door opened the clerk at the desk spotted us and shouted for help. They got Reid into a wheelchair and took his blood pressure. Tracy asked him what he had been eating and he said Cheerios and Jell-O and some tuna fish sandwiches that friends had brought him. She decided that he hadn't been drinking enough liquids, that his heart hadn't been pumping enough volume of blood to keep him from blacking out. She said they would readmit him to the hospital.

But Dr. Volberding had been right. Reid didn't want to go back to the hospital despite his friendship with the volunteers in the ward. Dr. Wofsy said if he stayed at least a little while they could get some nutrition into him. Reid said, "Do you really think so? I've eaten here before."

He meant it as a joke, more a commentary on the food than on his condition. Somewhere inside, Reid was still functioning.

Outside in the car, I told Tom what had happened. "I didn't think it would be like this," he said. He confessed having a mental image of Reid gradually fading away like the heroine in *Camille*. He hadn't suspected that death would come as a puffy-faced, emaciated man with purple splotches covering his arms and face and with his shirt and Levi's hanging on him like laundry on a clothesline.

Reid had been unable to dress himself without help, unable

to feed himself without assistance, unable to walk down a flight of stairs without aid.

His well-meaning friends and the doctors and nurses at the AIDS clinic had been even more helpless. In the things that really mattered, there was nothing any of us could do for him anymore.

Reid was going to spend the rest of his life, however long or short it might be, struggling against the side effects of chemotherapy, trying to keep down what little food he could eat, mustering enough concentration so he could follow the intricacies of the afternoon soap operas he watched from his bed, trying to work up enough enthusiasm for meaningless conversations with the few friends who dropped by to see him. Reid knew better than anybody else that he was never going to get well.

Henry Fielding had been right when he wrote: "It is not death, but dying, which is terrible."

Like everybody else, I was frightened—sticking my tongue out when I brushed my teeth in the morning, looking for the whitish splotches of thrush.

I was frightened but nowhere near as frightened as the people who had to work with AIDS patients every day—the doctors and nurses, who had no solid information yet on how HIV was transmitted. Could it be transmitted by water droplets, if the patient coughed or sneezed? Or even breathing the same air? What about bathroom sinks or clothes?

Some gays thought it could be transmitted by sitting on a wet bench in a bathhouse. For medical personnel, it was a lot more serious, and many began wearing masks and gloves when handling patients. And what about surgeons, cardiologists, and operating room teams? All high-risk jobs—who would want them? And ER personnel would have their own problems with patients with gunshot wounds or who had been in accidents.

Lots of blood would be splashed around—and there were no reliable HIV tests for blood until the middle 1980s.

Some hospitals refused to admit new patients, claiming they were full. Most stayed open, and the doctors and nurses and interns stayed on the job—warriors in the front lines.

A doctor friend told me of his problems with an obese, middle-aged drug patient with a respiratory infection and high fever. The doctor finally got a syringe with needle through folds of fat when the patient suddenly bucked, throwing out the needle, which punctured the back of the doctor's left hand. After sending the blood-filled syringe to the lab for an HIV test (the doctor forged the patient's signature for permission), he spent the rest of the day scrubbing the back of his hand. The test came back negative, but there was a two-to-six-week window before he could be sure.

My doctor friend came back for anonymous testing every six weeks for a year before he was reasonably certain he was clean.

I didn't ask him how close he thought he could get to his girlfriend. I knew the answer—not very.

The richest country in the world was no better than the poorest when it came to letting its citizens die for political and religious reasons. At the start, the only ones who stood between the country and medical catastrophe were those same citizens—their generosity and intelligence and in many cases being willing to put their own lives on the line to try to save the lives of others.

Checking my tongue every morning for the signs of thrush was small potatoes. I was frightened—but like a lot of gays, not nearly frightened enough. I picked up a kid at the Corner Grocery Bar and took him home. Dan Fuller was a handsome young man and showed me his model comp—like many handsome men he had wanted to be a model. The best photo was one that hadn't been used in the comp and is currently hanging above my desk. A straight shot, not pretending to be a model—just himself. If you looked in his eyes you could see his whole life story. He probably had a lousy family life—especially if his parents had found out he was gay—and was looking for a better life out here.

Dan gradually drifted away from me—I should have held on to him, but I was too busy writing bad fiction. He was the most handsome kid I'd ever met, with a sweet personality to match. He was picked up by an "A" gay and passed around the circuit.

He never found the better life he'd been looking for. He died a year later.

The last one was one of the worst. Steven Wallace was a dancer—not good enough to be a star, but happy in the chorus line. We hit the sack and a short time later stared at each other for a good five minutes. I think each of us had been waiting for the other to show some real affection. I should have made the first move and have regretted it ever since.

He was my tenant for a while, along with his lover, finally moving into a nearby hospice to spend his time taking care of the sick and the dying. Then it was his turn, and somebody at the hospice had to take care of him until he, too, died.

I regretted losing both Daniel and Steven more than I can say. That's one-sided—they might not have been interested in any event. But I should have tried. Love usually has two components—sex and concern. I should have showed that concern was what I really wanted. (Sex without concern and affection is fool's gold.)

Shortly afterward a young Latin kid took to flirting with me. He liked me a lot and called me "Dad"—to him that was the role I was playing. One time David got behind in his rent and was about to be evicted, and I and a friend went over, packed

him up, and put his belongings in storage. While tieing the draw-
ers of his bureau shut so they wouldn't slide open, I saw a photo
and picked it up. A bathhouse group shot with all the customers lined up on one side of the pool, stark naked. I didn't ask
David which one he was.

He vanished for a while, then showed up at the door. I took
one look at the panicked expression on his face and knew the
whole story. He ended up in a nearby hospice, and I went over
frequently to see him. One day he asked for some Disney films,
and I brought him over my tapes. The next day I heard he was
dying. His entire family came up to see him, but I didn't go. I
thought the family had seen enough of gays.

I wondered later if I should have said screw the family and
gone over to see David. I wondered if he would have wanted to
say good-bye to "Dad" if he were still conscious.

⚜ XXVII ⚜

I THOUGHT ABOUT writing a book about the young gays and what it was in their life that made them take the risk.

Randy Schilts heard about it and came over to check out what I had in mind. I told him and asked what he was planning.

Like a good reporter he said, "I'm going to follow the money." (It was published as *And the Band Played On* and was a damning critique of a government that valued money over lives.) Randy had an autographing party for the book on the balcony of the Castro Theater. When I saw him, I wanted to break into tears. Randy had finally become one of those he had written about— gaunt and feverish. He dictated the final lines of his last book— *Conduct Unbecoming* (a book about gays in the military)—from his hospital bed. A few days later, he slipped away.

What it was like for early homosexuals in the United States lacks historical context. To understand the reasons for the reactions of gay men to getting tested later for AIDS and what they considered infringements on hard-won rights, you have to go back a ways.

From the '40s through most of the '60s, homosexual acts were against the law, with penalties ranging from fines to life imprisonment. It was guilt by association at a time when blackmailers grew fat and murderers went free because society considered the murdered gay man to be less than human. In some states those convicted of homosexuality were issued an identity card. Local law enforcement kept records on all suspected sexual subversives and shared them with the FBI. You were forced to carry these cards for the rest of your life.

The government and much of the populace considered homosexuals traitors and enemies of the people. They were denounced from the pulpit, and many doctors were afraid to treat them. Those who did were known as "clap doctors" (you trusted them with your privates but not with the rest of you). "Dirty Commie faggot" was a common expression, and during the Eisenhower administration, a shakedown was held at the State Department in a search for "Commies" and homosexuals. Hundreds of homosexuals were found and fired, but the search came up with just three Communists.

In short, if you were a homosexual you were persecuted by the state, damned by the church, and considered sick by the medical profession. (Homosexuals weren't taken off the "sick" list by psychiatrists until the early '70s. Gay radicals from Chicago crowded the balcony of the meeting hall for a group of psychiatrists and hooted and hollered and the doctors below finally decided they weren't sick, they were just angry.)

There was no *Kristallnacht* for homosexuals, but no doubt there was a pogrom. Most people were unaware of it, but then most "good Germans" usually were.

But it wasn't that way for all homosexuals, especially for those who knew how to hide but still recognize each other. Many older gays looked at such times with a degree of nostalgia.

One of the first persons I interviewed for my projected book was Bob Ross, the publisher of the *Bay Area Reporter*. He had been discharged from the submarine service shortly after World

War II was over and never went home. The more he saw of San Francisco the more he liked it and the longer he stayed.

"Halloween in the late fifties and sixties was a parade of stars. People used to line up around the major bars—the Black Cat, the Five-Two-Four up on North Beach, the Tenderloin bars— to see whole troops of costumed gays arrive in buses and limousines. There were searchlights in the streets and the bars were always decorated for the event, and people waited to see the drags parade through the bars."

The growing gay community in San Francisco had adopted its first communal holiday.

It was a different community then. The bars were the equivalent of British pubs, where you met friends and made new ones. It was a far different atmosphere from a community of baths and people lining up outside the bars on the weekends to make throwaway friends with the strangers on the inside.

Paul Lorch, the editor of *B.A.R.*, moved in completely different circles. At the time I interviewed him, he was fifty-one years old, tall and graying, with a sardonic wit and abrasive opinions that weren't always appreciated by some of his readers. He was an impressively handsome man, and most of those who knew him twenty years before described him as "stunning."

Lorch took his discharge overseas, where he spent a year in Vicenza, Italy. His stay in Italy was a love affair in more ways than one.

On his return to the United States, Lorch worked for a bank in New York and later moved to California, where he got a job teaching school in Sacramento. On the weekends, he made excursions to both Los Angeles and San Francisco, preferring the former.

And then, in a gay bar in Sausalito, Lorch met a wealthy older San Franciscan who showed him a city he had never really seen.

The circles that Lorch now traveled in enjoyed dinner at Gordon's or the Sausalito Inn, pool parties elsewhere in Marin, and yacht parties on the bay. There were obviously two worlds for gays—the world of Pacific Heights and the world of the middle class and the Tenderloin and it was very seldom that the twain ever met.

I didn't become friends with Lorch—far from it; his life had been a fairy tale in which I had no interest. And there was a streak of the vicious in him.

Back on planet Earth things were happening that were of primary importance. Selma Dritz, the chief epidemiologist of the Health Department, had kept a map in which she marked the location of every case of AIDS. After a few months of collecting them, she told Dr. Silverman, the head of the department, that the foci of infection for AIDS were the bathhouses.

Larry Littlejohn, former owner of the Psychedelic Shop, found out and threatened to put closure of the bathhouses on the ballot in November. To some of us in the community it was a clear call to close the tubs. We approached Silverman, who refused to do it without support from the community. Twelve of us then drew up a letter and signed it as representing community support.

When word got out, the battle began. The bathhouses had played too important a role in the life of many gays. They protested that it was an invasion of their freedom, a warning of things to come. Four (or maybe more) of the bathhouse supporters appeared on the steps of city hall with white towels wrapped around their waists. They claimed they represented the community far more than we did.

The real threat had come from Larry Littlejohn, who said he could get enough signatures to put closure on the next electoral ballot. We knew there would be a battle then, and everything that happened in the tubs would become public knowledge, including slings, fisting, and a dozen other practices. The fallout would be a public relations disaster for the community—and the reason why a dozen of us had written the letter—to avoid a city vote on bathhouses, one that the gay community would surely lose.

Attitudes in the city were already changing. AIDS had spooked everybody—cops put on rubber gloves before arresting a gay man, a TV station interested in interviewing an AIDS patient was faced with an employee walkout. The solution was to put the AIDS patient in one room and the interviewer in another and then the patient would be interviewed via telephone. Concentration camps and identity cards were once again bugaboos that haunted gays.

Locally we had a debate between the doctors and members of the community at a lesbian bar, Valencia Rose. The purpose was to expose the very real dangers of going to the tubs. Several doctors were present, about fifty bathhouse devotees, and myself.

The *B.A.R.* had gotten hold of a copy of the letter, and all of us who signed it were listed as traitors in an editorial by Lorch. The list included Harry Britt, the supervisor, Randy Shilts, Bill Krause (a man who had spent years working for the community and was devastated by the criticism), and various other members of the gay political community, including myself.

On the way over to the bar I ran into Bob Ross, who said bitterly, "Frank, how could you betray us?"

At the meeting, the doctors gave their views, summing up the very real medical threat that faced all gays. The final doctor to speak, his shirt soaked with sweat, received a chorus of boos from the audience. I was the last gay to speak, pointing out the dangers of a ballot initiative. The audience was already walking out when I said that there were forty-seven members of the community who could not vote because all of them were dead.

When I got home I ran into my tenant coming out of the laundry room. I asked him if he had ever gone to the bathhouses, and he said "Once." I asked why only once and he wrinkled his nose in disgust. "The smell."

The position of the *B.A.R.* was strange—or perhaps not so stange. Every week they devoted a page or two to photographs and short bios of those who had died the previous week. (Some weeks later I paged through a copy of the *B.A.R.* and noted page after page of the deceased—perhaps four pages or more in all.)

Keeping them company were the usual dozen full- and half-page ads for the bathhouses—the main income for the paper and presumably a good chunk of Lorch's salary.

Silverman's initial response was to put posters in the bathhouses warning of the dangers and to install monitors to make sure that the doors to the cubicles were not completely closed. It was a futile gesture. The posters ended up gathering dust at the ends of hallways, and the monitors lounged by the entrance enjoying a joint.

A few months after that, Silverman reversed himself and closed the tubs by executive fiat—an authority he'd had the entire time. The numbers of those dying had become too great.

Medically, some progress had been made. One of the researchers discovered that an AIDS-free baby had been born to a mother who had AIDS. The conclusion was that AIDS was a bloodborne disease. The transfer of "bodily fluids," a euphemism that included semen as well as blood, was to be avoided.

Hemophiliacs were at risk—the blood banks had to test their blood (something they had rejected because of the cost and because a large number of their contributors were gays who objected to being tested and some were heroin abusers who frequently used the same needle). Gays were urged to use condoms—and to be tested. The latter was objected to by many members of the community who didn't want their names added to any list. They had spent too many years of their lives hiding and did not wish to add their names to a list accessible to a government they did not trust.

It wasn't all paranoia. Old-timers could remember when homosexual acts were against the law, with penalties ranging from fines to life imprisonment. It had been a world of first names and passwords, introductions by friends when it came to people you didn't know.

For me, I kept getting jobs where I thought I should be careful. One of the first was the Sunday supplement *Family Weekly* that went to small towns. In my own mind, to come out was risky. Ditto working for *Science Digest* and even *Rogue* and *Cavalier*. I was probably safer at *Playboy*, but a squib in a newspaper that the man giving out advice to the straight readers of *Playboy* was a gay man, and *Playboy* probably would have decided they didn't need me that badly.

The Eisenhower administration had cleaned house of suspected subversives but the Reagan administration tied the hands of researchers and doctors in a totally different way. The weapon was money. Early requests for research money are usually minor—but necessary. Few problems are cured by simply throwing money at them, but in 1982, when Congress appropriated the munificent sum of $500,000 for AIDS research, the appropriation was promptly vetoed by President Reagan.

Frequently money appropriations requested were cut in half, or sat for months on the desk of Margaret Heckler, the secretary of health and human services.

She was, of course, following the wishes of her boss. President Reagan's atitude toward gays and HIV was largely shaped by his political base. Pat Robertson and Jerry Falwell maintained that AIDS was a punishment from God. In Congress their attitude was pushed by Representative William Dannemeyer (R-CA) and Senator Jesse Helms (R-NC). It was reflected in the monies spent by the CDC: $1 million for AIDS, $10 million for Legionnaires' disease. (The Legionnaires had logged fifty deaths; AIDS, a thousand).

When Rock Hudson, a good friend of Reagan's, died in 1985, Reagan still didn't mention AIDS. William F. Buckley, Jr., a staunch conservative and friend of Reagan's, wrote an opinion piece for *The New York Times* in 1986 suggesting that HIV-positive gay men should have the information tattooed on their butt.

Considering the attitude of the government and its supporters, gay men paranoid about the possibility of concentration camps may not have been that far off the mark. The attitude of much of the government, and possibly the president, was "Let the pansies die."

In San Francisco, it was like a war was going on, with the casualties hidden from the general public. Gays with AIDS either stayed in their homes, tended by friends and lovers, or else ended up in hospices, where their stay wasn't all that long.

The community did its best to take care of itself. There were fund-raisers to help those who had locked themselves away, and for publicity and local education about how to have sex without dying from it.

The statistics were frightening. Almost three hundred deaths in 1983, twelve hundred in 1986. There was some progress being made on the medical front. AZT was an early drug that showed some promise, but many gays refused to take it on the grounds that it killed a number of its users.

AZT did not obliterate HIV; the most that can be said is that it postponed its effects. Some gays tried their own systems. One man I knew claimed that drinking his own urine was helpful.

A more practical approach was taken by Danny Nicoletta, a former helper in Harvey Milk's camera shop. He watched his diet, took a combination of pills from the health-food store, and staved off the infection for years. He finally switched to protease inhibitors, a better drug, when his doctor warned him that his regime was staving off the effects of HIV, but wasn't eliminating it. If his T-cell count fell below three hundred, then it was only a matter of time before he died.

Danny switched, his T-cell count rose to seven hundred, and there was no trace of HIV in his blood (which didn't mean it wasn't there—the virus was an expert at hiding).

After the death of her friend Rock Hudson, actress Elizabeth Taylor founded AMFAR (American Foundation for AIDS Research) along with Dr. Mathida Krim. Taylor concentrated on fund-raising and soon became an icon to the gay community. Before she died, she had raised $270 million, parceled out to researchers and different AIDS groups.

A turn in public opinion was engineered by Larry Kramer when he scripted *The Normal Heart*, which played for a year at the Public Theater in New York. It got rave reviews and reduced many in his audiences to tears. Kramer had been a gadfly for the *New York Native*, constantly suggesting that New York gays do more to pressure the government and the public to fight harder against AIDS. His main character, Ned, was patterned after himself, and other characters were similar to members of New York AIDS groups whom Kramer had pilloried in the *Native*. In a sense it was Kramer's revenge against some of the New York AIDS organizations that he considered slackers. Once the play received an overwhelming critical response, Kramer was a hero to some and at least tolerated by others.

Over the years, several of the actors in the play died of AIDS (including Brad Davis, who had the main role of Ned). The character of Ned was a plum role and was played by a variety of actors over the years, including Joel Grey, who played the role of the MC in the movie of *Cabaret* and later reprised it when *Cabaret* hit the road.

After his run in *The Normal Heart* and role in *Cabaret*, Grey wanted to play Harvey Milk in a movie. When *Cabaret* played in San Francisco he asked Anne Kronenberg and me to meet him in his dressing room and talk about Harvey. I had to give him credit for trying, but I didn't think it was ever going to happen. His voice wasn't right and he was six inches too short to be a convincing Harvey.

(He was the second straight man to whom I admitted I was gay. The first was Dr. John O'Brien, who had the courtesy to look interested but also bored when I told him. We were both collectors—I collected old magazines and Dr. O'Brien collected military miniatures. He had filled his basement with pool tables loaded with armies of military miniatures and I even managed to accumulate a small army of my own.)

In addition to Kramer, there were other "civilians" who contributed both time and effort to fighting the plague. One was Ryan White, a thirteen-year-old hemophiliac who had been given six months to live. When White tried to return to his school in Kokomo, Indiana, parents and students objected. He fought the school system and became a poster boy in the fight against AIDS.

Ryan White gave everything he had, including his life. He died when he was eighteen, but he didn't die in vain. Congress passed the Ryan White Care Act, which became the largest provider of services for people in the United States living with

HIV/AIDS. I'm sure Ryan was thankful for the act but would have preferred to be alive.

Cleve Jones, Harvey Milk's right-hand man with a bullhorn, was responsible for creating the greatest contribution to making the general public aware of AIDS. Jones had the idea for an AIDS quilt to be made by the parents and friends of those who had died. Each section was three feet by six on which memorabilia of the deceased were stitched to remind those who made it of the man they loved. Letters, photographs—anything that would serve as a memento.

In time the various quilts were stitched together to make a huge panorama of quilts. A few years later, when they unfurled it in Washington, DC, on the Mall before the Capitol, it covered the entire area—some eighty thousand quilts representing forty-five thousand gay men who had died of AIDS. It wasn't just hairdressers and actors who died of AIDS, it was also the butcher, the baker, the candlestick maker, the cook, and the construction worker. One thing for sure: each quilt was far superior to a small white headstone in some soon-to-be-forgotten cemetery.

Theaters on Broadway did their part when they dimmed their lights for a minute to pay tribute to all of those who had contributed so much to the plays and musicals their audiences had just watched.

I think some parents didn't want a quilt to remember their son because it might be a sign their son had been gay. But when Johnny came home in a casket, the neighbors could probably guess why.

Toward the end of the eighties, a number of survivors in San Francisco confessed that they had started to suffer funeral fatigue. Their friends would live on in their memory or in the quilt. But a funeral ceremony several times a week was hard to take, and a few refused to go.

One friend of mine threw a party before he died, inviting all his friends and telling them to take anything they wanted from his house as a memento. I couldn't bring myself to take a thing.

I was losing friends outside the city as well as in. Craig Musser had gone to Paris, as had Rock Hudson, because they'd heard that researchers there had found a cure. They hadn't, and Craig slowly died by inches on the East Coast. (His former lover Eric Ashworth died of AIDS at age thirty-nine.)

For myself it was like flipping over dominoes. One by one my friends disappeared, and Castro Street was looking strangely empty. They still had a parade every year, but eventually I couldn't bring myself to go.

The final total for the country of those who had died of AIDS from 1980 to 2012 was 636,000. That's roughly equal to the total who died in the Civil War (on both sides). The total of deaths from AIDS in San Francisco was close to 20,000. The community had been decimated.

They weren't old men—they were young men who had yet to contribute the most to their country. Eventually various states in the country repaid their sacrifice by making it legal for gays to marry those they loved.

The last one of my friends to go was Tom Youngblood, whose Indian heritage had been of no help at all. We had a small breakfast club that used to meet every morning, and Tom would always be there. He hadn't appeared for a number of days now and we'd begun to worry.

Then one morning he dropped in. Or rather, a shadow of him did. Gaunt, shaky, but determined to show up. All of us knew why. Tom had come to say good-bye.

We said all of the appropriate things, shook hands all around, and he left. That afternoon he went to his bedroom and took the pills. Who he got them from, I didn't know. But doctors who had dedicated their profession to saving lives were now in the position of watching every single one of their patients wither and die. There was nothing they could do. If they knew beyond a shadow of a doubt that their patient was terminal, they probably made it easier for them to slip away. The part of the Hippocratic Oath, *"I will neither give a deadly drug to anybody if asked for it,"* no longer applied.

A friend of Tom's sat with him as he died, then two weeks later did the same thing.

I had no tears left. I no longer went to funerals, I no longer searched for familiar faces on the street. There weren't any. I had lost every close gay friend I had since coming to San Francisco.

No exceptions.

There was no way that thousands of people didn't know somebody who had died of AIDS or of somebody who had lost a son to the disease. Being gay was no longer a subject of humor or of violence. They could be the boy next door or the man who fixed your car.

Cleve deserved a lot of gold medals for his work with Harvey, but the biggest medal of all should go to his creation of the AIDS quilt. If there was one single event that started the ball rolling to change the attitude of Americans toward homosexuals, the AIDS quilt was it. It wasn't just the hairdresser who had died. It was the son of your next-door neighbor or the kid who waited on you at McDonald's.

The quilt on the Mall was probably the first time that Americans realized the death toll among their fellow citizens numbered in the tens of thousands—and growing.

Tolerance and awareness of gays was also growing, but the gay community had paid a horrendous price.

AFTER THE LAST book we wrote together, Tom Scortia moved to Los Angeles to try to make his mark in Hollywood. He had made connections with Gene Roddenberry and said they were going to make a film (predictably a science fiction film) together. My guess was that Roddenberry was impressed with Tom's extensive experience in the aerospace industry. A few months later, Tom talked of a lawsuit against Roddenberry, claiming he was doing all the work and Roddenberry was doing nothing. I thought that when Roddenberry had lent his name to the project, he'd done his half.

Tom went back to writing books, the first of which was titled *Blowout*. It was not going well for him. Tom was sick and getting sicker by the day. Some days, according to his adopted son, JJ, he could only write a few lines and then go back to bed.

At first he refused to see a doctor. His brother had died in a hospital, which had left Tom with a deep prejudice against them. By the time he finally agreed to go, it was too late.

As a writer Tom was an "idea" man, expert in plotting and characterization. His only fault was that once the book was plotted, in Tom's eyes it was done. I was the cleanup man who did the elementary editing and polishing.

In many respects, he was a great man to work with. He drank too much and smoked too much, but that didn't affect his professional life. He was a heavyset man, not particularly athletic, "nice-looking" (as my mother might have said but not what she would have called handsome), a great raconteur to bullshit with. His major flaw, which I think affected his life, was that he was not the first man you'd look at in a gay bar.

Great abdominals and a handsome face were of much more appeal than the ability to hold your own in a conversation. (Conversing in a gay bar is usually at a mininum.) I once took him to one of my doctors, who later told me he'd never met a man who hated himself so much. Tom's friends had a much higher opinion of him than he had of himself. His background in aerospace was of immense help in writing science fiction, but of little interest to the man sitting next to him in a bar engrossed in his glass of beer and the hot number standing in a corner by himself.

I think Tom would have given a lot to be the man in the corner.

I finished Tom's novel for him, and that was the last of our collaborations.

I had written one novel by myself (*The Power*), which did well, and now I was faced with the prospect of working alone. I looked forward to it. Critics who reviewed the books by Tom and me had usually typecast them as "disaster" novels—what's the disaster, who lives, and who dies.

In my first solo effort after Tom had passed I swore to myself that it would be a story based largely on character. I hated the title—*The Dark Beyond the Stars* (suggested by fellow pulp collector Bill Trojan)—but with time learned to love it. It was about a spaceship looking for life among the stars. It's been traveling for two thousand years, which meant that the crew—who had an ordinary lifetime—had to breed the next crew.

There was one exception: the captain was immortal and had been brainwashed at launch not to come back to Earth until he'd found life on another planet. The crew wanted to go home—the ship was falling apart, and while they would never get back to Earth, their descendants might. The captain intends to take the ship across "the Dark"—a section of space with no stars in view for thousands of light-years, though there are some on the other side. The crew knows the ship will never make it and is ready to mutiny. But the captain is unable to change the indoctrination he'd received on Earth.

Any kind of a ship with a mutinous crew is hardly original—the *Bounty* had beat me by years. The fun—and original—part for me was what the crew would be like after two thousand years. How would they interact with one another? How different would they be from the original crew? There would be no divisions when it comes to sexuality—there would be straights, gays, and bisexuals among the crew, and all of them would be accepted as totally natural. Impregnation and the birth of babies would be a religious affair, with multiple impregnations so no man would know which baby he's fathered. My best line: "The father is the one who takes an interest."

It was the line that hit the closest to home.

I told the plot to an editor I'd met at a science fiction convention in New Orleans. He was wildly enthusiastic, saying "put it up for auction and I'll bid it in!" Unfortunately, he'd had too many hurricanes, which erased his part-time memory. When I got home I sent ten copies of the manuscript to my agent, asking him to auction it. Of the ten, six were returned unread. Three were rejected. The last was accepted primarily because a publisher's stringer editor in San Francisco (Debbie Notkin) liked it a lot.

The book received great reviews, won the first Lambda Literary Award for "Gay Men's Science Fiction/Fantasy" (I knew some of the judges so in part it was a put-up job), and was chosen as a "Notable Book of the Year" by *The New York Times*. It's still available from Amazon twenty-two years later.

The next one I liked almost as well. *Waiting*. What if Neanderthals (in the book called "the old people") were still living among us, breeding true so they remained a different species? And since they were here first, what if they wanted their world back?

That was long before researchers discovered that all of us have a few Neanderthal genes. For a while scientists thought we might have killed them all when Homo sapiens came up from Africa. It seems they interbred and Neanderthals were swamped by the (my hopeful guess) gorgeous-looking Homo sapiens women.

One benefit: Neanderthals had lived in Europe and the Levant for hundreds of thousands of years and had become immune to most of the local diseases. They passed that immunity on to us—otherwise Homo sapiens might be just a footnote in some other species' history book.

My last solo fiction book was something of a potboiler, a throwback to the type of book Tom and I usually wrote. Titled *The Donor*, it concerned the richest man in Boston, who has a disease and is doomed to die at fifty or sixty or so. He has himself cloned twice and plans on raising the two boys as a donor bank when needed. One boy, who's already been operated on for a spare kidney that the rich man needs, escapes and the story becomes who finds who first.

I thought it was a great idea. Unfortunately, the publisher forgot to set two pages of type, so I sent him hard copy on both. When I got the book itself I had a fit—they'd set the two pages, but nobody had read them; they'd relied on "spell check." All the words were spelled right, but five or six of them were the wrong words. Our heroine is talking to her boyfriend and suddenly breaks into fractured Greek (or whatever).

Predictably there were few reviews, no chance with Hollywood, and few sales or recommendations. Readers are usually alert even to typos, and this book was beyond the pale.

Most authors have friends who want to be writers, and I had two. The first, John Levin, was a winner. *The Great Divide*'s premise was as follows: The East has a political grip on the country but the West has most of the natural resources. The governor of California plots for the West to secede and support their economy by trading with Pacific nations, rather than letting the East bleed them dry. The president is a drunk, the veep has a bad ticker, and most of the action is carried by the veep's chief assistant.

Both of us thought it would be a winner and a cinch for a movie. And what could be more relevant with modern-day Texas making secession noises and California realizing that most of its trade is with Japan and China?

The book wasn't the first surefire hit that didn't make it in Hollywood. No musclebound heroes, no big explosions, no huge robots, no monstrous aliens—who's going to see it?

(No big studio picked up *Behind the Candelabra*, either. Who wants to watch a love affair between a gay piano player and a dumb but muscular farm boy? The answer was: a lot of people.)

The other book was *Death of a Marionette*, a mystery thriller by Paul Hull (a pseudonym) and me. Hull had done some work for me at one time and wanted to be an author. He mapped out an idea and asked me my opinion. It had possibilities and I made some sugestions. They didn't work. More suggestions and they still didn't work. I finally agreed to collaborate with him, thinking he would pick up pointers.

The book sold—not for a fortune—but Hull had disappeared

and I didn't have an address to give him the good news. I finally found him in Oakland, right across the bay, through the State Department. His wife was the chief medical officer for an embassy overseas.

I called him, gave him the happy news, and in a cold voice he told me he wanted to see me. He came over, sat in the big easy chair opposite my couch, and bitched at me for an hour, nonstop. It hadn't sold for a lot of money, there was no paperback edition tied in with the contract, it hadn't sold to Hollywood, and it was all my fault.

He had some ability—he was good at atmosphere (his wife worked for the embassy in Brussels, Belgium, and he had lived there for two years and had his description of the city down pat) but he couldn't put it all together. He couldn't tell a story. Like a kid who knew all the letters in the alphabet but couldn't write a sentence. Hull couldn't plot, he couldn't handle action.

Raymond Chandler summed it all up for me:

"I have done everything from plotting and rewriting stories for would-be writers and I have found it to be all waste. The people whom God intended to be writers find their own answers. Those who have to ask are impossible to help. They are merely people who want to be writers."

But in one sense, we came close. The book section of *The Washington Post* gave the novel a review on its front page and compared us to John Le Carré: "deservedly comparable to the classic *The Spy Who Came in from the Cold* . . . every line is sterling, and the whole is a small, laconic masterpiece."

We also got an enthusiastic review in *Kirkus Reviews* ("an updated version of *The Spy Who Came in from the Cold*.")

And still another rave in *Publishers Weekly* ("it all adds up to one tough spy thriller.")

And one more in the *Lansing State Journal*: "Robinson and

Hull are a great team, superbly maintaining tense suspense in a very controlled atmosphere."

The publishing company did no promotion, despite the glowing reviews—but it did get a second printing. (Note to film studios: the line forms on the right.)

My last effort at working with other people was with—of all the millions out there—Francis Ford Coppola.

One day my agent called saying that Coppola wanted to talk to me. Agents don't give out phone numbers of their clients, so I made the call and Coppola asked me to bring down all my "unencumbered" (meaning books not under contract for film) to his office on Columbus Avenue. There were a lot that were free: *The Dark Beyond the Stars*, *Death of a Marionette*, *The Great Divide*, the manuscript (at the time) of *Waiting*. I spread them out on a table in Coppola's office and he poked through them.

Coppola himself was a somewhat pudgy man, instantly likable (make that "lovable").

He picked out *The Dark Beyond the Stars* and I was thrilled. A science fiction film made by Francis Ford Coppola! I found out later that he wanted to make a movie in every genre that he had missed. I was not his first choice in science fiction—somebody had recommended Kim Stanley Robinson's *Red Mars*. Filed on the shelf next to it was *The Dark Beyond the Stars*. *The Dark* was a thinner book than *Red Mars*, and besides, Francis was familiar with my name. In film school (so I was told) he'd wanted to option *The Power* but had no money.

I was excited working with Francis on a science fiction film—no way could it miss. Coppola's first offer via the agency was so low I told the agent to tell Francis that I was not chopped liver, I was worth more than that. Francis upped the offer—no fortune, but I thought I could learn a lot from working with him.

He turned out to be much more than just a teacher. I was invited to the winery, had lunch with his crew, and was invited to the anniversary party for *The Godfather*. He wanted me to meet his son, Roman, in Hollywood, and invited me to the opening of the restored silent version of *Napoleon* by Abel Gance—shot partly in three-screen format, with a musical score by Carmine Coppola, father of Francis. One Christmas season Coppola's wife called to see if I had a copy of a 1913 *All-Story* as a Christmas present for Francis. They had started a literary magazine titled *Zoetrope All-Story*. I found a copy and sent if off. Soon after, *Zoetrope All-Story* published an excerpt from *Tarzan of the Apes*. (The novel had appeared complete in a single copy of the original *All-Story*. A copy of that issue in fine shape would now run you about $30,000.) I edited the excerpt and corrected the errors—a lot of them.

I finished the first draft of the script for *The Dark Beyond the Stars* and took it up to the winery. I had lunch—I felt like part of the family—and then Francis glanced over the script, running his eyes down the middle of the page to catch the dialogue. He tore out page after page that he didn't think worked. I wrote a second draft (not a bad one—I still have it and reread it recently), but no studio was interested in this one, either.

The impression I got from nosing around was that science fiction films cost a lot of money to make and nobody was willing to trust Francis at this point in his life with $100 million, despite his past successes.

Francis also submitted the manuscript copy of *Waiting* to Hollywood Pictures. They bounced it. Next season I noticed a new series on ABC—*Prey*. Soon after I started getting phone calls from friends who complimented me on peddling *Waiting* to TV.

I hadn't and neither had Coppola. I thought of suing ABC and Hollywood Pictures, then watched the second episode and shrugged. It wouldn't last and it didn't. The third episode was the last. (Just incidentally, Hollywood Pictures and ABC were both owned by Disney.)

This was my introduction to the "Hollywood haircut." Take a story you like, add and delete a few scenes, change the names of the characters and the title, and presto—a new project! And you didn't have to pay the original author. . . .

Francis faded out of my life for a while, then called and asked if I wanted to write a script based on a treatment he had written. It would be for Paramount, and this time it would be for real money. He wanted something of blockbuster stature, something like *The Guns of Navarone*. I had trouble putting the two concepts together, but what did I have to lose?

The treatment came in, and to my shock it was not quite two thirds of a page. Furthermore, the idea was hardly new—a takeoff on *Orpheus in the Underworld*. A Greek myth, it had been turned into an operetta by Offenbach and filmed as *Black Orpheus* (a remarkable movie that I didn't think anybody could ever top).

Orpheus's girlfriend is kidnapped by Hades, and Orpheus goes to Hell to retrieve her. At the top of the page Francis had written his hopes for it: "Blockbuster." I called my agent, who told me to go ahead and try it—that it was never going to be made into a movie. Take the money and run. . . .

To my eventual regret, that's exactly what I did. I tried twice, and failed each time (by contract, if you fail the first time you have a second chance—money accordingly). My first draft, a screenwriting friend told me, had failed because I had made hell into a version of Las Vegas, with Hades as the doorman to a casino (someting of a John Goodman type).

My friend broke it to me gently: Francis had lost a pot of money with *One from the Heart*, set in Las Vegas. I had never seen the film, but I could understand if Francis was unwilling to go there again.

(Francis might also have objected to my ending—the most grisly I had ever written. Even *Game of Thrones* would probably have bounced it.)

My second effort also bounced. I called Francis and told him I was willing to try a third time if he'd give me more directions on what he wanted.

Francis was surprisingly cool on the phone. Why didn't I talk to the man at Paramount who was the one who had really bounced it and get suggestions from him?

What was his name? I asked. Francis didn't remember.

How about his phone number? Francis said he didn't know that either and hung up.

(Sometime later it occurred to me that Francis and Paramount had wanted to break up their relationship and I was the fall guy. Shows you how far paranoia can take you.)

I sat there holding a dead phone while inside my head a hero crumbled. I stared at the phone and remembered that Francis had been very nice to me. And I could, of course, have turned the project down.

For most of his films made in the '70s and '80s, Francis deserves great credit. He used outstanding books as the skeletons for many of them, hardly a novelty in Hollywood. In the "research" that Zoetrope sent me was a sixty-to-seventy-page treatment with "Inferno" written at the top along with "Blockbuster."

Not exactly an outstanding treatment. But it was comforting to know that I wasn't the only one who had failed.

I stared at the phone and remembered how friendly Francis had been to me. And to be honest, I had been free to reject his initial offer.

Francis had used many popular books to serve as skeletons for his movies, which, of course, is standard practice. But I had been asked to create a "blockbuster" from the small bone he had sent me. I hadn't been able to do it, and I doubted that anybody could. (Francis now owns one of California's largest wineries, two or three hotels and resorts, a literary magazine, and I suspect a roomful of trophies and awards. I doubt that he's involved in making films anymore.)

I hung up the now dead phone and went straight to the hospital with a case of atrial fibrillation. This time the paddles burned off what little hair I had on my chest. I also had to learn how to walk all over again—one of the risks of modern medicine.

❧ XXIX ❧

MY NEXT BRUSH with filmmaking was far more pleasant and far more important to me.

I had gone to city hall for the funeral services for Jimmy Rivaldo, a former political advisor for Harvey. After the services I noticed a middle-aged man with a very handsome younger man at his side. Somebody had gotten lucky, I thought.

A friend of mine nodded at them and said, "The older man is Gus Van Sant, a movie director. The younger guy is a screenwriter—they're here to do a movie about Harvey Milk."

There had been a biography about Harvey, a local play about him, a TV special about him, a DVD, an opera, and now there was going to be a movie.

About damn time.

Later I heard they were going to do location shooting, including re-creating Harvey's camera store. I drifted down to the camera shop (on Castro, a few blocks from where I lived) to see how they were rebuilding the replica of the original. It had been something of a knickknack store, and all the display cases and shelving had been removed. The major restoration was primarily based on photographs that Danny Nicoletta had taken years before.

I couldn't have told the difference. To me, the store looked exactly the same as it had forty years before. Not quite, I was told. They'd had to hunt up an old red couch to replace the original, and the old dental chair had been replaced by one even older. A new black dog had replaced Kid, long since gone to doggie heaven, and was flaked out on the couch, relucantly moving when somebody wanted to sit down.

A few days later Anne Kronenberg called to say that Van Sant, the screenwriter Dustin Lance Black, and the star of the show, Sean Penn, wanted to interview me. They had already hired an actor to play me but apparently they were delighted to get the real McCoy. (I met the actor later on—nice guy.)

The three showed up and made themselves at home in the usual clutter in my living room. It seemed that Penn wanted to interview me as to how Harvey delivered his speeches—hand movements, if he changed the content, etc.

What I could remember was that Harvey copied the repetitious phrasing of black preachers, chopped my longer sentences into two and three parts, and—most important—never forgot the nature of the audience he was talking to.

After they finally broke I took them to dinner at the neighborhood Nirvana Restaurant—exotic foreign food. The headwaiter was a friend of mine and cleared out the back room (complete with potted palms) so we'd be alone. Everybody in the front of the restaurant knew perfectly well who was eating in the back room, and the buzz of conversation occasionally drifted back. But nobody came back to bother us—except the waiter's mother, who showed up with an autograph book and quickly made the rounds of the table. (I think my guests were secretly glad somebody had noticed them.)

I thought I'd be in awe of all three but I wasn't. One hard-working actor, the director who was the master of the show, and the handsome screenwriter who I wanted to get to know better.

I was, of course, boring them to death with my tales of experiences in Hollywood, and at one point said a few nasty things about Francis Ford Coppola. Penn glanced up from his plate and remarked, "Francis is one of my best friends." (As soon as I got home I wrote a note of apology and gave it to Lance to give to Penn.)

A little later Penn had to leave for an appointment, leaving me with Gus and Lance to entertain. I told them tales about gay life in Chicago, etc., which interested them, but after twenty minutes of my monologue Gus interrupted and asked, "How would you like to be in my movie?"

I felt embarrassed and told him I was no actor, that when I had been cast as the lead in my grammar school play I had forgotten every single line. Gus said it was only going to be one word: "dogshit."

I hesitated, then said, "I think I can manage that," and my career as a movie star was born.

On the way out, I told Lance that if I had a word—any word—in the movie I should have a copy of the script so I'd know how to say it. He choked back a smile, but I got a copy the next day.

I was what they call a background actor—just hang around in the background so the audience wouldn't think Harvey was a Pied Piper surrounded by a retinue of young kids. When we were all gathered in the front of the camera shop, Penn suddenly appeared in makeup. I gasped (so did everybody else), then broke into applause. He was Harvey to a T. A few inches too short, voice an octave lower—but Harvey Milk in the flesh.

So. Action. "Danny," young boy of all work, was filing photographs in the back—he would become one of the most skilled photographers in the city. (He was played by Lucas Gabreel, star of *High School Musical* on the Disney Channel.) Two of Harvey's political consultants were talking in the background, James Franco (playing Harvey's lover Scott), was sitting at the front desk, and I was slouched in a corner of the couch pretending to be wallpaper—I'm to be seen, not heard.

I could hear the cameras start and then Franco looked at me and said, "Hey, Robinson, did you get laid last night?"

Franco had decided to play agent provocateur.

I stared for a split second—I had no words—then remembered I had been writing dialogue before he was born.

"Yeah, I got laid last night."

"What's his name? Maybe I want to date him."

"You'd like him, Scott—he's got an inch for every letter in his name."

"Yeah, but what's his name?"

"Joe."

The back room erupted, and the cameramen and Gus and Cleve Jones came running out, Cleve saying, "Frank, I never thought you had it in you!"

They made me a member of SAG immediately. From a hundred bucks a day to a thousand . . .

Later in the movie I ad-libbed a scene or two with Penn, but they never got in the movie. The Writers' Guild of America was on strike, which meant that not a word of the script could be changed. (Maybe someday there'll be a director's cut!)

The only way I could trade lines with Penn—hey, an Oscar winner!—was to pretend that he really *was* Harvey Milk.

There were a few mob scenes at night shot at Castro and Market, and one time I popped out and went across the street to the Hot Cookie—a coffee and fresh baked cookie place. Lance Black came in afterward, and I told him that I had read his screenplay twice (he later won an Oscar for it) and thought it was great. "And I'm not blowing smoke."

He looked at me, grinned, and said, "Frank, you can blow smoke at me anytime" and kissed me. (It's the little things that make life bearable.)

Some months later, I watched the Oscars and cried when Lance gave his acceptance speech when receiving the Oscar on what it was like to grow up "different" before the audience of a thousand in the auditorium and perhaps a billion around the world.

I've read a number of screenplays by Lance since then, and for my money, he's an ace screenwriter. (*J. Edgar*—the screenplay of a man whom Americans almost universally hated—was a damned good character study. In the movie the makeup on Hoover's lover when he aged was atrocious, and one of the stars insisted on having Hoover put on a dress in a scene, apparently to fulfill the expectations of an audience that had bought into the myth. It had never happened in real life. Lance had done what could be done in explicating the personality of a man who had none.)

A few more scenes of sitting around, and then Gus asked Penn and me to improvise a scene where Harvey originates his most popular speech, about "hope." I had no idea how the speech came into being—I think it was one of those that just originated from a number of speeches. My contribution to the improvisation was to whine "We've got nothing to give the public, Harvey—not even hope." Penn turns and (as Harvey) walks away muttering to himself, "hope, hope . . ."

It was as good an origin as any but it didn't matter—the script was frozen, and our little improvised bit would never appear on-screen.

Penn was a generous man on filming. They had found the original longshoreman with whom Harvey had agreed to help boycott Coors beer—provided that the longshoremen's union would make room for gay drivers. But the original longshoreman was not the husky man he'd once been. He was small, thin, and the uniform they gave him hung on him.

The obvious thing was to let him go and hire an actor to take his place. But Allen Baird had desperately wanted to be in the movie, which, after all, honored a longtime friend whose death had been as much of a blow to him as it had been to everybody else. To fire him from the movie might be practical but very cruel.

I'm pretty sure it was Penn who suggested doing a long shot of Allen so you wouldn't see he was now an elderly man. Penn dubbed his lines in voice-over.

I never met Josh Brolin, who played Dan White, but everybody who had, said he was a sweet guy. I did see him act in one scene. It was a confrontation between White and Harvey— broken up by the sudden appearance of Harvey's lover, Jack Lira, who resented the attention Harvey was giving to White.

(Jack Lira was played by Diego Luna, one of the stars of *Y tu Mama Tambien*. I didn't recognize him when he came on set and asked him who he was. When he told me, I blurted, "You're a great actor!" He grinned and gave me a heartfelt thanks. Again, high praise from an unknown stranger is the best kind there is.)

It was a sensitive scene to shoot, so it was a closed set, with folding doors hiding the actors and the action. Fortunately for us would-be onlookers, there was a space between the folding doors and we had our eyes glued to it. White was drunk while trying to find common ground with Harvey and thought he was succeeding when Harvey's lover breaks in and tugs Harvey away. Harvey had to choose between White and his lover and he chose Jack, leaving White talking to thin air.

That was shot number one. The second one was a variation (the one that was used in the film). The third one was after Harvey was dragged away, White punches madly in the air, insulted that Harvey had chosen his street lover over him, and striking out at the empty air, wishing it were Harvey.

Tough scene to shoot. Brolin was as convincing at being White as Penn was at being Harvey. Brolin's anger was also genuine, as was Penn's growing realization that White was trying to be friendly but Harvey couldn't resist the attraction of his bed partner.

That was the scene that broke any thread of friendship between Harvey and White.

The next scene was a lot more cheerful. It was a big room with a dance floor at one end. Gus asked me if I wanted to dance, and I said I couldn't. He looked disappointed and it occurred to me that it wasn't very smart to disappoint the director. "Oh," I said, "you mean boogie."

"Yeah, Frank, boogie."

It had been a long time, but at least I was dressed for the part. A pair of brown, checkered pants with suitcoat to match and I was all set. Moving my arms was easy; moving my feet would have been disastrous.

At the back of the room, Sylvester (long gone but a double that made me believe in reincarnation) danced up the side of the room, followed by Penn and a few others. Penn, I decided, could do absolutely anything.

The occasion was a birthday party for Harvey, and several actors lugged in a huge faux cake while the rest of us sang "Happy Birthday." Penn put out a finger to fake tasting the frosting and somebody—unexpectedly—hit him in the face with a pie. He slipped on the dance floor, and I was the nearest to catch him before he hit the deck. (I figured that made up for my dishing Coppola in the restaurant.)

My last scene (I'm cheating—I had one before that) came

when I wasn't on camera (dammit)—I said "dogshit," and everybody in the theater heard it. Hot damn, I was now an honest actor—I had earned my SAG pay!

I asked Gus if he was going to give me a gold watch and instead he gave me a eulogy.

It was hugs all around, and for them I felt great.

I hung around and watched some other scenes being shot, one of which had Penn standing on the steps of city hall delivering a speech that mentions what's inscribed at the base of the Statue of Liberty. I had seen Penn standing in the wings apparently talking to himself and now realized he had been rehearsing his lines.

I was thrilled when he moved to the steps and started to deliver his speech. I recognized it immediately as one of the speeches I had written for Harvey. At the time I hadn't known what was inscribed on the base of Liberty and had to look it up in *Bartlett's Familiar Quotations.*

The very last scene was the funeral march for Harvey late at night. I knew it would be very emotional for me and I talked with my doctor first, who laughed and assured me I wouldn't die of a heart attack in the middle of the march.

Some of the film assistants were afraid for me and locked me in the actors' trailer. I got out, caught one of the film's vans, and made it to Market Street just in time to join the front of the parade. It was late at night, and it had been open casting—some four thousand extras showed up in street clothes, holding paper cups and candles in them. All of the major actors were in the front row for the camera shoot. I was at the far end and doubted that anybody would see me.

The parade started and passed through an underpass. For the film, Gus had spliced in actual newsreel footage of the parade before it reached the underpass. The final parade on-screen looked like it stretched all the way down Market to Castro with forty thousand marchers, almost all of them crying.

In the front row a man standing next to me had to hold me up. I was time traveling, and in my head, I was in the real parade, weak and sobbing.

Roll the credits, the film was done. I went home and went to bed and cried myself to sleep. (I would see the movie seven times and would cry at the ending every time. It had become a Pavlovian reflex.)

The "wrap" party at the end of major shooting was a real hoot. I invited a good friend of mine, Terry, who worked for a local radio station, to come along—he had a car and I didn't. All the way to the bar where the party was being held he complained how he had been to a number of these and it was always cheap wine and bad food and you'd be bored to death. He even stopped to pick up a slice of pizza at a hole-in-the-wall in the Tenderloin so he wouldn't go hungry.

The party was jammed with everybody who had been in or had worked on the film. The wine was good, the food was great. There was a short receiving line of Gus and Lance and I think one of the producers, and Terry was suddenly stagestruck. He knew that Lance had been a Mormon, and Terry, who once had a Mormon boyfriend, hurried over to make friends. The first thing he did was to get Lance's name wrong. He was talking a mile a minute, and an assistant casting director a few feet away noticed and came over to rescue Lance.

She smiled at Terry and said, "How would you like to be in the movie?" There were a few pickup scenes yet to be shot.

Terry, of course, was delighted. All the way to my house— he got lost three times, though he had visited me half a dozen times in the past—he talked constantly about "his" scene, a shot of Penn addressing a group of Teamsters. Would people see him? Terry wondered. Would they recognize him? (No and no, and Terry was vastly disappointed.)

Terry and I left the wrap party early, and Penn, who had been chatting up some dolly in the corner, came running over and gave me the biggest hug of my life. "It was great working with you, Frank!"

He had it all wrong, of course. It had been great working with *him*.

It was all over now, and the only thing left were some interviews with the original people who had known Harvey. Everybody had a twenty-minute tape, except for me. They used up three tapes, but only after Lance and a young PR man did a lap dance to warm me up. Thoughtful of them.

A prescreening was held at the Lucas Theater in the former military base on San Francisco's oceanfront, now taken over by Disney and Pixar. Half a dozen of us who had known Harvey were invited, and when it was over, we just sat there for a few minutes without saying anything. (Gus had been curious how we would react to it.) I finally turned around to Gus and said a simple, "Thanks."

The preview of the film was held at the Castro Theater, complete with a red carpet out front. Across the street was a small group of people protesting the anti–gay marriage initiative Proposition 8 and holding up "No on Eight!" signs. I wanted to show my solidarity, so I cupped my hands and shouted, "NO ON EIGHT!"

Penn was right behind me and upstaged me by walking across the street and shaking their hands.

The film, of course, received nothing but applause. I was sitting on the aisle, and as Cleve walked by, I turned my face into his shoulder because I couldn't stop from crying.

The studio had rented the whole first floor of city hall for a party, and that was jammed, too. A friend of mine—the soon to be much-married David Moloney—flew in from London for the premiere, complete with tux. He and his partner, Richard Link, were first married when San Francisco's mayor, Gavin Newsom, made same-sex marriage legal—for a short time—in 2004. (After the wedding, I made the huge mistake of taking the wedding party—all fourteen—out to lunch at the Garden Court in the Palace Hotel. I never went through half a grand so fast in all my life.)

David and Richard were Canadians who had worked in the States for ten years, but their green cards were pulled almost immediately after the wedding. They fled to London (David's father was British and he had citizenship), and when Canada made gay marriage legal, they went back to their hometown of Calgary and were married still again.

That one I *had* to attend—I was the only one around who had been at their first wedding. Unfortunately, I was the only single man among married couples of both gays and straights who attended the wedding, but David and Richard insisted I say something appropriate to the crowd about love. I forget what I said, but it drew great applause. Immediately afterward I de-camped for Lake Louise, Canada's most popular tourist trap. On board the bus, I speculated about where David and Richard would be married next.

David loved the film—he had once met Harvey in years past—and was glad to have made it to the party and premiere.

I stayed for about an hour at the *Milk* party and then left. On the way out, Lance hooked his arm in mine and we went skip-ping to the doors.

It was the first time since I was six that I had skipped any-place. I felt very foolish and at the same time very brave (I didn't fall once).

There was a part of one scene that never made it into the film (because of the WGA strike). Harvey (Penn) is addressing a roomful of radicals and telling them that if they wanted to change people's minds about gays, all of them had to come out. I was sitting in a sling chair, and Franco kept hitting my foot—he wanted me to ad-lib something. I got up and asked Harvey if he wanted me to tell my family that I was a fucking faggot. Gus came running over and said no, no, it's a statement, not a question.

I time traveled again. My family were all gone, but they still lived in the back of my head. I took a deep breath and finally told them that I was a *fucking faggot* and it was loaded with all the self-loathing I had felt back then. I started to shake, and Sean held me for an extra second before I went out—I think he was the only one who realized I was coming apart on set.

Outside, it was a cold night and I began to settle down. The world had changed for me. The words now meant nothing to me—I was what God and my family had made me, and the stone that had been in the middle of my heart for decades suddenly disappeared.

When the residual check came in half a year later, I cut it in two and sent $7,000 to UNICEF for Haitian relief. Sean Penn had been working down there for six months getting his hands dirty in the muck of that little country. The money wasn't much, but it was the only way I could thank him for what he had done for me, even if he hadn't known it.

Sometimes small things are really huge.

But there was more to it that I really didn't realize until a few days before writing this. For some people it's not easy for them to love themselves. In college there had been those who never considered themselves worthy of love (I was one). Most of them came from fractured families, kept their secrets to themselves, and if they couldn't find a way out, took another way out.

I was lucky. There were those who weren't. When I found Herb and his boys, it was usually a quick financial transaction. It satisfied part of me—for a while—but not the really important part. The Castro was, as Cleve Jones once put it, "all about sex." You could multiply the number of times you had sex and the next day be ready for more.

Everybody has their own opinion, but for me something was always missing. Marriage was looked down upon; "open" partnerships were tolerated. The answer was still, always, sex.

The first break came when Gavin Newsom made it relatively easy—for a short time—for those interested to get married. I was a best man at the marriage of David and Richard and noted that it was mainly women waiting in line for a license—most of them in their thirties or so, some bringing along children.

It didn't make much of a dent in public attitude and then—a miracle for me—more and more people were beating the drums for marriage. This last weekend (as I write this) the dam broke. There were a million and a half people gathered for the Gay Pride Parade. The number of people marching and bragging about either their present marriage or their coming marriage was staggering.

Suddenly it wasn't all about sex. It wasn't left out, but concern and affection and mutual help had been added.

There was, suddenly, another goal beyond the hot number standing on the corner.

Judge Vaughn Walker handed down the decision that broke the logjam in California. Lance Black wrote a play where the only dialogue was that taken from Walker's opinion. A lot of known stars wanted to act in it.

When it opened in San Francisco at the Castro Theater and Judge Walker walked in, there was a standing ovation. Walker's decision had been carefully crafted. Two out of three appellate justices passed it. Justice Anthony Kennedy and others on the US Supreme Court said the plaintiffs had no standing—they had failed to prove that if two persons of the same sex got married, that somehow it would endanger the marriage of those who had complained.

That's all I can write, Bob. For most of it I've been writing about dead people and it's been breaking my heart.

The next book I write will be full of aliens and spaceships and huge explosions. I'll make a million dollars and grab a friend and go to London and Paris and Venice—and Florence, to see if Michelangelo did as good a job on David's butt as he did on the rest of him. (I'm pretty sure he did.)

Right now I'm sitting on my front steps and it's a warm, sunny day and I've got my shirt open so the sun hits my far-too-white skin. I've been sitting here for maybe fifteen minutes and waving at the people passing by on the sidewalk, and this being San Francisco, they all waved back. I've seen a guy and his girlfriend walk by and then two women with a little boy between them, looking in wonder at the world around him. And two young men, maybe in their mid-twenties, strolling hand in hand. If they were open to advice I'd tell them to get married.

Maybe they already have; if not, they'll probably have to wait in line.

It's a different world now, and as I look at the couples passing by, I can't tell any difference between them in any ways that really matter.

All my love,
Frank

AFTERWORD

The Most Interesting Guy in the Room

BOB ANGELL

To be the recipient of a letter like this one is at once daunting, intimidating, and marvelous. It is, without a doubt, the longest and most wonderful letter I will ever receive in my lifetime, and from a man I considered to be one of my best friends.

Like so many people who knew Frank, I met him at a science fiction convention, World Con 2004 in Boston, just a couple of months after graduating from the Clarion West writing program. The year was also notable because on May 17, Massachusetts became the first state to allow same-sex marriage, and there was a general optimism floating through the gay community. Two thousand four was also the year that Tor published his thriller *The Donor*.

I dropped in late at the gay fandom party and there was this older guy wandering around and being ignored by all the young gays who were busy talking with one another.

"Whose the old guy?" I asked a friend.

"That's Frank Robinson," he said. "He wrote *The Dark Beyond the Stars*, a Lammie Award Winner. Oh, and the book that became the movie, *Towering Inferno*."

"So why isn't anyone talking with him?'

A shrug was my answer.

So I went over and said hello and discovered one of the most interesting people I would ever meet. Frank had a deep, sonorous voice with a decidedly Milwaukeean accent coupled with a nimble and articulate mind. He was captivating.

We talked for hours about books, movies, but most of all about gay activism. You see, Frank had been Harvey Milk's speechwriter, and at the time I was deeply involved in the marriage equality movement back home, and there were a lot of relevant current events that we had in common.

He asked me what I had written. I told him that I had a few short stories published and that I'd also written three unpublished novels and a collection of linked short stories mostly unpublished and mostly autobiographical about growing up gay, working for a defense contractor, being on a gay swim team, guarding the AIDS quilt the first time it came to DC, and so on.

"Send it to me," he said.

We began talking on the phone regularly, which wasn't the easiest of things because I was East Coast and he was West Coast. E-mails were easier, but it was more fun to talk with him.

I started reading everything he'd written that I could get my hands on. Through an interlibrary loan, I checked out a copy of *The Power*, his first book, published in 1956, the year I was born. It had been made into a movie with George Hamilton, Suzanne Pleshette, Michael Rennie, and other big names, but the movie, like the book, was out of print and impossible to find. Frank sent me a copy of the movie on DVD and a hardcover copy of the book.

Frank was incredibly generous, as all his friends know, and he sent me many things over the years: *Science Fiction of the 20th Century*; *Pulp Culture*; *Waiting*; *The Donor*; and *The Robinson Collection*, a coffee-table book containing images of the covers of all the pulp magazines he had collected since he was a kid. I was proud to lead a book discussion on his novel *Waiting* for my local gay science fiction and fantasy book club.

A few months into 2005 I got a call late one night and he started to say his usual greeting of my name in a long and drawn out, "Baaaaaaahb." But he hung up. He called back moments later and he was crying, apologized, and hung up again. A few minutes after that, he called back again and said, "Hold on until I can get this under control," and I listened to him sob and get it together.

"I finished your collection," he said. "It got to me." He then went on to tell me he'd been bawling on and off all afternoon. He was an emotional man, full of rare empathy, and he would cry at movies and at injustices in the world. He was a real man, honest about who he was, and unapologetic.

We talked almost every day for the last few years of his life. I'd ask him about Harvey, his early life growing up, the pulp years. We talked about aging. He answered every question I had with open honesty and then offered even more personal experiences. Ever aware that he was the elder statesman, and that someday it would fall on the next generation to tell the stories of the way it was, I urged him to write it all down.

Then on August 4, 2011, Frank called me and told me he's going to finally write his memoir, wants me to help edit it. Marriage equality was heating up, Prop 8 was angering a lot more people than just Californians, and state after state was signing up for gay marriage. It was time he wrote down what it was like before everyone forgot. Frank needed a framework on which to hang his life story, so he told me he would be writing it in the form of a very long letter. "Oh, and by the way, I'm writing it to you. Are you okay with that?" he asked.

For the next two years, he would tell me his stories, going over them again and again. This was not an old man's forgetfulness and retelling, but it was part of his writing process where he would tell the story over and over, with small changes in phrase or order, until he felt that he got it right. If he hadn't habitually done this in the past with other things he was writing, I might not have understood what was going on.

On Friday, June 26, 2015, the US Supreme Court ruled in *Obergefell v. Hodges* that gays and lesbians have a constitutional right to marry. Previously, when that right was granted on a state-by-state basis, Frank would invariably say to me, "I never thought I'd see this in my lifetime." Astonished and pleased, he would reminisce about the way it used to be.

Frank died on June 30, 2014, almost exactly one year before the Supreme Court ruling, and I wish that he had lived to see it.

That you and I *have* seen it in our lifetimes is a direct result of people such as Frank. Reading his memoir will help you understand not only the pivotal moments in which he had a hand, but also the evolving socioeconomic environment that roughly shaped gays and gay culture since 1926, the year Frank was born. Because of people such as Frank, many kids are growing up incapable of imagining the institutionalized oppression that was our peculiar history.

But this memoir is not just about gay history.

Herein are stories of Frank's life, vignettes woven together to make up the grand arc of an amazing man's productive life. He wasn't just pivotal in the gay movement, an activist in the AIDS pandemic, but he was also a pulp fiction connoisseur who arguably amassed one of the single most important magazine collections in the world. There was his career in the pulps and at *Playboy* magazine. There were his wonderful books that helped create the thriller genre in print and in the movies.

With a sharp eye for story and character, just as with his novels, he recorded in this autobiography the things he witnessed, participated in, history as it happened, all in his own engaging words. Read this book and, like me, you will understand why Frank M. Robinson will always be the most interesting guy in the room.

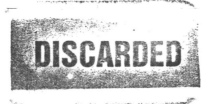